The McGraw-Hill Self-Study College Workbook

John C. Bean
Montana State University

Richard Marius
Harvard University

Harvey S. Wiener
The City University of New York
LaGuardia Community College

McGraw-Hill Book Company

New York St. Louis San Francisco Auckland Bogotá Hamburg
Johannesburg London Madrid Mexico Montreal New Delhi Panama
Paris São Paulo Singapore Sydney Tokyo Toronto

The McGraw-Hill Self-Study College Workbook

1234567890 SEMSEM 898765

ISBN 0-07-040382-1

See Acknowledgments on page 388.
Copyrights included on this page by reference.

This book was set in Times Roman by Progressive Typographers, Inc.
The editors were Emily G. Barrosse, Allan Forsyth, and David Dunham;
the designer was Merrill Haber;
the production supervisor was Joe Campanella.
Semline, Inc., was printer and binder.

Contents

Vickie

Preface

Overview

The McGraw-Hill Self-Study College Workbook is designed specifically for a process-oriented classroom. The exercises in this workbook are of two types: open-ended exercises requiring students to compose or revise text and self-study exercises with answers and explanations provided.[1] The open-ended exercises, which engage students as writers, eliminate as much as possible the "drill and practice" feel of traditional workbooks. In contrast, the self-study exercises provide extensive drill and practice in such matters as sentence structure, usage, and mechanics, but do so in a self-study format that eliminates the need for students to hand in tear-out sheets for grading. The answers and supplemental explanations provided by the self-study format give students immediate feedback on each exercise, allowing them to study at their own pace and to concentrate on material dealing with errors recurring in their own writing. If instructors wish, they can check students' progress by grading the short mastery exercises that conclude each self-study unit.

The McGraw-Hill Self-Study College Workbook has been designed to accompany *The McGraw-Hill College Handbook* and follows the handbook's organizational scheme, numbering system, and pedagogical philosophy.

Advantages of this workbook over competing texts

In comparing this workbook with others on the market, instructors will find noticeable differences. Among the advantages of *The McGraw-Hill Self-Study College Workbook* are the following features:

- Initial exercises that guide students through the composing process (Chapters 1 and 2).
- Self-study format for sentence-level problems.
- Supplemental explanations provided in the self-study units.
- A common-sense approach to grammar that combines the traditional system with insights from structural grammars (Chapter 3).
- Innovative exercises and explanations to teach students the concept of sentence completeness (Chapters 4 and 5).
- Plenty of open-ended exercises, including sentence-combining, that engage students as writers.
- A focus on rules, not as arbitrary points to be memorized but as conventions for enabling writers to control subtleties of meaning.

This workbook and the writing process

The McGraw-Hill Self-Study College Workbook emphasizes writing as a process. It has been shaped throughout by the assumptions about language associated with a process approach to composing. This approach assumes that writing is a means of

---

[1] For instructors who prefer a traditional workbook without the self-study features, an alternative version, called simply *The McGraw-Hill College Workbook,* is also available.

discovering and making meaning and that even the most seemingly product-oriented concerns, such as rules for punctuation or parallelism, should be explained to students in terms of the writer's intended meaning and audience.

The first two chapters of the workbook focus specifically on the writing process. Chapter 1, "Planning, Developing, and Revising Papers," guides students stage by stage through the process of composing an essay of their own. Instructors can ask students to do the exercises in Chapter 1 while drafting their first essays for the course. Then students can repeat the sequence for subsequent essays, seeking to adapt and modify the exercises to meet their own thinking styles.

Chapter 2, "Building Paragraphs," also takes a process approach to writing. Several exercises, particularly the paragraph assignments on the death rate table or the letters of recommendation (Exercise 2-3), help students learn how a writer's intended meaning controls both the shape of a paragraph and the writer's selection of details.

The remaining exercises in the workbook focus mainly on style, sentence structure, usage, and mechanics in a self-study format. Because students do not hand in numerous worksheets for grading, they can see their own writing as the center of interest in the writing course, while instructors can confidently reduce the amount of class time spent explaining sentence structure, usage, and mechanics. This self-study workbook allows students to learn this material on their own when they need it. In short, this workbook is a means of teaching rather than of testing.

Dictionaries and spelling

Chapter 22, "Using Dictionaries and the Thesaurus," and Chapter 29, "Spelling," differ from the other self-study units in this workbook in that answers are not provided. Because students should develop the habit of using their own dictionaries to check for word meanings and spelling, not having answers in these chapters encourages students to learn and practice good dictionary skills.

Acknowledgments

I would like to thank Richard Marius, Harvard University, and Harvey S. Wiener, LaGuardia Community College, The City University of New York, for inviting me to join them in producing a state-of-the-art handbook and workbook aimed at meeting the needs of contemporary writers. I wish also to thank the capable editors at McGraw-Hill who encouraged me to try out new ideas for the workbook, especially Phillip Butcher, Annette Hall, and Allan Forsyth. For marshaling an unusually complex set of exercises through production, David Dunham of McGraw-Hill also deserves special thanks, as do the following reviewers who gave me valuable insights into how to improve the exercises and explanations: Marilyn M. Cleland, Northern Illinois University; John Huxhold, St. Louis Community College at Meramec; Philip Keith, St. Cloud State University; Elizabeth Rorschach, New York University; Jay S. Vanatta, University of Southern California.

Finally, I would like to thank my son Matt for typing the manuscript, along with endless revisions, into the family computer, and my wife Kit, who rescued me from a missed deadline by writing the instructor's answer key for the traditional format version of the workbook. And to Andrew, Stephen, and Sarah, thanks for putting up with a grouchy dad.

John C. Bean

To the Student
How to Use This Workbook

The McGraw-Hill Self-Study College Workbook is designed to help you learn the process of writing, while also helping you learn the rules and conventions of English sentence structure, usage, and mechanics at your own pace.

This workbook contains two kinds of exercises. The first kind includes various open-ended exercises that ask you to compose or revise sentences, paragraphs, or even whole essays. Sometimes you will use your own paper for these exercises; at other times space will be provided for you to write responses in the workbook itself. Your instructor may ask you to hand this material in for checking or to bring your work to class for sharing with classmates in small group discussions.

The other kind of exercise in this workbook is designed for self-study. These exercises should help you avoid most of the errors that beginning writers sometimes make in constructing and punctuating sentences. These exercises are set in a two-column format with exercises in the left-hand column and answers, often accompanied by further explanations, in the right-hand column. To study this material, cover the right-hand column with a folded sheet of paper, and attempt to do each of the exercises in your head or on scratch paper. Then check your response against the answer or model provided in the right-hand column. Whenever your response to an exercise varies unexplainably from that in the workbook, be sure to discuss the matter with your instructor. Often there are several acceptable ways to improve a passage, especially if your improvement involves restructuring a sentence. The workbook will succeed best if you see it as expanding both your options and your sense of flexibility in using them.

Your instructor may ask you to work systematically through all the self-study exercises and may check your progress by assigning the short Mastery Exercises at the end of each self-study unit. Or your instructor may simply ask you to study those exercises that deal with problems occurring in your own writing.

1
Planning, Developing, and Revising Papers

Beginning writers sometimes think that experienced writers put a piece of paper in the typewriter and type out finished essays on the first try. This is a serious misconception. Experienced writers go through a long process of thinking about a topic, jotting down ideas, thinking some more, imagining their audience, considering their purpose, trying out a quick sketch of a first draft (often regarding it as an exploration or trial run rather than as a fleshed-out essay), "re-seeing" their ideas (*revision* means literally "re-vision" or "re-seeing"), writing a new draft, deciding on an organizational structure (which they often map out in a sketch outline, but seldom in a formal outline), drafting again, patiently revising, showing their drafts to trusted colleagues for feedback, patiently revising some more, editing their later drafts for sentence-level mistakes, checking spelling, and finally producing a neat, finished copy following the manuscript form appropriate for their purpose and audience. This final copy—the very copy that beginning writers think comes full-blown out of the typewriter on first try—is thus the result of a long, often arduous process.

Writing teachers have learned that students do a better job of writing in college if they practice following the processes used by experienced writers. The exercises in this chapter of the workbook are designed to guide you through the writing process, taking you stage by stage through the actual production of an essay of your own.

GENERAL DESCRIPTION OF THE EXERCISES IN THIS CHAPTER

The exercises in this chapter will guide you through the writing of an essay: the initial exploration of a variety of possible topics, the decision about a single topic, the discovery of a purpose and stance for your essay, the formulation of a tentative thesis statement, early decisions about the shape of your essay, the initial drafting, the later revising, and finally the editing and preparation of your polished manuscript.

You will begin these exercises by exploring three broad subjects: "education," "families," and a subject of your own choice. By a long-standing tradition among writing teachers, *subject* is the word used for broad, sweeping areas such as "education," "families," "love," or "crime." However, to write an actual essay you will eventually need to limit your subject to a much narrower area that is then called a *topic*—for example, "instituting merit pay at our high school" (instead of "education"), "my uncle Sam's love of practical jokes" (instead of "families"), my love/hate relationship with my father" (instead of "love"), or "the time my brother got arrested for shoplifting" (instead of "crime"). Obviously, within every broad subject there are hundreds of topics. How you can find your own narrow topics within a broad subject will be one of the things you will learn in this chapter.

The first subject you will explore is "education." Throughout this chapter you will watch a fellow student writer, Gail, do her own exploration of the subject "education"; her explorations will be used as examples throughout this chapter to illustrate the writing process.

The second subject you will explore is "families," a subject that will let you think both about your own family (what your childhood was like; your relationship with members of your own family; problems related to your own family life; your trials, tribulations, and triumphs as a family member) and also about issues relating to families in general (the decline of the traditional family, the effect of the economy on families, changing patterns of family recreation, and so forth). Since all of you using this workbook will be exploring "education" and "families" in common, you will be able to compare notes and share ideas with your classmates.

Finally you will choose a subject of your own, something that you think you would especially enjoy exploring. Here is a possible list of subjects. You can choose one of these or anything else that you would like to explore.

fishing	America's volunteer army
alcohol	urban pollution
college life	gun control
television	contact sports
advertising	pornography
fads	outdoor life
religion	emotion

Eventually you will write an essay on a very small piece of one of these subjects and will therefore necessarily choose *not* to write about dozens and dozens of other ideas you will have explored along the way. However, you may be able to use many of your other ideas for later essays in your college writing courses.

YOUR TASK FOR NOW

Write your choice for subject three in the space at the right.

Subject one: Education

Subject two: Families

Subject three: _____

1A Use prewriting techniques to explore what you know, believe, or feel about a subject before you write about it.

Prewriting covers all the time you spend thinking, jotting down ideas, and otherwise exploring your subject or topic before you write an actual first draft. Because many persons' first drafts are really more like intense explorations than attempts to compose a piece of writing for readers, some teachers even include first drafts as part of the prewriting process. The prewriting techniques you will practice in this chapter are thinking to yourself, discussing, making lists, questioning, writing nonstop, making clusters or subject trees, and doing library research. Some of these techniques, such as thinking to yourself, you will obviously be doing all the time with any essay. Other techniques work especially well for some people but not for others. Some writers, for example, find that list-making and nonstop writing are especially effective for them, while others prefer more visual techniques such as clustering and treeing. Try to discover what works best for you.

1 Think about your subject to yourself.

This may seem obvious, but many beginning writers sit down to write a draft without doing much prior thinking. Try this experiment. Get up from wherever you are now reading and walk around for five minutes thinking about one of your three subjects. What ideas about "education" or "families" or your own subject particularly interest you? What personal experiences come to mind? What might you like to write about and why? Get in the habit of thinking about ideas for essays as you walk around campus or take a shower. Each of the following prewriting techniques will stimulate your thinking. Keep playing with your subject.

2 Discuss your subject with other people; also watch for ideas about your subject while you read or watch television or movies in order to gather information and ideas.

Good writers are always on the prowl for ideas. Start noticing anything you see or hear about your subjects. Be on the lookout for newspaper and magazine articles, or for ideas from movies and TV and from dorm room bull sessions and other conversations. Strike up discussions about your subjects with your friends. For "families," try conversation starters like these: "parents shouldn't spank their kids." "Most old people prefer living in nursing homes." "Kids who spend their early childhood in day-care centers are better adjusted than those whose mothers stay home." "There should be a law against couples having more than two children." Make up your own conversation starters for your other subjects. The more you discuss your topics with others, the more you will be encouraged to think about them while walking to class or taking a shower and the more you will notice ideas about them when you read or watch movies or TV.

3 Jot down ideas in an informal list.

Any time an idea about your subject strikes you, write it down quickly so you won't forget it. Another way to stimulate thinking is to force yourself to jot down ideas in a list. Here is a list that one student, Gail, made while thinking about "education."

- Teachers, why do I like some of them and not others?
- Am I a good student? I used to be a good student in grade school, and then I kind of got out of being interested in being a good student until I got into my senior year of high school.
- Mr. Brown, what a jerk of a teacher. Maybe I could write a paper describing all the bad teachers I have had. I hated him with his boring lectures and his stupid pictures of his family up there on his desk. He must have put his kids to sleep at the dinner table if he was as exciting at supper as he was in class.
- Basketball games. I loved to go to basketball games and sit in the cheering section eating popcorn and yelling for the team. Sam Kreyler could dunk the basketball and he wasn't much taller than my brother. I also liked to watch the cheerleaders do their routines even though I think it is dumb to be a cheerleader. Why was cheerleading still popular at my school since women's liberation was getting stronger? Are cheerleaders women's libbers? Think about Molly.
- Expenses of going to college. My parents are paying through the nose.
- Should I get a work-study job?
- My adviser seemed pretty nice on registration day. I wonder if she likes working with freshmen?
- Will I do all right in college?

- Are grades really important in later life? I wonder if grades really screw up our educational system. Are the best students the ones who get the best grades?
- The special ed. kids at our high school. I remember the first time I saw Kathy, the mongoloid girl, when she came into the lunchroom. Everyone moved to another table when she sat down. They didn't exactly do it too rudely. They just ate faster and left or suddenly noticed a friend at another table. Remember the witch episode.
- I wonder how much mentally retarded kids are aware of how others are reacting to them. I wonder what they are really thinking.
- Are education requirements too low for high school students? The debates at the school board when those national reports criticizing education in America came out.
- Why don't kids study very much? You know who studies around here? The Oriental students. Why do they study harder than most other students? Have I stereotyped them?

Exercise 1-1 Making an informal list

Choose one of your three subjects and spend twenty minutes making an informal list of ideas. (Or choose two of your subjects and spend ten minutes listing ideas for each one.) Time yourself with a watch and try to get into a mood of intense concentration, jotting down ideas as fast as they come to you. Use your own paper.

4 Ask yourself questions about your subject.

This is one of the most powerful techniques you can practice for generating ideas on a subject. Not only does a series of questions set your mind thinking about a topic and cause you to look for information, but a question can also help you focus an essay because your answer to a question can serve as your thesis statement (more on this later).

A good way to ask questions is simply to list them on a sheet of paper, leaving some space to jot down later notes about possible answers to your questions. Here is a series of questions Gail asked about "education":

- Is our present grading system a good one?
- Is the curriculum at this college a good one?
- What is the best way to teach writing?
- Do these prewriting techniques really work?
- My comp. teacher said we won't be studying much grammar. Is that a good idea?
- Why do so many people oppose women's sports? (Note: remember the volleyball incident!)
- Do I really like school?
- Should teachers get merit pay?
- Who is my favorite teacher?
- What makes a good teacher? (I like that question.)
- Should retarded kids be mainstreamed in the school?
- Why do they have to have drug searches at dances?
- Why are some kids better spellers than others?
- Why don't the high schools know what to do with computers?

Exercise 1-2 Generating questions about your subjects

Make a list of questions (at least ten) for each of your three subjects. If you have trouble thinking of questions at first, try stimulating your thinking by using the journalists' questions *who? what? where? when? how?* and *why?* Try asking questions that begin with each of those words.

A. Ten questions about "education":

1.

2.

3.

4.

5.

6.

7.

8.

9.

10.

B. Ten questions about "families":

1.

2.

3.

4.

5.

6.

7.

8.

9.

10.

C. Ten questions about your third subject: _____

  1.

  2.

  3.

  4.

  5.

  6.

  7.

  8.

9.

10.

D. Choosing your favorite questions

Now go back over your list and pick out three or four questions you think it would be interesting or informative to explore in an essay for this course. If you think of your essays as answers to questions or as attempts to answer questions, you can often best visualize the focus or purpose for an essay. Write below your three or four favorite questions.

1.

2.

3.

4.

5   Write nonstop for a stated time period.

When you write nonstop, you put pen to paper for the stated period and write without ever letting your hand stop moving. If you can't think of anything to say, write your last word over and over again or repeat "this is dumb" or anything else that helps you relax. This exercise focuses entirely on the discovery of ideas. Don't stop to edit your writing by crossing something out or by worrying about spelling or grammar.

Nonstop writing causes your mind to work in a somewhat different way from the way it works during list-making or question-asking. In list-making, for example, you will jot down an idea and then leave it in search of another idea. In nonstop writing, however, you are more apt to keep exploring a single idea as your mind starts remembering details about it. You are apt, for example, to remember a story from your past and spend your whole nonstop writing session telling that story. This is fine. Let your pen follow your mind wherever it wants to go. Before starting your nonstop writing, look back over your list from Exercise 1-1 and your questions from 1–2. Start your nonstop writing with something that most appeals to you and then let your mind flow.

Here is Gail's five-minute piece of nonstop writing on the topic of "education." She looked back over her list from Exercise 1-1 before beginning.

> Let's see, what part of my list do I like the most. The special ed. kids interest me. I wonder if mainstreaming in our high school was good for them. I wonder if we really learned anything from them. I remember when Kathy called me a witch in sewing class and how I got really mad at her and then later felt guilty about it. Why should I have felt guilty about it? What kind of attitude are you supposed to have toward retarded kids? Why can't you get mad at them just the same way you would get mad at anyone else? Let's see what else interests me. This is dumb. I don't see how nonstop writing helps you learn anything. Who invented this stupid idea? Teachers. I hated a lot of my teachers, but I really liked some of them also. I think the best teachers don't get enough reward in our system. I really favor merit pay for teachers, but the teachers themselves don't seem to want it. My math teacher said the administration would use it to reward favorites and you can't really tell good teachers anyway.

Exercise 1-3   Writing nonstop

For this exercise you will do three different sessions of nonstop writing. Use your own paper. Begin by writing nonstop for five minutes about the topic "education." Look back over your previous prewriting activities to find an interesting starting point for your nonstop writing, such as a specific idea, memory, or question. After your nonstop writing, rest for at least ten minutes. Then write five minutes nonstop about "families." Try to write more words this time than you did the first time on "education." Then take another break. Then write nonstop for ten minutes on your third subject.

6   Use a visual prewriting technique such as clustering or making a subject tree.

Clustering is something like list-making except that you fill your page with circles and lines. To begin clustering, draw a circle in the middle of your page and write the name of your subject in it. Then branch off the circle writing new ideas as they come to you and placing these ideas in circles. Each circle becomes a new center of focus. You can later connect different circles with lines whenever you see interesting relationships. The point is to let one idea stimulate another, forming a kind of trail on paper. If one trail hits a dead end, you can start over again at your center circle or you can begin branching out from any of the satellite circles. Note the accompanying example of Gail's cluster on "education" in Figure 1. As she made her cluster, she looked back

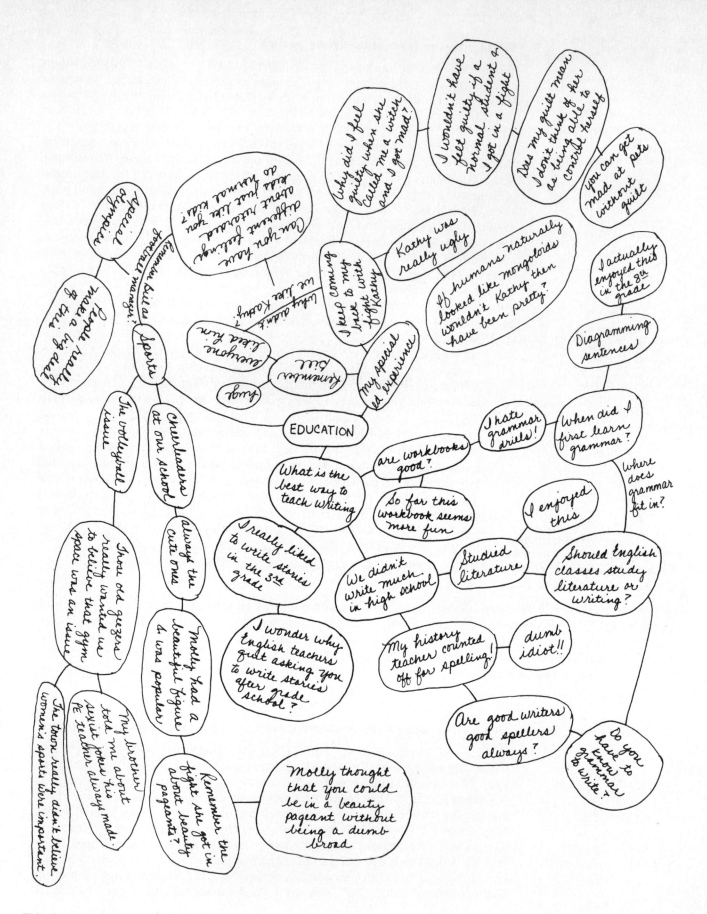

FIGURE 1   A cluster on "education."

over her previous prewriting to get new ideas whenever her mind temporarily hit a dead end.

A subject tree is like a cluster except that it tends to be more focused and structured. Subject trees are a good way of moving from a broad subject to a narrow topic. A subject tree starts with a broad area and then branches out into narrower and narrower areas. The further away you get from the root of your tree, the narrower and more specific (and of course more numerous) your topics become. Thus you could start with "education" at the root of your tree and branch out into narrow topics as shown in Figure 2.

Either technique, clustering or treeing, can be useful. Clustering tends to be more chaotic and thus might lead you to make an unexpected discovery. Treeing tends to be more logical and thus may help you see how to organize an essay. Because they are quite similar techniques, you don't need to worry whether you are doing exactly one or the other. If what you draw looks very random with lines going everywhere, you are clustering. If your lines clearly branch from the general to the specific, you are treeing. And if what you draw is something in between, it doesn't matter since the whole point is simply to help you think of ideas.

Exercise 1-4 Making clusters or subject trees

Make a cluster or subject tree for two of your three subjects. (Use your own paper.) Don't worry about the differences between the two techniques. As long as you fill your page with ideas connected in some way with lines, you are on the right track.

7 Browse in the library or do research on your topic.

Having gone through the previous prewriting steps, including drawing a cluster or subject tree, you may now have discovered what you know about your subject from your own experiences, observation, and discussions. You may also have discovered what you do not know, areas of your subject that need to be researched in order to strengthen your support of a possible topic: statistics, historical background, and so forth.

Not all college essays require research, of course. Many of your essays in a composition class can be based entirely on personal experience. On the other hand, many college essays will require extensive research (see Chapter 33 in *The McGraw-Hill College Handbook* for advice on writing research papers). Thus it is a good idea early in your college career to get to know your college library and to learn where some of its best resources are. You should find out where the periodicals are stored in your library and learn how to find newspapers and popular magazines as well as books. Even though you can often depend on personal experience for details, many of your essays can be strengthened if you also can add some insights, quotations, or statistics discovered through a brief period of research.

1B Limit your subject.

The subjects you are working with—especially "education" and "families"—are broad. (Many libraries, for example, will have hundreds of books written on the general subject "family" and even more on "education.") For writing short essays in college, you will need to narrow down your subject immensely, writing not about families in general but about how your family learned to help Grandpa keep up with the news when he could no longer read the paper or how you as a baby-sitter learned to handle a screaming two-year-old when her parents left the house for a movie. Writing teachers call this process "moving from a subject to a topic."

You can get the feel for narrowing a subject down to a topic if you see how, in the following example, the general topic "education" yields a great number of specific

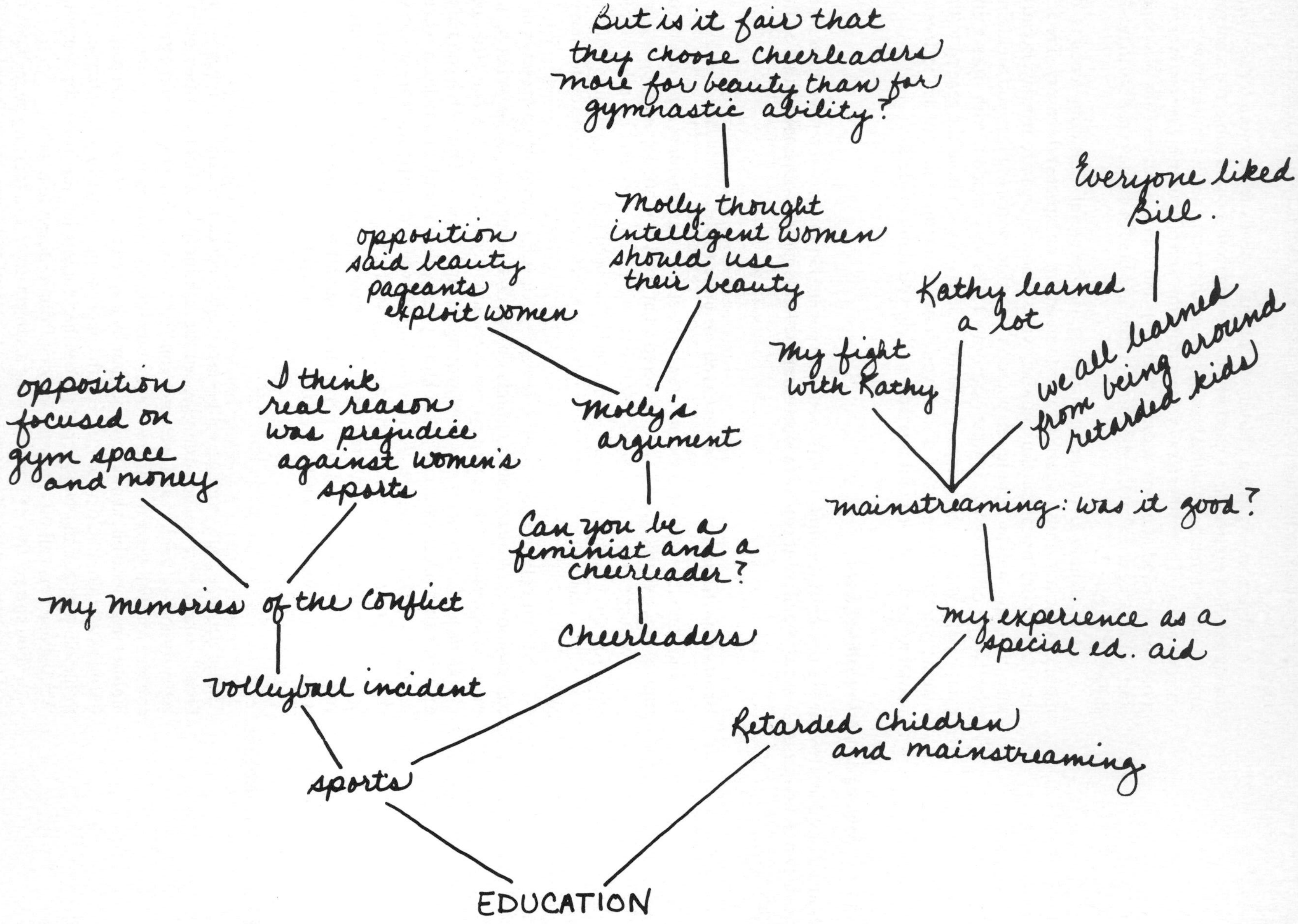

FIGURE 2 A subject tree on education.

topics when the field of focus becomes increasingly narrow. Figure 3 shows how Gail used a subject tree to narrow her subject into possible topics.

Exercise 1-5   Narrowing your subject

Using the "education" example as a model (as shown in Figure 3), narrow down your three subjects in steps, going from the very broad to the very specific. Identify at least eight narrow, specific topics for possible essays within each of your three subjects—education, families, and the subject of your choice. Use your own paper for this exercise. Be sure to include the headings that are at the top of Figure 3.

1C   Decide upon the purpose of your paper, using one of the four traditional rhetorical categories as an aid to formulating your intentions.

There is a long-standing tradition of four major rhetorical categories: description, narration, exposition, and argumentation. Although these categories aren't entirely satisfactory as a way of classifying the kinds of essays writers can compose, they are nevertheless useful as a way of seeing the various purposes an essay might have.

Description

A descriptive essay provides a verbal picture of a place, person, or event. In description, details are usually taken from the five senses and are arranged in some kind of spatial order.

Narration

A narrative essay tells a story, with its details usually arranged in chronological order (this happened, and then this happened).

Exposition

An expository essay informs, explains, and analyzes. This is the most common kind of essay you will write in college. Typically an expository essay might examine the causes or effects of an event, the strengths and weaknesses of an idea, the purpose or point of something, the meaning of a poem or work of art, the significance of the findings in a scientific experiment, and so forth. In exposition, details are arranged in some kind of logical, hierarchical order, as opposed to a simpler space or time order as in description and narration.

Argumentation

An argumentative essay presents a position on a controversial issue and attempts to persuade those with opposing or uncommitted viewpoints to accept the author's position. Typically, argumentation tries to change readers' minds about something.

These categories, in conjunction with an analysis of your audience, will help you see possibilities for various kinds of essays you might write on any given topic.

1D   Consider your intended audience.

As you decide on the purpose of your essay, you must also make decisions about your intended readers. An essay on drug searches at a school dance will have an entirely different arrangement of ideas, choice of details, and tone depending on whether you are writing a complaint letter to the superintendent of schools or a humorous feature story for your school paper.

A decision about the purpose and audience of your essay will go a long way

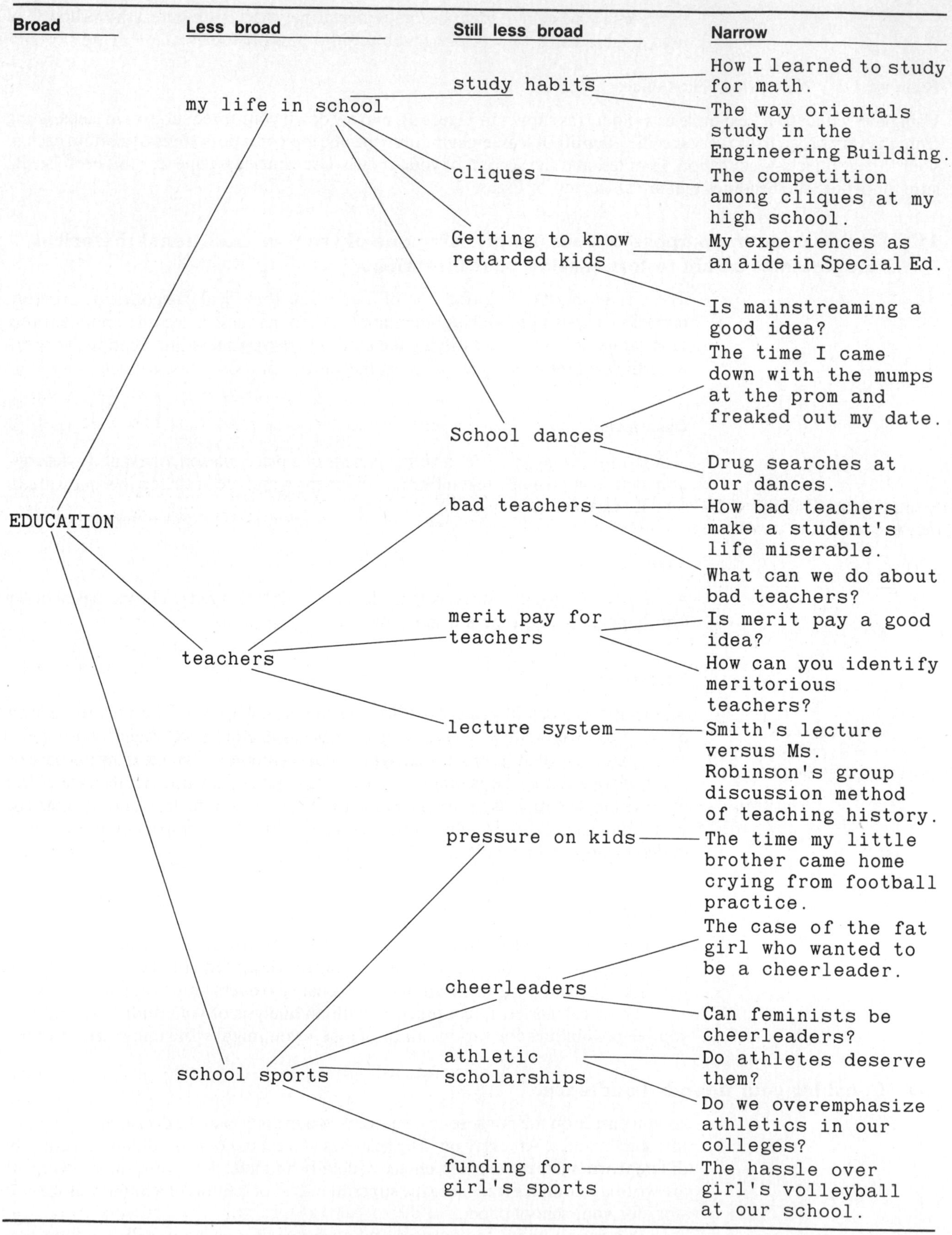

Broad	Less broad	Still less broad	Narrow

my life in school

study habits → How I learned to study for math.

study habits → The way orientals study in the Engineering Building.

cliques → The competition among cliques at my high school.

Getting to know retarded kids → My experiences as an aide in Special Ed.

Getting to know retarded kids → Is mainstreaming a good idea?

School dances → The time I came down with the mumps at the prom and freaked out my date.

School dances → Drug searches at our dances.

EDUCATION

teachers

bad teachers → How bad teachers make a student's life miserable.

bad teachers → What can we do about bad teachers?

merit pay for teachers → Is merit pay a good idea?

merit pay for teachers → How can you identify meritorious teachers?

lecture system → Smith's lecture versus Ms. Robinson's group discussion method of teaching history.

school sports

pressure on kids → The time my little brother came home crying from football practice.

cheerleaders → The case of the fat girl who wanted to be a cheerleader.

cheerleaders → Can feminists be cheerleaders?

athletic scholarships → Do athletes deserve them?

athletic scholarships → Do we overemphasize athletics in our colleges?

funding for girl's sports → The hassle over girl's volleyball at our school.

FIGURE 3   An example of how a subject tree is used to narrow a subject into possible topics.

toward helping you see what you need to do when you begin drafting your essay, so it is worth your while to spend time making these decisions. Note how Gail's specific topic areas discovered within the general topic of "education" can yield various kinds of essays.

Topic: School Dances

Descriptive purpose: To describe a typical drug search at a typical dance. (Audience: school board members who don't appreciate how humiliating this can be.)

Narrative purpose: To tell the story of the time I was searched at the junior prom and my ensuing fight with a teacher that led to a bad grade in history. (Audience: fellow classmates who can appreciate my dilemma and anger.)

Expository purpose: To compare dances at my high school with the dances my parents used to go to when they were in high school. I can show how the innocence of their old sock hops was a different world from the drug scene we are now in. (Audience: a general audience of people interested in social change.)

Argumentative purpose: To argue that the current drug search policy is humiliating to many students and should be changed. (Audience: school officials who believe that the drug searches are necessary—I will have to portray myself as a responsible student who shares some of their values, not as a hophead.)

Topic: My Experiences as an Aide in Special Ed.

Descriptive purpose: To describe the physical appearance, personalities, and typical activities of some of the special ed. students at our school. (Audience: general audience of people who have never been around retarded or severely handicapped students.)

Narrative purpose: To tell the story of the time Kathy, a mongoloid child, called me a witch and how I got mad. (Audience: special ed. teachers and other pro-mainstreaming people who believe special ed. students can be placed in the schools without unpleasant incidents.)

Expository purpose: To explore both sides of the controversy over mainstreaming retarded and physically handicapped students and analyze the strengths and weaknesses of the arguments. (Audience: general audience who haven't thought through the issue for themselves.)

Argumentative purpose: To support mainstreaming. (Audience: people who are skeptical about mainstreaming, especially parents.)

Topic: Girls' Volleyball

Descriptive purpose: To describe the action during an exciting moment of girls' volleyball. (Audience: people who have never seen a competitive volleyball game. I want to convince them it is exciting.)

Narrative purpose: To tell the story of how our school finally got girls' volleyball accepted as a varsity sport. This story would show a lot about the politics of a small town. (Audience: readers of a newspaper. This would make a good feature story.)

Expository purpose: To analyze why so many people in our town opposed girls' volleyball and whether the reasons they gave were their real reasons. (Audience: general audience of people interested in why other people take the positions they do.)

Argumentative purpose: To support the adoption of girls' volleyball as a varsity sport at my high school. (Audience: all opposed people. Essay could be an open letter to the school board but published in our town newspaper.)

It should be noted that few essays are pure examples of any one of the rhetorical categories, which often overlap. Thus an argumentative essay supporting mainstreaming of special ed. kids could include a description of several special ed. children (description), the story of how the author got mad at the girl who called her a witch (narration), and also an analysis of the weaknesses in some of the opposing arguments (exposition).

Exercise 1-6   Deciding upon a purpose and audience for your essay

Using the "education" examples as a model, decide upon the purpose and audience for possible essays within your three broad subjects. This exercise will ask you to think of possible essays in each of the rhetorical categories of description, narration, exposition, and argumentation. Begin each exercise with one of the narrow topics you discovered in Exercise 1-5. For example, in Figure 3 Gail narrowed the broad subject "education" down to a whole list of narrow topic areas, including "drug searches at dances," "my experiences as an aide in special ed.," and "the hassle over girls' volleyball at our school." These narrow topics were then used on pages 15 and 16 to develop ideas about the purpose and audience for possible essays. This exercise asks you to follow the same process for your own topics. Under each subject you can use the same narrow topic for each of the different purposes (description, narration, exposition, and argumentation), or you can choose different topics for each of the purposes.

Example:

Major Subject: Education

Narrow topic: *Teaching kids to swim.*

Purpose—description: To describe the physical behavior of Andy in the water and then to compare that with a description of the physical behavior of Martie. (Andy hated water and was nervous; Martie loved it.)

Audience:

A group of parents who haven't watched young kids learning to swim.

Major Subject: Education

Narrow topic (from Exercise 1-5): _____
Purpose—description:

Audience:

Narrow topic (either the same one or a different one): _____
Purpose—narration:

Audience:

Narrow topic: _____
Purpose—exposition:

Audience:

Narrow topic: _____
Purpose—argumentation:

Audience:

Major Subject: Families

Narrow topic (again, from Exercise 1-5): _____
Purpose—description:

Audience:

Narrow topic (either the same one or a different one): _____
Purpose—narration:

Audience:

Narrow topic: _____

Purpose — exposition:

Audience:

Narrow topic: _____

Purpose — argumentation:

Audience:

Major Subject: Your Own (No. 3)

Narrow topic: _____

Purpose — description:

Audience:

Narrow topic: _____

Purpose — narration:

Audience:

Narrow topic: _____
Purpose—exposition:

Audience:

Narrow topic: _____
Purpose—argumentation:

Audience:

1E   Determine the kinds of details you will need to make your points.

Whatever topic or purpose you choose, you must support your ideas with plenty of details. Sources of details include your own personal experience and observation (concrete sensory images, dialogue); books, magazines, and other media (quotations, summaries of arguments, or paraphrasing of authorities); and statistics (data from graphs, tables, and so forth).

Before doing the next exercise, you will need to decide on the topic you will choose for your formal essay and to make a preliminary decision on your purpose and audience. Go back over all the material you have written so far for this workbook and select the topic that you find most appealing and that will let you do your best job of writing. Your topic will probably be one of the narrow topics you wrote about in Exercise 1-6, but you are free to choose something else. The next exercise will help you explore details for that essay.

Enter below the topic on which you wish to write your essay. If you have already written a purpose and audience statement for your topic in Exercise 1-6, then recopy below what you wrote (or revise what you wrote, if you wish). If you decided on a different topic, then write a purpose and audience statement following instructions from Exercise 1-6.

Narrow topic for my essay: _____
Purpose:

Audience:

Exercise 1-7   Brainstorming for details

In this exercise, you will begin discovering the ideas and relevant details you will need in order to develop a formal essay on the narrow topic you have just chosen. Brainstorm ideas for your essay by listing all the ideas you can think of for each of the following questions.

1. What experiences in my own life will help me make this topic interesting? (Include at least one very specific scene that you can describe with details appealing to touch, sight, sound, and even taste and smell.)

2. What have I read recently in books, newspapers, or magazines that will relate to my topic? (If nothing comes to mind, try browsing through your library, reading an article or two you could locate through the *Reader's Guide*.)

3. What television shows, movies, popular music lyrics, and so forth, have I observed recently that might relate to my topic? How so?

4. What have I learned in recent conversations with friends, parents, relatives, teachers, and associates that will help me support my topic? (Give specific details.)

5. What do people in my audience already know about my topic? What will interest them? What will bore them? What can I say that will be new to them?

6. What are the major points I want to make in my essay?

7. What details, taken from all the sources I explored in questions 1 to 4, will be needed to support these points?

1F Think through the main idea of your composition and formulate a tentative thesis statement.

A thesis statement is a one-sentence summary of the main point of your essay. Whether you place your thesis statement in your actual essay itself is often a matter of choice, but you should always be able to state your thesis "for yourself." Because thesis statements are such valuable focusing tools, many writing instructors ask students to place their thesis statements prominently in the introduction—either as the opening sentence or as the last sentence of the opening paragraph. Although some writers are able to compose a well-developed thesis statement before writing a rough draft, most writers find that their thesis changes with succeeding drafts, since each draft helps writers understand their ideas more clearly. The thesis statements you compose early in the writing process should thus be seen as exploratory, tentative, and subject to revision later.

A thesis statement always does two things and sometimes does a third. It always identifies the narrow topic of the essay, and it always makes an assertion about the topic—the main point that the essay will develop and support. Occasionally, the thesis sentence also summarizes the main supporting ideas of the essay, thus previewing the essay's shape. The features of a thesis statement will vary somewhat, depending on an essay's purpose:

Descriptive Essays

A thesis for a descriptive essay usually contains a key attitude word that identifies a unified impression that the description is supposed to convey. (If a description of a room had no thesis, then the writer might include every sort of detail from the size of the walls to the number and make of the light fixtures.) A descriptive essay with a thesis, however, would make a point: "Professor Rinaldo's office is the messiest room on campus." All the details would then focus on the messiness of the office.

Purpose: To describe the action during an exciting moment of girls' volleyball.

Thesis statement: Girls' volleyball, with its stunning smashes, its diving saves, and its dramatic teamwork, is an exciting spectator sport. [This thesis predicts details focusing on the excitement of volleyball.]

Purpose: To describe a typical drug search at our high school dances.

Thesis statement: The rudeness of the security officers and their arrogant use of authority make drug searches at our high school dances a humiliating experience. [This thesis predicts a description of scenes focusing on unpleasant rudeness and use of authority.]

Narration Essays

Narrative essays sometimes don't have a thesis since the essay might simply tell a story for its own sake. Often, however, the narrative will be used either to make or to illustrate a point, and in those cases the point can be summarized in a thesis statement.

Purpose: To tell the story of the time Kathy, a mongoloid child, called me a witch and how I got mad.

Thesis statement: My fight with a mongoloid teenager, Kathy, lasted only a few seconds, but it changed my attitude toward retarded people forever.

Purpose: To tell the story of how our school finally got girls' volleyball accepted as a varsity sport. This story could show a lot about the politics of a small town.

Thesis statement: The saga of instituting girls' volleyball as a varsity sport at our high school reveals the hypocrisy of many of our town's citizens.

Exposition

Thesis statements for expository essays can take a variety of forms, but once again they are one-sentence summaries of an essay's central idea. Often a writer's analysis in an expository essay competes with opposing analyses. A thesis statement is sometimes sharpened if the writer summarizes opposing views in an "although" clause.

Purpose: To compare dances at my high school with the dances my parents used to go to when they were in high school. I can show how the innocence of their old sock hops was a different world from the drug scene we are now in.

Thesis statement: A comparison of the innocent sock hops of my parents' era with the drug scene at today's high school dances suggests that my world is much different from my parents'.

Purpose: To analyze why so many people in our town opposed girls' volleyball and whether the reasons they gave were their real reasons.

Thesis statement: Although our town elders claimed that lack of gym space and lack of money were their main reasons for opposing girls' volleyball, their real reason seemed to be a resistance to the social change symbolized by women's sports.

Argumentation

Thesis statements for argumentative essays take a clear position on a controversial issue. The opposing position can often be summarized in an "although" clause, and the supporting reasons for the author's position can often be summarized in a series of "because" clauses.

Purpose: To support mainstreaming of physically and mentally handicapped students in the public schools.

Thesis statement: Although some people claim that the physically and mentally handicapped can get better attention and care in institutions, mainstreaming of these children in the public schools benefits both handicapped and normal students.

Purpose: To support the adoption of girls' volleyball as a varsity sport at my high school.

Thesis statement: Our school should adopt girls' volleyball as a varsity sport because the gym schedules can be worked out, because the sport is surprisingly inexpensive, and because the addition of another women's sport would make our athletic programs fairer to both sexes.

If you have trouble constructing thesis sentences, it is sometimes helpful to think of them as one-sentence answers to questions:

Question: Should a school be allowed to kick a girl off the cheerleading squad for being too fat?

Thesis: Weight should not be a criterion for selecting cheerleaders; rather the criteria should be a cheerful "on-stage" personality, enthusiasm, and the ability to do the dance and acrobatic routines gracefully.

Question: How can schools identify meritorious teachers?

Thesis: Meritorious teachers can be identified by use of an improved student-evaluation form.

Exercise 1-8   Composing thesis statements

The following exercises will ask you, as practice, to create some tentative thesis statements on topics you haven't explored. Although it is somewhat unnatural to compose thesis statements under these conditions, practicing on topics that you haven't personally explored can be helpful if you see your thesis statements as "attempts" rather than as correct answers.

A. In the next four exercises design a possible thesis statement on topics in "education."

> *Example:*
> **Topic: Poor spelling**
> *Thesis statement with narrative purpose:* The time I lost the spelling bee in the fifth grade turned out to be one of my most embarrassing moments.
>
> *Thesis statement with argumentative purpose:* Teachers should not count off for spelling errors on an essay exam.

1. Topic: Merit pay for teachers
Thesis statement with expository purpose:

Thesis statement with argumentative purpose:

2. Topic: Pressure on kids in grade school sports
Thesis statement with narrative purpose:

Thesis statement with expository purpose:

3. Topic: High school cliques
Thesis statement with descriptive purpose:

Thesis statement with narrative purpose:

Thesis statement with expository purpose:

Thesis statement with argumentative purpose:

4. Topic: Cheerleading and feminism
Thesis statement with descriptive purpose:

Thesis statement with expository or argumentative purpose:

B. In the next eight exercises you will approach the writing of thesis statements from a slightly different direction by seeing a thesis statement as an answer to a question. For each of the following questions compose a thesis statement that would represent your tentative answer to each. If you think other people might disagree with your thesis, try summarizing an opposing view in an initial "although" clause. This time the subject is "families."

5. Should parents reward their children with money or gifts for getting good grades? (Write an argumentative thesis; summarize your reasons in your thesis.)

6. What is the significance of the word *fall* in the phrase *fall in love?* (For example, why do we say "fall in love" and not "fall in friendship"?) (Write an expository thesis.)

7. Should parents force a child to practice a musical instrument if the child doesn't want to? (Argumentative thesis; write two versions—one without a summary of your reasons and one with a summary of your reasons.)

8. What are the greatest mistakes that parents make in raising children? (Write an expository thesis.)

9. What is the effect on preschool children of spending four to eight hours per day in a day-care center? (Write an expository thesis.)

10. When you get old, would you rather live with your children or in a nursing home? Why? (Write an expository thesis.)

11. What is a typical holiday meal like in your family? (Think of a specific scene at a specific time and write a descriptive thesis.)

12. What story could you tell that illustrates what you mean by kindness? (Write a narrative thesis.)

C. In the next seven exercises, ask questions based on your explorations in Exercises 1-5 and 1-6 and then answer them in single sentences that would serve as thesis statements. Have at least one thesis in each of the rhetorical categories of description, narration, exposition, and argumentation.

Example:
Question: Can a cheerleader be a feminist?
Answer: Any girl who allows herself to be chosen for a position on the basis of beauty rather than the skill actually needed to do the job is violating the principles of feminism. (argumentive thesis)

13. *Question:*

   Thesis:

14. *Question:*

   Thesis:

15. *Question:*

   Thesis:

16. *Question:*

   Thesis:

17. *Question:*

Thesis:

18. *Question:*

Thesis:

19. *Question:*

Thesis:

D. Finally, devise a preliminary, tentative thesis statement for the essay you plan to write.

Example:
Here is the question and tentative thesis for the essay Gail decided to write:

Question:

Should schools mainstream handicapped students?

Thesis:

Mainstreaming handicapped students in the schools is a good idea.

Now do the same for your own essay.

20. *Question:*

Thesis statement:

1G To develop your paper, expand your informal written ideas, group them by subject, and organize these ideas in a rough outline.

Before you begin drafting your essay, you will need to make some sort of informal plan about what to say first, what next, and so forth. Very few writers make formal outlines, but almost all writers devise some sort of organizational plan, either keeping their ideas in their heads or sketching them out on paper.

Now that you have a tentative thesis statement, as well as a page or so of idea notes on your essay, look back over your notes and make an initial organizational plan. Here is Gail's preliminary organizational sketch for the topic she chose: mainstreaming of handicapped children.

Preliminary thesis: Mainstreaming handicapped children is a good idea.

1. Give background about mainstreaming. (Note: I've got to go to the library and get some facts and figures.)

2. Show that this is a controversial issue.

3. Summarize some of the opponent's views—kids don't get care they need. They will be ridiculed in public schools.

4. Give my own position and thesis.

5. Say that both handicapped and normal kids will benefit.

6. Retarded will learn appropriate behavior by watching normal kids. Give my Kathy example. Maybe use example of Anita and Dianna too.

7. Normal kids will learn lessons too. Give example of Bill.

8. Conclusion

Once an informal outline is completed, you can use it as a preliminary check for unity and coherence in your essay. If your essay has *unity,* then all parts of it pertain clearly to the thesis statement. (The above outline is unified—every part relates to Gail's argument in favor of mainstreaming handicapped children.) If your essay has *coherence,* the flow of ideas makes sense as the reader goes from sentence to sentence, paragraph to paragraph. (The above outline promises coherence because the parts seem arranged in a logical order.)

Exercise 1-9   Writing your own informal outline

On this page write your own informal outline to help guide you through your first rough draft. If you have a great deal of difficulty finding order in your ideas, set your alarm clock for forty-five minutes and on separate paper write a "discovery draft" of your whole essay (try writing almost nonstop). This will sometimes clarify for you the organizational problems you need to solve. Then write your informal outline on this page. Use the back of this page if necessary.

Tentative thesis:

Outline:

• Do all parts of your outline relate logically to your thesis sentence? (unity)
• Does the ordering of parts seem logical? (preliminary check on coherence)

1H Prepare the first draft of your composition.

The important thing to remember as you write a rough draft is to concentrate initially on the creation of ideas and the fleshing out of general statements with specific illustrations, examples, statistics, quotations, or other details. Do not worry at the rough draft stage about spelling or grammar. Double-space your rough draft, writing on one side of the page only. This will leave you plenty of room to make changes and to cut and paste your pages if you later want to rearrange the order of the parts. Try to write your rough draft rapidly and then put it aside for a while. Promise yourself that what you write now will be changed substantially several drafts later.

Here is the first rough draft of Gail's essay on mainstreaming handicapped children.

In 1950 (?--go to library) mildly mentally handicapped people were in state institutions. Today, nearly every mildly to moderately handicapped person has been ''mainstreamed'' into group homes or into public schools.

Many people question the rationalaty (?) of placing mentally retarded students in public schools with the so-called ''normal'' students. They believe that, by placing the ~~slow~~ *slower* handicapped students ~~who are slower~~ in the same school with the normal students, the quality of the education that the normal students receive will be ~~lowered~~ *reduced.* In such a fast-paced world, students of average intelligence cannot afford to be slowed-down by other students who require (more time to learn with a totally different set of learning objectives.) The handicapped students' learning may also be hindered. Those who oppose mainstreaming claim that the handicapped student may feel ill-at-ease with the other students. The student may even be subject to ostrisism (?) from other students because he's different. The alienation the retarded student suffers may ~~do more harm than~~ defeat the pupose of mainstreaming however because I worked for a year as an aide to the special education class in High school I have become I am convinced that mainstreaming *the handicapped kids* is very valuable.

Students on both ends of the spectrum of intelligence can benefit from mainstreaming. First, ~~I think that normal students~~ I think that the mentally retarded students can learn many things from being directly integrated with normal students. These things are very hard to learn in an institutional setting such as socialization. The retarded students (what should I put--Kimmy lost weight, dressed more normal; we helped Anita make charts for grooming.--what is my point here?) Kathy, a 14-year old mongoloid, began the school year with no friends. She was very rude, she often told others to ''shut up''. During a sewing lesson one day she even told me I looked like a witch. *This made me so mad!* Kathy was a very spiteful ~~little~~ girl. By interacting with other students, Kathy learned that her behavior was socially unacceptable. Kathy is only one example. Many other handicapped students learned to modify their behavior to fit into society also. (Should I add others here?)

Normal students learn too from mainstreaming. Many of them are nervous around the retarded people they don't know what to expect from them to treat them as people retarded kids or even how to treat them.

For instance, many normal students learned a very valuable lesson from Bill. Bill was very big and students treated him as though he was almost a Frankenstein. After attending school with him for a few weeks, everyone began to see the real Bill, a kind, gentle, considerate person. The high school students learned that most retarded students are people just like them.

In conclusion, I think that mainstreaming handicapped kids serves to better the lives of both the handicapped and normal kids.

Exercise 1-10   Writing your first draft

Write your first draft. Use your own paper for this exercise.

1I Revise your first and subsequent drafts for clarity and correctness. Give your draft to a friendly reader for comments and suggestions.

An injunction to remember is that "writing is rewriting." As a general rule, the more you see your draft changing and growing, the more you will be following the writing process of mature writers. Such revising is messy. Most writers make pen-and-ink changes on their drafts, adding and deleting words, taping in inserts, cutting pages apart to rearrange them, until their drafts are finally too messy to work from any more. Then they type out a fresh copy. (If you are fortunate enough to be able to write and revise at a word processor, these tasks are made much easier.)

Always read your drafts aloud to "hear" the rhythm of your sentences. Mistakes that look fine on paper are often easily detectable when you read aloud. Whenever possible, have someone else read your drafts and alert you to confusing, undeveloped, or boring passages. At the early draft stages, focus mainly on the development and arrangement of your ideas. At later draft stages, worry also about grammar and sentence correctness.

Here is a revised version of Gail's essay on mainstreaming handicapped students.

Kathy and Bill: Two Arguments in Favor of Mainstreaming

It is a typical day in the Senior High School cafeteria. Kim, a short, chubby girl with Down's syndrome waddles over to her table carrying a carton of chocolate milk. Kim grunts, sits down, and begins the sloppy process of eating. A few of the regular students glance over, but they pay little attention to her. To them, Kim is just another student.

This scene is not an unusual one. Since the early 1970s nearly 85 percent of the mildly to moderately mentally handicapped people in state institutions have been moved from those institutions and mainstreamed into the community. They have been placed in group homes and, more controversially, into special classes in our public schools. Many people question the rationality of placing the mentally retarded in public schools with the so-called ''normal'' students. They believe that, by placing the slower, retarded students and the normal ones in the same school, the quality of the normal students' education will be lowered. In such a fast-paced world, students of average intelligence cannot afford to be slowed down by students who require so much more time to learn. They also believe that the handicapped students will feel ill at ease and even be subject to ostracism when placed in a setting with the other, more intelligent students. The alienation the retarded student suffers may even defeat the purpose of mainstreaming. However, because I worked for a year as an aide in the special education class in my high school, I am convinced that mainstreaming of most handicapped students is very valuable for both handicapped and nonhandicapped students alike.

First, I think that handicapped students will benefit because they will learn appropriate behavior by following examples set by the normal students. Because institutions provide no realistic role models to follow, public schools are the best places for handicapped children to learn about appropriate social behavior. Kathy, a fourteen-year-old girl with Down's syndrome, is a very good example. She started the school year with virtually no friends because she treated others so rudely. She often told others, ''You're ugly!'' or ''Shut up!'' One day, during a sewing lesson, Kathy looked up at me and said, ''You look like a witch!'' I glared back at her and snapped that she had no right to talk to me like that. My negative reaction helped Kathy realize that her behavior was socially unacceptable. By watching other normal students, she even learned to apologize after her rude outbursts. Many of the other handicapped students encountered similar problems. They, too, learned more appropriate behavior which eventually helped them fit into our society.

My second major reason for supporting mainstreaming is the positive effect it has on the normal students. For instance, many of the students in my high school learned a very valuable lesson from Bill, a retarded boy who was about 6 feet 3 inches tall and weighed over two hundred pounds. At first, his appearance caused many students to fear him, this Frankenstein's monster in our midst. After attending school with him for a few weeks, however, everyone began to see the real Bill--a kind, gentle, and very considerate person. Bill was even chosen by the varsity football and basketball teams to be their team manager. The high school students learned that most retarded students can be treated the same way you would treat a normal person. As adults, the normal students will probably be more likely to be friendly and supportive of the handicapped people in their community instead of trying to ignore them.

It has been said that a society is only as strong as its ability to care for its poor, sick, and handicapped members. Perhaps by attempting to integrate the mentally retarded people into our society instead of trying to hide them away, our society is working toward our goal of being an open-minded and wise society that is able to do the best for all its members.

Exercise 1-11   Observing how a draft grows

In this exercise you will be comparing the first draft of the example essay on mainstreaming handicapped students with the revised draft. Our goal is for you to observe the kinds of changes the student made in the draft and to appreciate the rationale for the changes. (Actually the revised version you see here is Gail's fourth draft; drafts two and three have not been included.)

1. Write out the thesis statement for the first draft.

2. Write out the thesis statement for the final draft.

3. What changes did the writer make in the thesis statement? Why?

4. Does the thesis statement in the final version preview the shape of the essay? How so?

5. Identify all the additions the writer made to the first draft (that is, what material appears in the final draft that is not in the first draft?). What function do these additions serve?

6. Identify any deletions that the writer made (that is, identify passages that appear in the first draft but not in the final draft). Why did the writer delete this material?

7. What changes have been made in paragraphing? Look at the opening sentences of the body paragraphs in the first draft and the final draft. How have the original opening sentences been changed? Why?

8. Identify all passages that use concrete, descriptive details that enable you to visualize a specific scene. What do these passages add to the essay?

9. What other changes has the writer made in going from the first draft to the last draft?

10. Pretending that you are a teacher, write an appropriate end comment to place on the final version of Gail's essay.
Strengths:

Suggestions for improvement:

Exercise 1-12   Critiquing a classmate's essay

For this exercise, exchange rough drafts with a classmate. You are to fill out the following critique sheet on your classmate's rough draft, and your classmate will fill out a similar critique sheet on your rough draft. In "doing a critique" for a fellow classmate, you are to act out the role of a caring, attentive reader who wants to help the writer improve his or her essay. Critiques are seldom valuable unless they offer clear suggestions on ways the draft should be revised.

Your name _____   Author's name _____

1. Copy the thesis statement for this essay exactly as it appears in this draft. (If you have trouble locating a thesis, discuss the problem with the author.)

2. Write out the question that this thesis statement appears to answer.

3. How many paragraphs does the essay have? Number the paragraphs in the margin for later reference.

4. Make an informal outline of the essay. For each piece of information on the informal outline, identify which paragraph the information comes from using the paragraph numbers added in entry 3 above. (Use a separate sheet of paper.)

5. Does the thesis statement predict the shape of the essay as revealed in your informal outline? Make suggestions on how the essay can be better organized.

6. Is the thesis clear? What improvements are needed?

7. Does the essay speak consistently to the same audience?

8. How many main points does the essay make? List the main points below even if you previously entered them on the informal outline.

9. Are there enough details to support the main points? Place a + in the margin next to any passages with especially good supporting details. If you don't place any +'s in the margin, make suggestions on how the use of details could be improved.

10. Does the essay show unity? Do all the ideas clearly relate to the thesis statement? Are there any parts of the essay that should be omitted? Explain.

11. Is the essay coherent? Do ideas flow logically and smoothly from one to the other? Were you ever lost? Explain.

12. Are ideas stated in precise language so that you are certain what the writer means? Note confusing sentences on the draft.

13. When you read the essay aloud, do the words and sentences sound right to the ear?

14. Reread the opening sentences of the opening paragraph. What strategy is used to capture the reader's interest right off? Were you immediately "hooked," or is the opening ho-hum? How would you improve the opening?

15. Does the conclusion complete the ideas established and supported in the essay?

16. Does the essay have a good title that identifies the subject of the paper and yet arouses reader interest?

17. Check the essay very carefully for sentence completeness. Are there any run-ons, comma splices, or fragments? (See Chapters 4 and 5.)

18. What do you like best about this essay? Please be specific and write at least three complete sentences.

19. What is the most important change the author should make on the next draft to improve the essay?

20. What other advice would you give?

1J   Proofread your paper for errors.

1K   Prepare the final copy carefully, according to the manuscript form specified by your instructor.

Often writers spend so much time drafting and revising their essays that they run out of steam near the end and submit their final copies without proofreading. The result is often a sloppy presentation that annoys the reader and creates a bad first impression for you the writer.

The later chapters of this workbook are devoted to helping you learn to recognize and avoid common sentence-level errors. However, this early in the term you should nevertheless get in the habit of careful proofreading before you turn in final copy.

Exercise 1-13   Proofreading

The following essay was typed at two o'clock in the morning while the author was bleary-eyed and caffeine-charged. It is now the next morning, one hour before the essay is due, and the author looks at it with fresh eyes. Unfortunately, there is not enough time to retype the essay. Fortunately, the teacher has said that corrections can be made neatly in ink on the finished copy. Proofread this essay carefully, making neat corrections that will leave a good impression on the teacher.

OK, Teachers, Get Off Our Backs

We students hear about an educatin crisis all the time. Teachers tell us that we wathc to much television that we dont' study enough, that many of us haven't learned the basic skils, and that we are interested only in grades rather than education. But if their really is an educatin crisis, then may be teachers should except part of the blame also, perhaps we would be better studetns if our instructors were better teachers. After much discussion about the best and wors teachers we have had, our group believes that teacher's could help us become better learners if they followed three simple principles of good teaching.

First, teachers should allow more class time to discuss and examine assigned homework. Rick one of the group members, gave an example. ''Mr. Anderson a fast talking algebra teacher always assigned us too pages of problems that we knew nothing about. This always resulted in me going home and setting for hours not learning anything. Id get so frustrated that I'd slam my book down and give up.'' A solution to this kind of problem wuld be to have the teacher set aside time to review the homework. Allowing class time to ask questions about the problems the students might have. Another member of the group illustrated a better method for conducting class. ''My calculus teacher always gives time to examine our homework and gives us hints to problems that he feels will give us trouble.''

Second, teachers should add creativity to their lectures, which might have otherwise been boring. A negative example is Mr. Owens, Greggs English teacher who would talk very slow and quiet in a monotone way that would put the students to sleep, on the other hand, Mr. Barlow, Shannon's psychology teacher, was just the opposite. ''Mr. Barlow would draw pictures on the chalkboard and make up stories which centered around the students in the classroom when he did this we would become involved in his lectures because we were his lectures. If teachers would involve studnet in lecures and add some humor at the same time. The students would become more absorbed in the class and perhaps learn better.

Finally, teachers should control their distracting habits in class. Bob particularly remembmers the annoying habits of Mr. Garrick, a tall scrawny man who wore thick round glasses and continuously gnawed on his chalk. ''Not only were his pencil-like fingers white,'' Bob told us, ''but his mouth was also. It didn't really become distracting until he started spitting white flakes of chalk on the students. Additionally, several student explained about the ''uh,uh,uh'' habit which Shannon remembers most vividly in Mr Dickerson who expounded the annoyance by dressing in ugly green and slicking his hair back like Jerry Lewis. But the most annoying habit of all was one Greg reported. ''Mr. Reynolds distracted the class by reading <u>Playboy</u> he would try to cover it up but we wuld just ask dumb questions so we could get a glimpse of the pictures.''

So the next time teachers tell us about an education crisis, we are going to hold up a mirror and let them see themselves. For every student who doesn't study, there is a teacher who does'nt prepare for class. For every student who goes off and does his own thing instead of knuckling down to homework, there is a teacher doing his own thing in class without caring a fig whether students' are learning or not. Maybe we would be better students if teachers were better role models for us to follow.

1L   When you get your essay back from your instructor, make the changes and corrections that your instructor suggests.

Some students seem interested primarily in the grade they receive on an essay and don't spend much time considering the comments placed on the essay by the instructor or reading and studying those portions of a handbook that explain how to correct errors that the instructor notes.

To benefit the most from your composition class, you should plan to spend at least an hour studying the comments your instructor places on your essay. Learn the instructor's marking system, especially any symbols that allow you to cross-reference the instructor's comments with explanations in this workbook or *The McGraw-Hill College Handbook.* When the instructor notes an error, study the appropriate explanations in your workbook or handbook and try to correct your error. (If you have trouble, be sure to see your instructor.) Additionally, keep a log of the kinds of errors you make so that you can alert yourself to any consistent patterns. When you write a second essay, be sure to check your draft carefully for the kinds of errors you made on your first essay.

Exercise 1-14   Keeping a sentence-correctness log

When you get your graded essay back from the instructor, use the chart in Appendix A (page 387) to begin a log of your sentence-level errors. On later essays, continue this log, adding additional sheets as needed.

2

Building Paragraphs

A **paragraph** is a unit of thought identified on a printed page by indentation of the first sentence. To convey meaning clearly to readers, paragraphs should display *unity, coherence,* and *sufficient development.*

2A Build unified paragraphs.

A paragraph is said to have *unity* when all its sentences support a controlling idea.

1 Achieve unity by giving each paragraph a controlling idea.

A controlling idea for a paragraph (often stated in a sentence called the **topic sentence**) is analogous to the thesis statement of an essay (see pages 25 to 27). Topic sentences occur most often near the beginning of a paragraph, but they can occur also in the middle or at the end. Sometimes a topic sentence does not appear within the paragraph, in which case the controlling idea is implied rather than stated.

Like thesis statements for essays, topic sentences have two functions: First they identify a topic:

> The grading system
>
> Grasshoppers
>
> Writing essays

and second they make an assertion about that topic:

> A problem with the current grading system is that is fosters conventional thinking rather than risky thinking.
>
> Although grasshoppers probably serve a useful function in some animal's food chain, they are for me a great source of stress.
>
> The pain of writing essays can be lessened if you practice three techniques.

Often a topic sentence is an arguable proposition, forcing the writer to defend a position, as in the first example above on the grading system. Sometimes, however, the topic sentence simply identifies an attitude toward the topic (as in the second example, where the writer is committed to show how grasshoppers are a source of stress). And at other times the topic sentence sets up a reader's expectation by suggesting the shape of the paragraph to come, as in the last example where we expect to learn about three techniques that will make writing essays easier. The essence of a good topic sentence is that it in some way sets up a reader's expectations, which the rest of the paragraph then fulfills.

In order to create a sense of expectation or anticipation, a topic sentence should be a generalization requiring support as opposed to a specific statement of fact that leads nowhere.

Specific statement:

Sam is a student at Boffo High School. ["So what?" we ask. "Where does this lead us?" As a statement of fact, it requires no further development. It doesn't set up any expectations for what must follow.]

Generalization:

Sam is the most imaginative thinker at Boffo High School. [This is a generalization that demands support, since the reader now needs evidence that Sam thinks imaginatively. This evidence could become the body of a paragraph, while the generalization could serve as its topic sentence.]

Exercise 2-1 Judging and writing topic sentences

A. In the following groups of sentences, select the sentence that would best serve as the topic sentence of a paragraph.

Example:

_____ In the 1984 Olympics the United States won more gold medals than any other country.

_____ Mary Lou Retton scored a perfect "10" in the vault.

X Television coverage of the 1984 Olympics seemed like jingoistic propaganda for the United States. [The first two sentences are merely facts that demand no further support. The last sentence is an arguable proposition that needs support. Thus is could serve as a topic sentence.]

1. _____ Word processing programs will operate on most kinds of microcomputers.

   _____ Word processing can encourage people to revise their essays.

2. _____ The state education association should endorse soccer as a varsity sport for high school students.

   _____ Throughout the state thousands of youngsters play soccer in community-run youth soccer programs.

3. _____ The taxicab driver wouldn't take us to the Bronx.

   _____ We got lost on the subway system.

   _____ For us, getting around in New York was nothing but frustration.

4. _____ I counted twenty-five old lunch sacks strewn around the floor of Professor James' office.

   _____ Professor James' office is an unbelievable mess.

   _____ On his bookshelf were two rotting apples.

5. _____ It is time for a new core curriculum at this university.

   _____ A recent survey showed that only 10 percent of our students take philosophy courses.

   _____ Two-thirds of the students in an advanced math class didn't know whether Aristotle lived before or after Thomas Aquinas.

6. _____ At a recent little league game two fathers got in a fistfight over an umpire's call.

   _____ The little league season should be canceled for two years.

   _____ Parents won't volunteer their time to help keep the playing fields mowed.

7. _____ Most students today have relatively neat hair and clothes.

   _____ The youth rebellion of the 1960s seems to have passed.

   _____ The most crowded majors in college are those leading to high salaries.

8. _____ Further development of hydroelectric power in the United States offers little hope for solving the energy crisis.

   _____ A recent public utilities bulletin points out that almost all possible locations for hydroelectric dams have already been used.

   _____ Environmentalist groups strongly oppose the building of more dams.

B. For each of the following topics write two sentences. Make the first sentence a statement of fact that leads nowhere; make the second sentence a generalization that could serve as a topic sentence for a paragraph.

Example:
Beauty pageants
Statement of fact: *A recent Miss America was forced to resign because she appeared nude in a men's magazine.*

Possible topic sentence: *Beauty pageants exploit women just as much as outright pornography.*

9. **Sports**
   Statement of fact:

   Possible topic sentence:

10. **Growing old**
    Statement of fact:

    Possible topic sentence:

11. **Parents**
    Statement of fact:

    Possible topic sentence:

12. Military defense
Statement of fact:

Possible topic sentence:

13. Writing classes
Statement of fact:

Possible topic sentence:

14. The presidency of the United States
Statement of fact:

Possible topic sentence:

15. Jobs for teenagers
Statement of fact:

Possible topic sentence:

2 Achieve unity by making all sentences in a paragraph support the controlling idea.

Paragraphs should show a clear relationship between the intended meaning and the details used to support the meaning. For example, if you wanted to write a paragraph about how grasshoppers cause you stress, there are only a limited number of things you could say. For instance, it is true that grasshoppers, like all insects, have tough outside shells that serve as their skeletons. But this fact tossed into a paragraph about stress would probably be irrelevant.

Irrelevant point:

> Each year grasshoppers ruin my garden. Last year these monstrous insects devoured two-thirds of my plants. *Like all insects, grasshoppers have a tough external shell which serves as their skeleton.* Scientists estimate that nine grasshoppers per square yard will do more damage than a grazing cow, and yesterday I counted seventeen grasshoppers on one head of lettuce.

However, apparently irrelevant points can often be revised to support a controlling idea. For example, the point that grasshoppers have a tough outside shell would be relevant if the writer related that fact to the theme of stress.

Passage revised for unity:

> . . . Last year these monstrous insects devoured two-thirds of my plants. Scientists estimate that nine grasshoppers per square yard will do more damage than a grazing cow, and yesterday I counted seventeen grasshoppers on one head of lettuce. If the destruction of my garden weren't source of enough stress, grasshoppers are also like a Chinese water torture. When I walk through the fields in late August, giant, thumb-sized grasshoppers crash into my face and chest. *Their tough external shells* make them pebble-sized missiles, hard and stinging against my skin. They don't inflict the physical pain of a horsefly bite but the psychological pain of an incessant enemy beating me down with dull thuds, like the relentless dripping of water. I can't even lie in my hammock without a dozen or so grasshoppers crashing into my forehead as I try to doze off. [In this version the writer uses the fact that grasshoppers have tough external shells to increase the reader's appreciation of the impact as they crash into the writer's body; thus the shells become relevant to the paragraph's point about stress.]

Exercise 2-2 Recognizing irrelevant details

The following passages, originally written by professional writers, have been altered through the addition of irrelevant details. Cross out the irrelevant sentences.

Example:
It is essential to use good videotape if you hope to preserve the video recordings you make for a long time. ~~For example, some people I know have made copies of TV movies which they plan to keep for ten or twenty years.~~ Even if you just record TV shows for one-time later viewing, poor grades of tape can cause premature head wear, leading to replacement of the entire head assembly, or, at the very least, may shorten the number of hours you can operate your VCR without having to clean the tape heads. Not surprisingly, some of the manufacturers of high-quality audiotape also produce videotape of superior quality and durability. [Len Feldman, *Science Digest* (July 1983).]

1. There are three major risk factors that increase your chances of having a stroke or heart attack—cigarette smoking, high blood cholesterol, hypertension or high blood pressure. Along with heredity and diabetes, these in large part determine whether you are at high or low risk for having cardiovascular disease. Of course cigarette smoking also plays a major role in the onset of lung cancer. Obesity, physical inactivity, and stress play a lesser role in determining your susceptibility to heart disease.

2. Of these three major risk factors, hypertension is the most common and perhaps the most dangerous. About 60 million Americans have a blood pressure above 140/90—the dividing line between a normal and high pressure. There are currently fewer statistics on the incidence of high blood cholesterol, and doctors aren't completely sure yet of the effect of high cholesterol on our susceptibility to heart disease. A normal pressure for an adult male may be as low as 90/60, though 120/80 is the usual level. As the pressure rises, the heart must pump harder, and the blood vessels are pounded harder with every heartbeat. After many years, the heart may enlarge and finally weaken, while the blood vessel walls roughen or rupture. Thereby, a heart attack or stroke will develop. Perhaps a vigorous exercise program will retard these effects. [Paragraphs 1 and 2 based on Norman M. Kaplan, *Saturday Evening Post* (October 1982).]

3. In fact, television has helped to create a comeback for magic in America. Of course television has also revolutionized children's education through such programs as *Sesame Street*. The adaptation to television of the ancient arts of illusion, escape, and conjuring is producing the first superstar magicians since Houdini died in 1926. Houdini is still probably the most famous magician who ever lived. The three top magic acts—Doug Henning, David Copperfield, and Siegfried & Roy—have all starred in primetime network-television specials. More people have seen their magic in one night than saw Houdini in his lifetime. [John Culhane, "Magic's Amazing Comeback," *Reader's Digest* (April 1983)].

Exercise 2-3 The relationship between details and meaning

A paragraph has meaning only because the details in the body of the paragraph support the point expressed in the topic sentence. The following exercises will help you appreciate how the meaning you intend must shape your selection of details. Each of the exercises asks you to write two paragraphs that are based on the same set of data. However, because the paragraphs begin with different topic sentences, you must select and arrange the data differently.

Pair 1: The Death Rate Table

Write two paragraphs — A and B below. Both paragraphs are based on the accompanying table showing death rates for selected diseases from 1910 to 1966. However, the paragraphs must begin with the different topic sentences provided. Select data from the table to create paragraphs that appropriately support each of the assertions.

The following table lists the death rates (per 100,000 population) and the causes of death from 1910 to 1966 in the United States. Fetal deaths are not included.

Death Rates Per 100,000 Population

Year	All causes	Cardiovascular diseases	Malignant neoplasms	Certain diseases of early infancy	Influenza and pneumonia	Diabetes	Bronchitis and emphysema	Accidents	All other
1910. . . .	1,468	287	76.2	73.0	155.9	15.3	—	84.2	776
1920. . . .	1,299	283	83.4	69.2	207.3	16.1	—	70.0	570
1930. . . .	1,132	328	97.4	49.6	102.5	19.1	—	79.8	456
1935. . . .	1,095	353	108.2	40.2	104.2	22.3	—	77.8	388
1940. . . .	1,076	407	120.3	39.2	70.3	26.6	—	73.2	340
1942. . . .	1,032	409	122.0	41.4	55.7	25.4	—	71.3	309
1943. . . .	1,087	439	124.3	41.3	67.1	27.1	—	73.4	315
1945. . . .	1,058	444	134.0	38.3	51.6	26.5	—	72.1	292
1948. . . .	989	437	134.9	42.1	38.7	26.4	—	66.9	243
1949. . . .	971	485	138.8	43.2	30.0	16.9	2.8	60.6	194
1950. . . .	964	494	139.8	40.5	31.3	16.2	2.8	60.6	178
1951. . . .	967	499	140.6	41.2	31.4	16.3	3.0	62.5	173
1952. . . .	961	499	143.4	40.9	29.7	16.4	3.1	61.8	168
1953. . . .	959	503	144.8	40.1	33.0	16.3	3.6	60.1	158
1954. . . .	919	485	145.6	39.4	25.4	15.6	3.6	55.9	149
1955. . . .	930	496	146.5	39.0	27.1	15.5	4.1	56.9	145
1956. . . .	935	501	147.8	38.6	28.2	15.7	4.6	56.7	142
1957. . . .	959	515	148.6	39.1	35.8	16.0	5.5	55.9	143
1958. . . .	951	516	146.8	39.8	33.1	15.9	6.2	52.3	141
1959. . . .	939	509	147.3	38.5	31.2	15.9	6.6	52.2	138
1960. . . .	955	515	149.2	37.4	37.3	16.7	7.6	52.3	139
1961. . . .	930	505	149.4	35.9	30.1	16.4	7.8	50.4	134
1962. . . .	945	515	149.9	34.5	32.3	16.8	9.2	52.3	135
1963. . . .	961	521	151.3	33.2	37.5	17.2	10.9	53.4	137
1964. . . .	940	509	151.3	31.5	31.1	16.9	11.1	54.3	135
1965. . . .	943	511	153.5	28.6	31.9	17.1	12.6	55.7	133
1966. . . .	954	520	154.8	26.1	32.8	18.1	—	57.3	146

Here are your two topic sentences. (Use your own paper to write the paragraphs.)

A. "As the table shows, death rates from some diseases have declined sharply from 1910 to 1966 while the death rates from other diseases have increased just as sharply."

B. "Although the death rates for most diseases followed predictable patterns from 1910 to 1966, the death rate pattern for one disease — diabetes — seems mysterious."

Pair 2: Two Letters of Recommendation

You are an assistant professor of management in the School of Business at Whacko University. Three years ago you had a student, Randy Smith, who left a strong impression on your memory. Here are some facts and impressions you recall about Smith.

- Very temperamental student (not a typical business type), seemed moody, something of a loner.
- Long hair and very sloppy dress — seemed like a misplaced street person; looked like he was on drugs.
- Absolutely brilliant mind; took lots of liberal arts courses and applied them to business.
- Wrote a term paper comparing different management styles and relating these to modern theories of psychology.
- This was the best paper you had ever received. You gave it an A+ and remembered learning a lot from it yourself.
- The paper was very well written. Smith had a strong command of language.
- Smith was also good at mathematics and could handle all the statistical aspects of the course.
- Frequently missed class and once told you that your class was boring.
- Didn't show up for the midterm. When he returned to class later, he explained only that he had been out of town. You let him make up the midterm, and he got an A.
- He didn't participate in a group project required for your course. He said the other students in his group were jerks.
- You thought that Smith didn't have a chance of making it in the business world because he had no "human relationship" skills — a genius but no talent at getting along with people.
- Other professors had the same opinion of Smith — brilliant, but rather odd and hard to like; a strange duck.

Now select details from this list to support assertions for letters of recommendation in each of the following cases. (Use your own paper.)

1. Randy Smith, still as sloppy as ever, approaches you to write him a letter of recommendation for graduate school in economics at a prestigious university. He tells you that he has a 3.85 grade point average and that his ambition is to become a college professor. The graduate school limits your recommendation to one paragraph. Write your recommendation beginning with a topic sentence that you must compose yourself.

2. One day you receive in the mail a request from the Whacko National Bank. Randy Smith has applied for a job as a management trainee, and the bank seeks your confidential recommendation. It especially wants your assessment of Smith's dependability, attitude, and ability to work with people. You haven't seen Randy for three years. You are in a dilemma because you want to give the kid a chance (maybe he has had a transformation in his personality), but you also don't want to damage your own professional reputation by falsifying your true impressions. Once again, you are limited to a single paragraph. Write your recommendation to the bank.

2B Use a variety of methods to achieve coherence in an essay.

A paragraph is said to have *coherence* if the reader can readily follow the chain of thought from the beginning to the end, seeing how each sentence connects to preceding and following sentences and also to the topic sentence. An illustration of the difference between unity and coherence will be helpful.

Version A: Passage without unity or coherence

The grading system doesn't help us develop thinking skills. Grasshoppers also annoy me. When flying in airplanes, you can practice strategies for making essays easier to write. Apples don't have Nutrasweet. [Here the order and selection of sentences is totally random.]

Version B: Passage without unity but with apparent coherence

The present grading system doesn't help us develop thinking skills. Thinking skills are of course important for success in most kinds of jobs. Success in a job also depends on one's personality and physical appearance. You will look best in clothes tailored to fit your own personal shape. You can improve your body shape with exercise. Perhaps the best kind of exercise is aerobics. . . . [Here each sentence is linked to a previous sentence by the repetition of a key thought (one of the attributes of coherence), but the sentences don't stay focused on a single point. The passage wanders from thinking skills, to physical appearance, to choice of clothes, to exercise. Thus the passage lacks unity and has only the surface appearance of coherence.]

Version C: Passage with unity but without coherence

The present grading system doesn't promote risky thinking. Paul gets almost straight A's. He takes careful notes in class and always sides with the teacher during class discussions. He also takes good reading notes. He is very good at taking objective tests. Another example of this is Sam. He once tried to invent a perpetual motion machine, and he always argues with his teachers during class discussions. He is genuinely imaginative and has the characteristics of a creative problem-solver. [This passage seems to focus on a central idea — that the grading system doesn't promote risky thinking — but it lacks coherence because the reader can't see how all the parts fit together. Important links seem to be missing from the argument; the meaning doesn't flow smoothly and clearly from beginning to end.]

Version D: Same passage revised to show both unity and coherence

The present grading system fosters conventional thinking rather than risky thinking. Paul, for example, gets straight A's, but he doesn't seem to exhibit truly imaginative thinking. Rather, he has mastered the skills for getting good grades. He listens carefully to lectures and takes elaborate reading notes from his textbooks. In class discussions, he regularly sides with the teacher and doesn't risk voicing his own opinions. He thrives on machine-gradable objective tests, which reward students who absorb information. In test after test Paul's careful assimilation of facts pays off. In contrast is Paul's fellow student Sam, who seems to struggle to get B's and C's. Sam would rather daydream than listen to a lecture, yet on many occasions you will get from Sam a spark of imagination seldom seen in Paul. Sam will argue with his teachers — "Mr.

Jones, I don't think your explanation accounts for this point"—and he once spent two whole days trying to invent a perpetual motion machine when his science teacher told him such machines were impossible. Sam seems to be genuinely imaginative, a natural question-asker and problem-solver, yet our present grading system makes him look less intelligent than Paul. [Now the passage is both unified and coherent: It focuses on a single point (unity), and the reader can now see how each of the sentences contributes to the point (coherence).]

1 Achieve coherence by arranging paragraph ideas in a logical order.

There are dozens of ways to arrange ideas logically within a paragraph. Descriptive paragraphs are often arranged by spatial order and narrative paragraphs by time order. Expository paragraphs often begin with a general statement followed by supporting details, but sometimes they begin with the details and eventually lead up to the general statement. Many kinds of paragraphs begin by announcing their shape ("The present grading system creates three kinds of problems"; "I support Senator Snorkle for two reasons"), so that the paragraph divides neatly into the number of predicted subparts.

The previous example paragraph on the grading system arranges its details into two parts—a section on Paul, who represents conventional thinking and high grades, and a section on Sam, who represents imaginative thinking and low grades.

2 Create coherence by using pronouns to link ideas.

An effective way to show the reader that you are sticking to the same topic within a chain of sentences is to use pronouns that refer to a noun used earlier. In the paragraph about Paul and Sam, note how often the pronouns *he* and *him*, referring to Paul in the first section and to Sam in the second, help the reader keep the sections distinct and focused.

3 Achieve coherence by repeating important words and phrases.

Within most coherent paragraphs, the central idea will receive frequent repetition, either by a direct repetition of key words or by the use of close synonyms. In the Sam and Paul paragraph, the section on Sam, who represents imaginative thinking, contains a variety of words and phrases associated with imagination—*daydream, spark of imagination, argue, invent, genuinely imaginative.*

4 Achieve coherence by using parallel structures.

This method cannot be used in all paragraphs but is useful whenever the writer develops two or more related points or supports a single point with several similar details. By casting the sentences in grammatically parallel structures, the writer emphasizes the way their meanings are related. (See Chapter 14.) The Sam and Paul passage above uses parallelism extensively in the Paul section, where the series of sentences about Paul all have a subject-verb opening ("Paul gets. . . ." "He has mastered. . . ." "He listens . . . and takes. . . ." "He . . . sides. . . ." "He thrives. . . .").

5 Achieve coherence by using appropriate transitional expressions.

In version C of the Paul and Sam paragraph, the writer calls Sam "another example" of how the grading system does not promote risky thinking. This transition implies that Paul and Sam are similar, when in fact they are supposed to be different. To make the logical connection clear, in version D the writer uses the phrase *in contrast* when introducing Sam.

>*In contrast* is Paul's fellow student Sam, who seems to struggle to get B's and C's.

Transition words are thus important ways of helping readers see the connection between one part of a paragraph and another. Here is a short list of transitions.

To show addition

also, and, and then, as well, besides, beyond that, furthermore, in addition, moreover, what is more

To show sequence

first (second, third), next, then, following, finally, last

To show similarity

also, as well, both, in the same way, likewise, similarly

To show contrast

although, be that as it may, but, even though, however, in contrast, nevertheless, on the contrary, on the other hand, yet, whereas

To show concession (concede a point)

although, granted, of course, no doubt, to be sure

To show emphasis

above all, especially, in fact, in particular, indeed, most important, surely

To show an example

as a case in point, as an illustration, for example, for instance, in particular, one such, yet another

To show location

above, beside, below, beyond, further, here, inside, nearby, next to, on the far side, outside

To show consequence

as, because, for, since, as a consequence, as a result, consequently, for this reason, hence, so, therefore, thus

To summarize

all in all, finally, in brief, in other words, lastly, on the whole, to sum up, in sum

To show time

after a while, afterward, at last, at present, before, briefly, currently, during, eventually, finally, gradually, immediately, in the future, later, meanwhile, previously, simultaneously, recently, soon, suddenly

---

6 Achieve coherence by linking ideas together from one paragraph to the next.

Just as ideas must be clearly linked within a paragraph, so must ideas be linked between paragraphs. In a short, tightly constructed essay, the beginning of a new paragraph will typically make three kinds of links: Some part of the transition will refer to the previous paragraph; some part will refer to the thesis statement of the essay; and some part will point to the topic of the upcoming paragraph.

Let's assume for the moment that the Paul and Sam paragraph occurred in the middle of an essay with the following thesis statement:

The current grading system has three major disadvantages.

Given this context the opening sentence of the Paul and Sam paragraph might become:

Another problem with the present grading system is that it promotes conventional rather than risky thinking.

The word *another* is a link to the previous paragraph, reminding readers that that paragraph also was about a problem with the grading system and that the present paragraph will be about *another* problem. The words *problem with the grading system* refer to the thesis statement, which predicted that three such problems would be addressed. Finally the words *conventional rather than risky thinking* point to the new argument about to be revealed in this paragraph.

Given this plan, the paragraph following the Sam and Paul paragraph might begin as follows:

. . . Sam seems to be genuinely imaginative, a natural question-asker and problem-solver; yet our present grading system makes him look less intelligent than Paul.

A third major problem with the grading system is that it leads to excessive cheating. . . .

OR

Besides its tendency to promote unhealthy competition and to encourage conventional thinking, the grading system also leads to excessive cheating. [The first version uses the transition *third* to link backward, telling the reader that we are now moving to the last of the three predicted "problems with the current grading system." The second version ties the argument even more tightly together by briefly summarizing the first and second problems. What do you think was the topic sentence of the paragraph discussing the first problem?]

Exercise 2-4   Use of linking and transitional devices within a paragraph

To improve your skills at creating coherent paragraphs, you should get the feel of how transitions work. This exercise should help. Write a sentence, clause, or phrase of your own that could logically follow each of the transitional expressions below.

Example:
I like living in the dorm; however, *I wish they would enforce quiet hours more.*

1. I like living in the dorm, so

2. I like living in the dorm; nevertheless,

3. I like living in the dorm, but

4. I like living in the dorm. For example,

5. I like living in the dorm because

6. I like living in the dorm. On the other hand,

7. I like living in the dorm. In addition,

8. Although I like living in the dorm,

9. I would like living in the dorm if

10. I like living in the dorm; moreover,

11. I like living in the dorm. For this reason

12. I like living in the dorm for a variety of reasons. First,

13.

In sum, I like living in the dorm.

14. I like living in the dorm. Similarly,

15. I like living in the dorm this term. Last term, however,

Exercise 2-5   Appreciating linking devices in a paragraph

A. In the following paragraph, various kinds of linking devices have been omitted. Fill in the blanks with words or phrases that would serve to make the paragraph coherent. Clues are provided in brackets.

Example:

Molly is a friendly person. *For example* [example], _____*she*_____ [pronoun] recently invited a foreign student to dinner and _____*also*_____ [addition] invited along two students from her math class. *In addition* [addition], _____*she*_____ [pronoun] was voted the "most friendly senior" for her caption in the high school yearbook. *However* _____ [contrast], when _____*she*_____ [pronoun] gets mad, _____*she*_____ [pronoun] is a vixen.

1. Writing an essay is a difficult process for most people. _____ [contrast] the _____ [synonym for "difficult process"] can be made easier if you learn to practice three simple techniques. _____ [sequence] learn the _____ [repetition of key word from previous sentence] of nonstop writing. When you are first trying to think of ideas for an essay, put your pen on your paper and write nonstop for ten or fifteen minutes without ever letting your pen leave the paper. *Being loose and free is an advantage. You can let your pen follow the waves of thought in your mind. Grammar and spelling shouldn't be worried about.* [Recast the preceding italicized sentences so that their structure is parallel to the previous imperative sentence "put your pen on your paper. . . ."] _____ [concession] this technique won't work for everyone, it helps many people get a good cache of ideas to draw on. ⋀ _____ [sequence] _____ [repetition of key word from topic sentence] is to write your rough draft rapidly without worrying about being perfect. Too many writers try to get their drafts right the first time. _____ [contrast] you will save yourself headaches and a wastepaper basket full of crumpled paper if you learn to live with imperfection. Think of your first rough draft as a path hacked out of the jungle—as part of an exploration, not as a completed highway. As a _____ [sequence] _____ [repetition of key word from topic sentence], try double-spacing your rough drafts. Many beginning writers don't leave enough space to revise. _____ [consequence] these writers never get in the habit of crossing out chunks of their rough draft and writing revisions in the blank spaces. After you have revised your handwritten rough draft until it is too messy to work from any more, you can _____ [addition] type a fresh draft setting your typewriter on triple space. The resulting blank space invites you to revise.

B. Another technique for appreciating linking devices within a paragraph is to reorder a "scrambled" paragraph. The following passages are paragraphs written by professional writers. However, the order of the sentences has been scrambled. Place the sentences in the correct order, indicating your answer by writing the correct sequence of sentence numbers in the space provided.

2. (1) Some birds, such as the ibis of Egypt, were considered sacred. (2) The dove long has been a symbol of peace. (3) The legend that storks bring babies is a modern vestige of this old myth. (4) Ancient peoples regarded the arrival and departure of birds as omens of future events and thus as creatures of magical powers. (5) Many sailors still believe that it is bad luck to harm one of these great soaring birds. (6) Many European peoples believe that a stork nest on a roof means good luck. (7) (Of course, the owl isn't more or less wise than any other bird.) (8) The owl is often regarded as a symbol of wisdom. (9) Since ancient times, sailors have had many superstitions about the albatross.

Correct order (list sentence numbers):

3. (1) There are also a number of cases where one or two people claim to have been taken aboard an alien spaceship, prodded and probed with unconventional medical instruments, and released. (2) To the best of my knowledge there are no instances out of the hundreds of thousands of UFO reports filed since 1947 in which many people independently and reliably report a close encounter with what is clearly an alien spacecraft. (3) Flying saucers, or UFO's, are well known to almost everyone. (4) It might, for example, be an automobile headlight reflected off a high-altitude cloud, or a flight of luminescent insects, or an unconventional aircraft, or a conventional aircraft with unconventional lighting patterns, such as a high-intensity searchlight used for meteorological observations. (5) But seeing a strange light in the sky does not mean that we are being visited by beings from the planet Venus or a distant galaxy named Spectra. (6) But in these cases we have only the unsubstantiated testimony, no matter how heartfelt and seemingly sincere, of one or two people. [Based on a paragraph from Carl Sagan, *Broca's Brain.*]

Correct order (list sentence numbers):

2C Develop paragraphs in sufficient detail and with appropriate form.

1 Develop your paragraphs adequately by using concrete sensory details, statistics, cases, examples, quotations, paraphrases, or summaries to support your points in a paragraph.

Perhaps the most frequent source of unsuccessful student writing is the lack of specific detail. Compare the Sam and Paul paragraph in the previous section with the following version, which is weak on detail.

> The present grading system fosters conventional thinking rather than risky thinking. Proof of this assertion is that Paul, who is a conventional thinker, gets high grades, while Sam, who is a risky thinker, gets low grades.

This writer makes the mistake of believing that readers are convinced by dogmatic assertions rather than by details and evidence. What is the evidence that Paul is a conventional thinker? How do we know that Sam is a risky thinker? Note how the previous version of this paragraph (pages 71–72) fleshes out these assertions with details.

2 Choose an appropriate form to develop your paragraphs.

Although no one can identify all possible ways of developing paragraphs, a few conventional methods are useful to consider, such as description, narration, process analysis, comparison, classification, causal analysis, and definition. Examples of these kinds of paragraphs can be found in *The McGraw-Hill College Handbook* as well as in most other handbooks.

2D Construct opening and closing paragraphs that suit your thesis and that hold your readers' attention.

Paragraphs that open and close essays usually use different strategies from those of body paragraphs.

In an introductory paragraph you usually have three goals:

1. To attract the reader's interest and attention. (You can begin with a colorful story or quotation or use some other technique to hold your reader's interest.)
2. To provide background and other preliminary information to set the stage for your argument. (How much background you need depends on your intended audience and the complexity of your essay.)
3. To provide your thesis statement. (A powerful position for a thesis statement is the last sentence of the opening paragraph, but of course you have many other options.)

Concluding paragraphs are sometimes tricky. Occasionally a conventional essay will use a simple summary of the argument as the conclusion, but most essayists strive for a more imaginative conclusion. One technique is to relate your topic to a broader context of issues, in effect answering the question "Why is my essay important?" "What larger issues have I raised?" Another technique is to conclude with an appropriate anecdote or quotation to create a memorable final impression.

Exercise 2-6   Expanding underdeveloped paragraphs

The following paragraphs are promising but underdeveloped. Expand them appropriately, inventing any details you need. Use your own paper for this exercise.

1. As a result of the university's faculty development program, Professor Hopkins has improved considerably as a classroom teacher. Several years ago students complained a lot about him. Now he says he feels a lot more comfortable in the classroom. These improvements are the result of the specific training he received in conducting a class.

2. Current TV ads create "superwomen" who are impossible role models for most women to live up to. One ad shows a beautiful woman who is a successful lawyer by day and glamorous lover by night. Thus the women's liberation movement took us out of one stereotype and has thrust us into an even more disheartening stereotype.

2E Revise a loose paragraph for unity, coherence, and development.

The principles in this chapter should now help you revise paragraphs in your own essays. Look carefully at the paragraph units in your rough drafts and ask yourself the following questions about them.

- Does each paragraph have a controlling idea? Have I stated it clearly in a topic sentence?
- Do all the sentences in this paragraph develop this controlling idea? Do I have any irrelevant sentences?
- Is my paragraph easy for a reader to follow? Have I provided transitions and other linking devices to make my ideas coherent?
- Is my paragraph sufficiently developed? Can I make it more convincing by adding specific details?

Exercise 2-7 Revising loosely constructed paragraphs

The following student paragraphs are promising but exhibit problems in unity, coherence, or development. Revise the paragraphs using the strategies suggested in this chapter. (Use your own paper for the revisions.)

1. You don't have to vote regularly. You can be a good citizen by doing other things. Volunteering to coach youth soccer or little league baseball is one thing. You can spend Saturday afternoon helping to clean up the trash in a vacant lot. Organizations such as Big Brothers and Big Sisters need volunteer help. I think the editorial is wrong in complaining that people who don't vote are necessarily poor citizens.

2. Writing summaries of class lectures improved my thinking and learning habits in several ways. I weed out most of the questions I have about the subject. I noted in my summary any uncertainties I found in the lecture material and then quickly found the answers through further research. Another thing is that summaries helped me to learn the subject matter by tying up loose ends and bringing the material into a more organized pattern. At times my lecture notes tend to wander and not make much sense—especially when looking at them after a few weeks. Simply being forced to organize my thoughts into one general idea while the material is still fresh in my mind has helped me understand the subject a lot better. Making summaries of lectures has helped me to realize how very methodical and boring taking lecture notes can be. After reading through and writing the summary for a lecture in music, I realized how dull and Mickey Mouse the course really is. The notes showed nothing more than simple regurgitation of definitions. I feel this is the professor's fault, because music should be fun and interesting, not just something immaterial on paper. In general, summarizing lectures has helped me to learn the subject matter better. I found myself looking deeper into what was being said instead of seeing the facts on a surface level.

Exercise 2-8 Revising paragraphs in context

The following draft of a student essay might well be developed into a superior piece of writing. At this stage, however, the writer has problems with paragraphing and development. Write the next draft of the essay, focusing on creating unified, coherent, and sufficiently developed paragraphs. You can either add details to paragraphs or combine paragraphs as you see fit. Use your own paper.

What Makes a Good Teacher?

Imagine yourself scurrying across campus on a rainy, spring morning. Although you would rather be at home watching soap operas, you would feel guilty about missing class. And yet the class is so boring that you feel angry about going.

After locating a seat in the crowded room, you watch your professor shuffle in and begin his lecture in a droning, monotone voice. Because he reads straight from note cards, he mumbles and hesitates whenever he misplaces one of them. Professors like this are all too common.

The university needs to establish a training program to help lecturers. This training program should give a teacher good public speaking techniques and also show teachers ways to involve students more actively in a lecture.

The art of public speaking combines varied techniques. One such technique is the use of many references, such as guest speakers. Another technique is to use your own experiences. This helps the listener to better visualize the point being made. In Biology 105, Dr. Jefferson often uses humor to relieve the tension and make a potentially boring subject come alive. If instructors can incorporate these things into a lecture, they will make their lectures more interesting.

You can involve students in a lecture by using the ''feedback system.'' This technique is used by my chemistry lecturer.

After twenty minutes or so the instructor stops and asks students to write for five minutes on what is confusing them. Then he collects about ten of the writings. At the beginning of the next class he answers questions raised in the feedback.

Another teacher asks students to work in small groups for a while.

In conclusion, teachers would be better if they learned better public speaking techniques and involved students more actively in the class.

3
Sentence Grammar

By *grammar* we mean the set of rules in any language for combining words into patterns that can convey meanings. In English, these rules govern both the order of words and the endings we place on words. Students often complain that they don't understand grammar, but the truth is that all of us learned grammar when we learned to talk. If we didn't know grammar, neither of the following groups of words would make sense:

a. Complain don't that grammar often they understand all at students.

b. Students often complain that they don't understand grammar at all.

If group b makes more sense to you than group a, you understand grammar. What people mean, then, in saying that they don't understand grammar is that they don't understand the terms and concepts that language teachers use to describe grammatical rules, even though their minds internalized those rules when they first learned to talk. The rest of this chapter will help you understand the way language teachers describe the patterns that can occur in English sentences.

3A   Learn the basic structure of the English sentence.

A sentence is a group of related words that names something (the *subject*) and then makes an assertion about the thing named (the *predicate*).

Name something	Make an assertion about it
Cheese	tastes good on crackers.
Lizards and snakes	are both kinds of reptiles.
Capital punishment	has been outlawed in many countries.

A sentence tells you that the subject does something or that something is done to the subject or that the subject exists in a certain way. Sentences can also ask questions or give commands.

Are lizards and snakes both reptiles?

Put some cheese on this cracker. [In commands, the word *you* is an understood subject.]

1 Learn to recognize subjects and predicates.

By definition every sentence must include at least one subject and one predicate. One way to locate subjects and predicates is to ask two questions about a sentence.

> **1.** Who or what is the sentence about? (subject)
> **2.** What assertion does the sentence make about the subject? (predicate)

Tree ants in Southeast Asia construct nests by sewing leaves together.

What is this sentence about? *Tree ants in Southeast Asia* (subject). What assertion is made about tree ants? [They] *construct nests by sewing leaves together* (predicate).

NOTE: Grammarians sometimes distinguish between simple and complete subjects and between simple and complete predicates. In the above sentence *ants* is the simple subject, while *tree ants in Southeast Asia* is the complete subject (the simple subject plus all its modifiers). A simple predicate is the verb phrase that makes the assertion about the subject. In the above example, *construct* is the simple predicate, while *construct nests by sewing leaves together* is the complete predicate (simple predicate plus modifiers and nouns needed to complete its meaning).

Another way to locate subjects and predicates is to begin by finding the verb at the heart of the predicate. There are several ways to find verbs:

By Meaning

Look for the words that express an action (tree ants *construct* nests) or a state of being (tree ants *are* interesting).

By Structure

> **1.** Look for the word that changes form when you change the time of a sentence. (Yesterday tree ants *constructed* nests; tomorrow tree ants *will construct* nests.)
> **2.** See if the word you are testing makes sense in combination with the pronouns *I; you; he, she,* or *it; we; you;* and *they.* (I *construct,* you *construct,* he *constructs.*)
> **3.** Check for the presence of helping verbs (and helping verb clusters) that are often used as part of a verb phrase. Although a single word by itself is often used as a verb (tree ants *construct* nests), more often verbs are preceded by helping verbs, which together with the main verb form a verb phrase. (Tree ants *might contruct* nests; *should construct* nests; *will have constructed* nests; *are constructing* nests; and so forth.) The common helping verbs and helping verb clusters are *am, is, are, was, were, shall, will, could, would, have, had, has, do, does, did, be, been, might, must, may, am (is, are) about to* (a helping verb cluster, as in "I am about to cry"), *am (is, are) going to* (as in "I am going to cry"), and *ought to* (as in "I ought to cry").

Once you find the verb in a sentence, you can usually locate the subject by asking a question beginning with *who* or *what* followed by the verb.

> Some insects *attract* mates by smell. [What attract mates by smell? Some insects. *Insects* is the simple subject of *attract.*]
>
> A termite fortress, walled and buttressed, *can contain* ten tons of mud. [What can contain ten tons of mud? A termite fortress. *Fortress* is the simple subject of *can contain.*]

Ordinarily a sentence begins with the subject, followed by the verb. But sometimes the word order can be changed. In the following examples, the subjects are underscored once and the verbs are underscored twice.

Normal word order:

> The most terrifying insects wander through the countryside seeking prey.

Question:

> What are the most terrifying insects?

Inverted order:

> Across the jungles of Africa marched the driver ants.

"There" opening:

> There are various kinds of terrifying insects.

Sentences can also have more than one subject or predicate:

Compound subject:

> The army ants of South America and the driver ants of Africa march in long columns.

Compound predicate:

> The hunters at the head of a column discover prey, swarm all over it, and eventually cut it apart.

Exercise 3-1 Self-study: Locating subjects and predicates

A. In the following sentences, draw a line between the complete subject and the complete predicate. Then underline the simple subject once and the simple predicate twice.

Answer column

1. The college radio station broadcast an unusual message.

2. Susan laid her head upon her husband's shoulder.

3. The man in the blue suit walked slowly toward the elevator.

4. A disagreement between an employer and an employee can often be resolved through communication.

5. The framing of the United States Constitution is one of the most amazing achievements in all of history.

1. The college radio station|broadcast an unusual message.

2. Susan|laid her head upon her husband's shoulder.

3. The man in the blue suit|walked slowly toward the elevator.

4. A disagreement between an employer and an employee|can often be resolved through communication.

5. The framing of the United States Constitution|is one of the most amazing achievements in all of history.

B. In the next sentences, underline the simple subject once and the simple predicate twice. All these sentences will have a word order different from the normal subject-predicate pattern.

6. Where has Sam gone?

7. Under the shade of the cottonwood tree on the old, broken-armed lawn chair sat my Uncle Jake.

8. There are many reasons for the failure of this year's basketball team.

9. In the final games of the season did Coach Jones use an appropriate strategy to break the opponent's zone press defense?

10. There can be no doubt about the team's complete loss of morale.

6. Where <u>has</u> <u>Sam</u> <u>gone</u>?

7. Under the shade of the cottonwood tree on the old, broken-armed lawn chair <u>sat</u> my <u>Uncle Jake</u>.

8. There <u>are</u> many <u>reasons</u> for the failure of this year's basketball team.

9. In the final games of the season <u>did</u> <u>Coach Jones</u> <u>use</u> an appropriate strategy to break the opponent's zone press defense?

10. There <u>can be</u> no <u>doubt</u> about the team's complete loss of morale.

C. The following sentences have compound subjects, predicates, or both. Underline simple subjects once and simple predicates twice.

11. Long lines at the gasoline pumps and skyrocketing fuel costs shocked Americans into a recognition of the energy crisis.

12. In desperation about the declining prospects for jobs, thousands of unemployed workers milled about aimlessly in front of employment offices or gathered in saloons and pool halls to discuss the grim future of their country.

13. The chattering sound began out in the neighbor's barn but then moved mysteriously from the barn to the house and then across the field to the old tool shed.

14. The Corps of Engineers and the Bureau of Reclamation are both paying more attention to environmental considerations as a result of lobbying by conservation groups.

15. The fighter plane dove, turned, darted, climbed, and then dove again toward the asphalt runway.

11. Long <u>lines</u> at the gasoline pumps and skyrocketing fuel <u>costs</u> <u>shocked</u> Americans into a recognition of the energy crisis.

12. In desperation about the declining prospects for jobs, <u>thousands</u> of unemployed workers <u>milled</u> about aimlessly in front of employment offices or <u>gathered</u> in saloons and pool halls to discuss the grim future of their country.

13. The chattering <u>sound</u> <u>began</u> out in the neighbor's barn but then <u>moved</u> mysteriously from the barn to the house and then across the field to the old tool shed.

14. The <u>Corps of Engineers</u> and the <u>Bureau of Reclamation</u> <u>are</u> both <u>paying</u> more attention to environmental considerations as a result of lobbying by conservation groups.

15. The fighter <u>plane</u> <u>dove</u>, <u>turned</u>, <u>darted</u>, <u>climbed</u>, and then <u>dove</u> again toward the asphalt runway.

D. The following series of word groups are all punctuated like sentences. Some of the word groups are sentences because they have at least one complete subject and one complete verb. However, some of the word groups are not sentences because they lack either a subject or a predicate or both. Identify which word groups are sentences and which are not.

16. His fears were irrational.	**16.**	sentence
17. Flying home from college on vacation after the last of the final examinations.	**17.**	nonsentence
18. By the late seventies, people began taking occasional shooting incidents as just facts of life.	**18.**	sentence
19. In talking to my teacher about my grade on the last paper.	**19.**	nonsentence
20. I settled into a seat near the aisle.	**20.**	sentence

E. Write sentences of your own that contain each of the following word groups.

Example:
in the cupboard are

The dishes in the cupboard are quite valuable.

21. on the shelf of the closet Ralph

22. has been lying to me every day

23. rapidly across the street

24. there are three

25. down the hill sped

2 Learn to recognize the basic English sentence patterns.

All sentences by definition must have a complete subject and a complete predicate. However, the predicates of sentences can take several different shapes depending on whether or not there is a noun or adjective in the predicate needed to complete the sense of the verb. These words are called **complements.** The kinds of complements that can occur in sentences are direct objects, indirect objects, subjective complements, and objective complements.

Pattern one: subject + verb

The dog barked.
The eagle soared gracefully across the summer sky.

In pattern one, no complement occurs in the predicate, which contains only a verb phrase and various adverbial modifiers. Because the verb in this pattern does not transfer any action from a doer to a receiver, it is called **intransitive.**

Pattern two: subject + verb + direct object *(DO)*

DO
The dog chased the cat.

DO
Peter was fixing a flat tire over in Bronco County at the very moment of the crime.

Direct objects occur with transitive verbs, which transfer action from a doer (the subject) to a receiver (the direct object). **Transitive verbs** don't seem complete in themselves; they need a noun or pronoun *following* the verb to answer the question "what?" or "whom?" The dog chased what? The cat. Peter was fixing what? The flat tire.

Pattern three: subject + verb + subjective complement *(SC)*

SC
My mother is a professor.

SC
The engine in this car seems sluggish.

Verbs in pattern three sentences are called **linking verbs,** which are followed by subjective complements rather than direct objects. Unlike direct objects, which receive the action of the verb, subjective complements either describe or rename the subject. You can best understand a subjective complement if you think of the linking verb as an equals sign (=). The following example shows the difference between a direct object and a subjective complement:

Direct object:

DO
My mother slaps the professor.
[Mother and professor are two different people. Mother does the action of slapping, and the professor receives that action.]

Subjective complement:

SC
My mother is a professor.
[Mother = professor.]

Subjective complement:

SC
My mother is extremely intelligent.
[Mother = intelligent.]

Pattern four: subject + verb + direct object + objective complement (OC)

$$\text{That } \underline{\text{woman}} \; \underset{DO}{\underline{\underline{\text{called}}}} \; \underset{OC}{\text{me an idiot.}}$$

That <u>woman</u> <u><u>called</u></u> ^{DO}me an ^{OC}idiot.

Last summer <u>we</u> <u><u>painted</u></u> ^{DO}our house ^{OC}green.

Whereas a subjective complement describes the subject of the sentence, an objective complement describes the direct object, either by modifying it or by renaming it. Compare the patterns:

^{SC}
<u>I</u> <u><u>am</u></u> an idiot.
[pattern three]

^{DO} ^{OC}
The <u>woman</u> <u><u>called</u></u> me an idiot.
[pattern four]

^{SC}
Our <u>house</u> <u><u>is</u></u> green.
[pattern three]

^{DO} ^{OC}
We <u>painted</u> our house green.
[pattern four]

Pattern five: subject + verb + indirect object (IDO) + direct object

My <u>mother</u> <u><u>sent</u></u> the ^{IDO}professor an angry ^{DO}letter.

My <u>father</u> <u><u>baked</u></u> ^{IDO}me a ^{DO}cake on Valentine's Day.

Sometimes transitive verbs take an indirect object as well as a direct object. Whereas the direct object answers the question "what?" or "whom?" following the verb, the indirect object answers the question "to what or whom?" or "for what or whom?" My mother sent what? A letter (direct object). She sent a letter to whom? The professor (indirect object). My father baked what? A cake (direct object). My father baked a cake for whom? For me (indirect object).

Exercise 3-2 Self-study: Identifying sentence patterns

In the following sentences underline simple subjects once and simple predicates twice. Then label direct objects *DO*, indirect objects *IDO*, subjective complements *SC*, and objective complements *OC*. Finally, identify each sentence as pattern one, two, three, four, or five.

Answer column

1. The owner of the bakery closed the shop early on this cold winter's night.

1. The <u>owner</u> of the bakery <u><u>closed</u></u> the ^{DO}shop early on this cold winter's night. (two)

2. The dog walked slowly across the yard toward the alley.

3. The woman walked her dog slowly across the yard toward the alley.

4. I am very happy for you.

5. I am dedicating this song to you.

6. I will write you a new song.

7. That man called my new song a disaster in the key of G.

8. With a twinkle in her eye, the mother gave her married daughter some advice about the meaning of cooperation.

9. He has a reputation for bullheadedness on issues like these.

10. Even his friends call him bullheaded.

11. In his own mind, however, he is the very picture of cooperation and compromise.

12. Few of the truly great leaders in history were great or popular in the eyes of their comtemporaries.

13. Except for a two-hour break, Jefferson, Sam, Lurinda, and Molly had been working on the project for twenty-three hours straight.

2. The <u>dog</u> <u>walked</u> slowly across the yard toward the alley. (one)

3. The <u>woman</u> <u>walked</u> her dog *DO* slowly across the yard toward the alley. (two)

4. <u>I</u> <u>am</u> very happy *SC* for you. (three)

5. <u>I</u> am <u>dedicating</u> this *DO* song to you. (two)

6. <u>I</u> will <u>write</u> you *IDO* a new song. *DO* (five)

7. That <u>man</u> <u>called</u> my new song *DO* a disaster *OC* in the key of G. (four)

8. With a twinkle in her eye, the <u>mother</u> <u>gave</u> her married daughter *IDO* some advice *DO* about the meaning of cooperation.

9. <u>He</u> <u>has</u> a reputation *DO* for bullheadedness on issues like these. (two)

10. Even his <u>friends</u> <u>call</u> him *DO* bullheaded *OC*. (four)

11. In his own mind, however, <u>he</u> <u>is</u> the very picture *SC* of cooperation and compromise. (three)

12. <u>Few</u> of the truly great leaders in history <u>were</u> great *SC* or popular *SC* in the eyes of their comtemporaries. (three)

13. Except for a two-hour break, <u>Jefferson</u>, <u>Sam</u>, <u>Lurinda</u>, and <u>Molly</u> <u>had been working</u> on the project for twenty-three hours straight. (one)

14. Sarah Clemson, the leader of this temporary group of pranksters, saw the van and both trucks in a vacant lot on 7th Street.

14. <u>Sarah Clemson</u>, the leader of this temporary group

                                  DO   *DO*

of pranksters, <u>saw</u> the van and both trucks in a vacant lot on 7th Street. (two)

3B Learn the traditional eight parts of speech.

The traditional eight parts of speech are *verbs, nouns, pronouns, adjectives, adverbs, conjunctions, prepositions,* and *interjections.* Many words can serve as different parts of speech in different sentences, so you can determine what part of speech a word plays only within the context of the sentence you are examining. Each part of speech serves a different meaning function in a sentence and also possesses structural features that distinguish it from the other parts of speech. Thus we can talk about both the *meaning* and *structure* of a part of speech.

Verbs

Verbs are identified by *meaning* as words expressing action *(run, laugh)* or state of being *(is, seem).* They are identified by *structure* as words that change form to indicate tense and sometimes to indicate person and number. Verbs also occur commonly in verb phrases beginning with helping verbs. (See 3A, section 1.)

In two tenses, the simple present and the simple past, the main verb of a sentence can be conveyed with one word only.

I *run.* I *laugh.* I *ran.* I *laughed.*

In all other tenses, the main verb of a sentence needs helping verbs to convey its meaning.

I *have run.* I *will have laughed.* I *ought to laugh.* She *had been running* for two hours. I *will have been laughing.* We *must laugh.*

See Chapter 7 for a full discussion of verb tenses.

Nouns

Nouns are identified by *meaning* as the names we give to persons *(Samuel, mechanic),* places *(Yellowstone,* the *forest),* things (a *rock,* two *potatoes),* or abstract concepts *(love, happiness).* Nouns can be identified by *structure* as words which follow the articles *a, an,* or, *the;* as words which change their form to indicate number; and as words which change their form to indicate possession.

Three Tests for Nouns

1. Use *a, an,* or *the* before the word.
   a *frog* [yes]   an *apple* [yes]   a *went* [no]   a *because* [no]
2. Make the word plural.
   Two *frogs* [yes]   two *apples* [yes]   two *wents* [no]   two *becauses* [no]
3. Make the word possessive.
   the *frog's* warts [yes]   the *apple's* taste [yes]   the *went's* ? [no]   the *because's* ? [no]

Pronouns

Pronouns take the place of nouns in sentences. The noun replaced by a pronoun is called the pronoun's **antecedent. Personal pronouns** refer to people *(I, you, she, he, we,* and *they)* and to animals or things *(it, they* and sometimes *he, she).* **Indefinite pronouns** *(anybody, someone)* do not have definite noun antecedents. **Reflexive pronouns** serve as indirect or direct objects and refer to the subject, indicating that the subject is doing action to itself. (I hit *myself* with the hammer.) **Intensive pronouns** also end in *self* and give special emphasis to the preceding noun or pronoun. (I *myself* will select the next committee.) **Demonstrative pronouns** *(this, those)* point out or emphasize the following noun. **Possessive pronouns** *(my, his)* show ownership or special relations. **Interrogative pronouns** *(who, which, what)* ask questions. **Relative pronouns** *(who, whom, whose, which,* and *that)* introduce subordinate clauses used as adjectives.

Adjectives and Adverbs

Adjectives and adverbs are said to *modify* other words, that is, to describe them more fully by adding special qualifications to them.

Adjectives modify nouns by answering such questions as "which ones?" *(those* rabbits), "what kind?" *(gentle* rabbits), "how many?" *(four* rabbits), "what size?" *(tiny* rabbits), "what color?" *(white* rabbits), "what condition?" *(contented* rabbits), or "whose?" *(Sally's* rabbits).

A special class of adjectives is called **articles** *(a, an, the). A* and *an* are indefinite and singular. They precede nouns that name a whole class of objects without indicating that a particular one is meant *(an* apple, *a* pickle). *The* is definite and can be either singular or plural. It always specifies that a particular object is meant *(the* apple, *the* pickles).

Adverbs modify verbs, adjectives, or other adverbs. They answer the questions "how?" (He petted the rabbit *gently*), "how often?" (He petted the rabbit *frequently*), "where?" (He petted the rabbit *there* in the corner of the room), "when?" (He petted the rabbit *early*), and "to what degree?" (He petted the rabbit *very* gently).

A distinctive structural feature of adjectives and adverbs is that they take *positive, comparative,* and *superlative* forms.

Positive:

> This is a quick turtle.
>
> It moves quickly.

Comparative:

> My turtle is quicker than yours.
>
> It moves more quickly than yours.

Superlative:

> Of the three turtles, mine is the quickest.
>
> Of all the turtles in the race, mine moves most quickly.

Some adverbs modify whole clauses by showing logical relationships between clauses or sentences. These are **conjunctive adverbs** (such as *therefore, however, moreover).*

Conjunctions

Conjunctions join elements within a sentence. **Coordinating conjunctions** *(and, or, nor, but, for, yet,* and *so)* join elements of equal importance.

> John *and* Mary went to town.
>
> Exhausted *but* happy, the team returned home.
>
> The city rejoiced, *for* the rats had finally been exterminated.

Subordinating conjunctions (such as *when, unless, if, because, after, while, although*) turn an independent sentence into a subordinate clause and then join it to a main clause. (See section 3C following.)

> *After* I get off work, I will buy you a Coke.
>
> She won't fix his typewriter *unless* he apologizes.
>
> *If* you are going to the city, please get me a new album at Caesar's.

Prepositions

Prepositions show the relationship between a noun or pronoun (called the **object** of the preposition) and the rest of the sentence. The preposition and its object are called a **prepositional phrase.** Common prepositions include *about, above, across, among, behind, between, from, in, into, of, on, toward,* and *with.*

> The cat walked *under* the table.
>
> The vase was *on* the table.
>
> I inherited the table *from* my grandmother.
>
> The table is a mixture *of* cherry and walnut woods.

Interjections

Interjections *(yippee, baloney, ouch)* are forceful expressions, usually followed by exclamation marks, that express emotion. They can be removed from a sentence without affecting the sentence grammatically.

> *Hooray,* school's out!
>
> *Ah, shucks,* I'm sorry!

> Remember that in the English language words can often serve as different parts of speech depending on the slots they fill in a sentence.

> I just finished the wash. [*Wash* is a noun.]
>
> I will wash the dishes. [*Wash* is a verb.]

Exercise 3-3   Self-study: Identifying parts of speech

In the following exercises, identify the parts of speech as indicated.

1. Identify the words in the following list that could serve as verbs in a sentence. Test each of the words by seeing if you can add *ed* to change it from present time to past time *(juggle, juggled)* or by seeing if it makes sense when joined with personal pronouns *(I juggle, you juggle, she juggles, we juggle, you juggle, they juggle).* The answers are on the right.

of	morsel	touch	laugh	shove
bunny	destroy	play	destroy	listen
ugly	butterfly	gopher	touch	play
laugh	terrible	jump	jump	wash
shove	listen	wash		

2. Identify which words in the following list could serve as nouns in a sentence. Test each word by seeing whether you can place *a, an,* or *the* in front of it (*the* gopher); whether you can make it plural (*two* gophers); or whether you can make it possessive (the *gopher's* hole).

beautiful	although	daughter	chain	shoe
chain	for	hasten	pickle	book
eat	book	quickly	daughter	log
shoe	happily	crystallize		
pickle	forever	log		

3. In the following list identify possible adjectives and adverbs. Adjectives and adverbs answer the questions listed on page 92. Most adjectives and adverbs can also be identified by seeing if they will fit in the following slots:

Adjectives:

It/she usually seems _____ . [It usually seems *hot.* She usually seems *happy.* It usually seems *ugly.*]

Adverbs:

It/she will do the task _____ . [She will do the task *tomorrow.* She will do the task *reluctantly.*]

In the following list, first locate all potential adjectives; then find all potential adverbs.

cold	happily	stupid	*Adjectives:*	cold
unusual	soon	stupidly	unusual	quiet
cow	quiet	stupidity	stupid	friendly
lady	matter	although		nervous
hit	friendly	nervous	*Adverbs:*	happily
			soon	stupidly

4. In the list below, find all potential prepositions. It is somewhat more difficult to find single tests for prepositions, but the general concept of prepositions becomes clear if you try these two tests. Prepositions identifying spatial relationships will fit this slot:

The cat walked _____ the table. [*on* the table, *under* the table]

Prepositions identifying time relationships will fit this slot.

We will talk _____ dinner. [*after* dinner, *during* dinner]

Not all prepositions will fit these slots, but all of them will be followed by a noun or pronoun (the object of the preposition) to form a prepositional phrase. Many prepositions can be more than one word (*next to, along with*).

ugly	because	bullet	beside	under
beside	when	comfort	before	after
under	after	toward	of	toward
golf	of	beneath	beneath	next to
before	if	next to		

5. In this exercise identify conjunctions. Like prepositions, conjunctions indicate relationships, and so no one pattern sentence will provide a sure test for all conjunctions. However, you can get a feel for conjunctions by trying the two following patterns.

Conjunctions that indicate a time relationship will usually fit the following slot.

You can call Susan _____ you finish dinner. *[as soon as, after]*

Conjunctions that indicate a logical relationship will usually fit the following slot.

You want (don't want) to buy a car _____ you have (don't have) the money. *[and, but, for, because]*

butterfly	if	garbage	when	before
happily	of	laugh	because	if
when	yet	soon	yet	while
before	tomorrow	although	although	
because	while	do		

6. Write a sentence of your own that follows this pattern:
Article adjective noun preposition article noun helping verb adverb main verb article noun.

Example:

The large cow in the field was contentedly munching the grass.

7. Write a sentence that follows this pattern:
Adjective adjective article noun verb preposition article noun conjunction verb article noun.

Example:

Tired, lost, the hunters sat on the ground and consulted a map.

In the following sentence identify the part of speech played by each word by placing the appropriate symbol above the word:

N = noun   *PN* = pronoun   *ADJ* = adjective   *AV* = adverb   *V* = verb   *P* = preposition
C = conjunction
Label articles *(a, an the)* and possessive pronouns *(my, his, our,* etc.) as adjectives.

Example:

    PN V V   V   N AV   P ADJ ADJ ADJ N

8. She has been skipping rope happily for the last two hours.

    ADJ   N   P ADJ N   V   ADJ   P

9. The students in my class seemed unhappy about
the test and complained to the dean.

(Answer column)

    ADJ   N   P ADJ N   V   ADJ   P

9. The students in my class seemed unhappy about

    ADJ N   C   V   P ADJ N

the test and complained to the dean.

10. Because the six oak chairs were too expensive,
we bought a simple rocking chair instead.

    C   ADJ ADJ ADJ   N   V   AV   ADJ

10. Because the six oak chairs were too expensive,

    PN   V ADJ ADJ   ADJ   N   ADV

we bought a simple rocking chair instead.

3C Learn the difference between phrases and clauses.

Phrases and clauses are both groups of related words. However, a phrase does not contain a subject and a complete verb, while a clause does. Some clauses can therefore stand alone as sentences *(main clauses)*. All phrases, as well as those clauses that cannot stand alone as sentences *(dependent clauses),* operate as a part of speech within a sentence.

1 Learn to recognize the basic kinds of phrases and to appreciate their uses.

Prepositional Phrases

A preposition connects a noun, pronoun, or group of words acting as a noun to the rest of the sentence, thereby creating a prepositional phrase that serves as a part of speech within the sentence, usually as an adjective or an adverb. Prepositional phrases usually begin with the preposition and end with the noun or noun substitute, called the object of the preposition.

> We watched the baby crawl *under the table.* [*Under the table* serves as an adverb, telling *where* the baby crawled.]

> The man *in the gray suit* is my father. [*In the gray suit* serves as an adjective describing *man.*]

Verbal Phrases

Verbals are *incomplete* forms of verbs that can't function as predicates in a sentence. They function instead as other parts of speech — nouns, adjectives, and adverbs. Verbals act partly like verbs in that they can show tense and can take complements; but they also act like nouns, adjectives, or adverbs in that they serve as other parts of speech in a sentence. When a verbal is accompanied by modifiers or complements, the word group is called a **verbal phrase.** There are three kinds of verbals and verbal phrases:

Participles and participial phrases

Participles are of two kinds: the present participle, which is the *ing* form of a verb *(swimming, laughing),* and the past participle, which is the *ed* form of the verb for regular verbs *(laughed)* and an irregular form for irregular verbs *(laughed, swum)*. Participles and participial phrases always act as adjectives in a sentence.

> I saw some ducks *swimming in the lake.* [The participial phrase *swimming in the lake* modifies ducks.]
>
> *Laughing happily,* Molly squeezed Jake's arm. [*Laughing happily* modifies *Molly.* See Chapter 10 for a discussion of participial phrases at the beginning of sentences.]
>
> The 100-meter freestyle, a race *swum by more than twenty competitors last year,* was won by a thirteen-year-old boy. [*Swum by more than twenty competitors* modifies *race.*]
>
> *Having swum more than 100 meters,* Molly suddenly got a cramp. [The opening participial phrase modifies *Molly.* In this example, the participle *swimming* is placed in the past tense, *having swum.*]

Gerunds and gerund phrases

Gerunds are always the *ing* form of the verb, and they always serve as nouns in a sentence.

> *Swimming* is my favorite sport. [Gerund serves as subject.]
>
> I love *swimming in the lake.* [Gerund phrase serves as direct object.]
>
> I am not happy about *losing my chemistry notebook over in the Student Union.* [Gerund phrase serves as object of preposition *about.* In this example the gerund *losing* has a direct object *notebook.*]

Infinitives and infinitive phrases

An infinitive is the dictionary form of a verb preceded by the word *to (to run, to swim, to laugh).* Infinitives or infinitive phrases can serve as nouns, adjectives, or adverbs in a sentence.

> *To complete college with a major in electrical engineering* is my primary goal at the moment. [Infinitive phrase serves as a noun in the subject slot. *College* is the direct object of the infinitive *to complete.*]
>
> She wants *to dance.* [Infinitive serves as the direct object of *wants.*]
>
> The person *to help you with that math* is Molly Malone. [Infinitive phrase acts as an adjective modifying *person. You* is the direct object of *to help.*]

NOTE: Like all verbals, infinitives regularly have complements such as direct objects or subjective complements. However, infinitives also can take subjects.

> Molly wants *Jim to do the typing.* [At first it might seem that *Jim* is the direct object of *wants* and that *to do the typing* modifies Jim. However, Molly doesn't want Jim; she wants the typing done. Moreover she wants Jim to do it. For this reason most grammarians call *Jim* the subject of the infinitive *to do.* This distinction matters when you choose the case of a pronoun (see Chapter 8, where subjects of infinitives take the objective case—"Molly wants *him* to do the typing").]

Absolute Phrases

An absolute phrase begins with a noun or noun substitute followed by a participle. An absolute phrase may seem like a sentence because it appears to have a subject; however, the phrase lacks a predicate because the verb form is a verbal instead of a complete verb.

Sentence:

His face is flushed with sweat.

Absolute phrase:

His face flushed with sweat, the runner headed down Grant Street.

Sentence:

The wind whipped her parka.

Absolute phrase:

The wind whipping her parka, Ruth Jensen tucked into the turn and swooped toward the finish line.

Exercise 3-4 Self-study: Identifying phrases

A. In this group of sentences identify all prepositional phrases by underlining them. (In the answer column, the phrases will appear in italics.)

Answer column

1. Under the branches of the old apple tree in back of the house are two buckets of apples and a box of pears.

   1. *Under the branches/of the old apple tree/in back of the house* are two buckets *of apples* and a box *of pears.*

2. Please go into the shed and find the jar of nails that I left when I was roofing the house.

   2. Please go *into the shed* and find the jar *of nails* that I left when I was roofing the house.

3. The little girl in the green dress just asked me if I had seen her box of crackers.

   3. The little girl *in the green dress* just asked me if I had seen her box *of crackers.*

B. In this group of sentences identify verbals and verbal phrases and label them as gerunds, participles, infinitives, or absolutes. Underline the verbal itself and place the whole verbal phrase in brackets. (In the answer column, the verbals will appear in italics.) Then write *P, G, I,* or *A* above the verbal to indicate participle, gerund, infinitive, or absolute. Finally, explain what function the verbal serves in the sentence.

4. The singing birds warbled in the trees planted fifty years ago by my grandfather.

   P (modifies "birds")   (modifies "trees") *P*

   4. The [*singing*] birds warbled in the trees [*planted* fifty years ago by my grandfather].

5. Right now I want to see Bertha more than anything else in the world.

6. To see Bertha is all I ask.

7. Seeing Bertha is all I ask.

8. Watching carefully as she crossed the street, my little sister headed for the post office, a letter clutched in her hand.

9. Wishing for a new job, George decided to go to the employment agency.

10. Becoming a major league baseball player was all my cousin Joe ever thought about, even though his older brother told him to put his energy into becoming a boxer.

I (direct object of "want")

5. Right now I want [*to see* Bertha] more than anything else in the world.

I (subject)

6. [*To see* Bertha] is all I ask.

G (subject)

7. [*Seeing* Bertha] is all I ask.

P (modifies "sister")

8. [*Watching* carefully as she crossed the street], my little sister headed for the post office, [a letter

A

clutched in her hand].

P (modifies "George")   (direct object of "decided") *I*

9. [*Wishing* for a new job], George decided [*to go* to the employment agency].

G (subject)

10. [*Becoming* a major league baseball player] was all my cousin Joe ever thought about, even though his

I (direct object of "told")

older brother told [him *to put* his energy into

G (object of preposition "into")

[*becoming* a boxer]].

Exercise 3-5 Self-study: Creating verbal phrases

A. In the following exercise, combine the short sentences into a single sentence that contains the kinds of verbal phrases specified. Your answers may vary from the models.

Answer column

1. The cowboy leapt into the saddle. Then he rode off into the sunset. (participle)

1. Leaping into the saddle, the cowboy rode off into the sunset.

2. The little girl tried something. She turned a somersault. (infinitive)

2. The little girl tried to turn a somersault.

3. She turned a somersault successfully. She jumped up. Her teeth flashed a happy smile. (participle, absolute phrase)

3. Turning a somersault successfully, the little girl jumped up, her teeth flashing a happy smile.

4. The girl skated on the pond. The pond was snow-covered. She began something. She did figure eights. Her body spun with perfect coordination. (participle, infinitive, absolute)

4. The girl skating on the snow-covered pond began to do figure eights, her body spinning with perfect coordination.

5. The family believed in Santa Claus. This was a strong tradition. (gerund)

5. For this family, believing in Santa Claus was a strong tradition.

B. In this exercise, combine the short sentences in any way that seems appropriate. Include at least one verbal phrase in each response. Your answers may vary from the models.

6. The speaker said the following: People have their traditions. These traditions are snatched from them. This happens when these people live under communism.

6. According to the speaker, people living under communism have their traditions snatched from them.

7. Some people cling to their family traditions. This can give them comfort. But this can also limit their freedom.

7. Clinging to family traditions can be both comforting and limiting.

8. The airplane touched down on the runway. It then lost a wheel. Then it began to fishtail. Its left wing came dangerously close to the ground.

8. Touching down on the runway, the plane lost a wheel and began to fishtail, its left wing coming dangerously close to the ground.

2 Learn the basic kinds of clauses and their uses.

Unlike phrases, clauses have subjects and complete predicates. *Main,* or *independent,* clauses can stand alone as a sentence. *Subordinate,* or *dependent,* clauses, however, cannot stand alone because they are introduced with a subordinating word such as a subordinating conjunction or a relative pronoun.

Main clause

> Sam broke the window.
> Lucy studied the violin for thirteen years.

Subordinate clause

> because Sam broke the window [Subordinating conjunction *because* reduces main clause to a subordinate clause.]
> who studied the violin for thirteen years [Replacement of *Lucy* by relative pronoun *who* reduces main clause to a subordinate clause.]

Subordinate clause attached to main clause

> *Because Sam broke the window,* he had to pay for it out of his allowance. [Subordinate clause modifies *had to pay,* answering the question *why.*]
> Lucy, *who studied the violin for thirteen years,* won a music scholarship to a prestigious college. [Subordinate clause modifies *Lucy.*]

> Subordinate clauses always act as nouns, adjectives, or adverbs in another clause.

Noun clauses

Noun clauses act as subjects, objects, or complements.

> He promised *that he would study harder.* [direct object of *promised*]
>
> *Why he came here* is a mystery. [subject of *is*]
>
> He lied about *what he did last summer.* [object of preposition *about*]

Adjective Clauses

Adjective clauses are formed with the relative pronouns *who, whom, whose, which,* and *that.* For this reason they are sometimes called **relative clauses.**

> Peter, *who is a star athlete,* has trouble with reading. [modifies *Peter*]
>
> The man *whose car was stolen* is the deputy sheriff. [modifies *man*]

Adverb Clauses

Adverb clauses are introduced by subordinating conjunctions, such as *although, because, if,* and *when.* (See page 114 for a list of subordinating conjunctions.)

> *Because he had broken his leg,* he danced all night with crutches. [an adverb telling *why* he danced with crutches]
>
> *When he got home,* he noticed unusual blisters. [adverb modifying *noticed*]

3D Learn to identify sentences as simple, compound, complex, or compound-complex.

A sentence is *simple* if it consists of a single independent clause. The clause can contain many modifying phrases and can also have a compound subject and a compound predicate.

> John laughed.
>
> John and Mary laughed and sang.
>
> Laughing happily and holding hands in the moonlight, John and Mary walked along the beach, wrote their names in the sand, and threw pebbles into the crashing waves.

A sentence is *compound* if it consists of two independent clauses linked either by a semicolon or by a comma and a coordinating conjunction. Again, each clause can contain many modifying phrases as well as compound subjects and predicates.

> John laughed, and Mary sang. [Compare with "John and Mary laughed and sang," which is a simple sentence.]
>
> Laughing happily, John took Mary's hand and led her toward the beach, for the night was beautiful. [The coordinating conjunction *for* links the two independent clauses.]

A sentence is *complex* if it contains one independent clause and one or more subordinate clauses.

> John laughed while Mary sang. [*While Mary sang* is a subordinate clause.]

After they walked along the beach, laughing and singing in the moonlight, John and Mary returned to the campfire, where they snuggled together in the shadows. [The main clause *John and Mary returned to the campfire* is modified by two subordinate clauses beginning with *after* and *where*.]

A *compound-complex* sentence has at least one subordinate clause and two or more main clauses joined by a semicolon or by a comma and coordinating conjunction.

John laughed while Mary sang, for he was happy.

After John and Mary walked along the beach in the moonlight, they returned to the campfire; later, they roasted marshmallows over the glowing coals.

Exercise 3-6 Self-study: Identifying kinds of clauses

In the following sentences, underline all subordinate clauses and then write above them whether they are noun, adjective, or adverb clauses. (In the answer column, the clauses will appear in italics.)

Answer column

1. Kate walked into the room with tears in her eyes.

2. She smiled at one of her sorority sisters and then sat on a davenport and began crying uncontrollably.

3. When Susan saw Kate in tears, she put her arms on Kate's shoulders and asked if she could help.

4. Then Kate, who had been studying at the library until it closed, began telling her story.

5. As she was walking back from the library, she had to cross the old faculty parking lot, which had been unlighted ever since the repair crew damaged an electrical cable two months earlier.

6. A man wearing a dark T-shirt and jeans had leaped at her from behind a parked car and threatened to hurt her if she didn't do what he asked.

Answer column
1. Kate walked into the room with tears in her eyes.
2. She smiled at one of her sorority sisters and then sat on a davenport and began crying uncontrollably.

3. *adverb clause*
When Susan saw Kate in tears, she put her arms on
noun clause (direct object of "asked")
Kate's shoulders and asked *if she could help.*

4. *adjective clause*
Then Kate, *who had been studying at the library/*
adverb clause
until it closed, began telling her story.

5. *adverb clause*
As she was walking back from the library, she had
adjective
to cross the old faculty parking lot, *which had been*
clause   *adverb*
unlighted/ever since the repair crew damaged an
clause
electrical cable two months earlier.

6. A man wearing a dark T-shirt and jeans had leaped at her from behind a parked car and threatened to
adverb clause   noun clause (direct object of "do")
hurt her *if she didn't do/what he asked.*

7. That he had a knife wasn't all that terrified Kate. He also had a wild look in his eye that made him seem wicked and irrational.

noun clause   adjective clause
7. *That he had a knife* wasn't all *that terrified Kate.*

adjective
He also had a wild look in his eye *that made him*

clause
seem wicked and irrational.

8. At first Kate didn't know how she should respond.

noun clause (direct object of "know")
8. At first Kate didn't know *how she should respond.*

9. Then suddenly she screamed and kicked her assailant just below the belt; he bent over, cursing violently, while she started running toward the lighted entrance to the science building.

9. Then suddenly she screamed and kicked her assailant just below the belt; he bent over, cursing violently, *while she started running toward the lighted*

adverb

clause
entrance to the science building.

10. When she was safe in her sorority house, Kate, with Susan's help, called the police to report what had happened and then called the RAPE hotline, which had been recently installed by the women's resource center.

adverb clause
10. *When she was safe in her sorority house,* Kate,

noun
with Susan's help, called the police to report *what*

clause (direct object of "to report")
had happened and then called the RAPE hotline,

adjective
which had been recently installed by the women's

clause
resource center.

Exercise 3-7   Identifying and creating simple, compound, complex, or compound-complex sentences

A. Identify the next five sentences as simple, compound, complex, or compound-complex.

	Answer column
1. Kate was brave to report the assault suffered in the old faculty parking lot.	simple
2. However, her sorority sisters still argue about whether she made the right decision to kick her assailant and then run for safety.	complex
3. Because the assailant had a knife and because he seemed so irrational, the assailant was clearly dangerous, and therefore Kate risked death in attacking him.	compound-complex
4. Some rape counselors believe that it is better to go along with the assailant, even if that means rape, than to try to overpower the assailant or to escape if the assailant seems likely to inflict serious injury.	complex
5. However, Kate believes in the rightness of her actions, for she acted on instinct, not on the ground of a rational decision.	compound

B. In this exercise, combine the short sentences into a single sentence of the type indicated. Answers may vary.

6. He staked out a plot of ground. After that he cleared away the trees. (simple)

6. After staking out a plot of ground, he cleared away the trees.

7. He asked three girls to the senior prom. They all turned him down. (compound)

7. He asked three girls to the senior prom, but they all turned him down.

8. She discussed her problem with an attorney. She was uncertain about her legal rights. However, she didn't have much money. (complex)

8. Although she didn't have much money, she discussed her problem with an attorney because she was uncertain about her legal rights.

9. Carrie Nation had a belief. God had called her to destroy saloons. This belief was widely applauded in her time. She influenced the thinking of many Americans in the prohibition movement. Undoubtedly she seems ridiculous in retrospect. (compound-complex)

9. Although Carrie Nation may seem ridiculous in retrospect, her belief that God called her to destroy saloons was widely applauded in her time, and she influenced the thinking of many Americans in the prohibition movement.

10. The female belted kingfisher lays six to eight pure white eggs. She lays them on a bed of regurgitated fishbones. This bird is distinguished by a rusty band across her breast. (simple)

10. The female belted kingfisher, distinguished by a rusty band across her breast, lays six to eight pure white eggs on a bed of regurgitated fishbones.

Exercise 3-8   Mastery exercise: Sentence grammar

A. In the following sentences underline the simple subject once and the simple predicate (complete verb) twice. Then identify all complements by placing *DO* above direct objects, *IDO* above indirect objects, *SC* above subjective complements, and *OC* above objective complements.

Example:

She showed the crowd her dog's new trick.
(IDO above "the crowd", DO above "trick")

1. Slowly, sadly, the woman behind the counter showed her driver's license to the police and admitted the truth.

2. That man in the sweat pants and Adidas shirt called me a liar.

3. I am not a liar, so I will steadily deny any accusations to the contrary.

4. The billowy white clouds floated gracefully across the deep-blue Kansas sky.

5. Across the shadows of the long auditorium aisle came the limping janitor, yet his partner did not even notice him.

B. In this exercise, which uses the same sentences as in the preceding exercise, identify the part of speech of each word by placing *N* above nouns, *PN* above pronouns, *ADJ* above adjectives, *AV* above adverbs, *P* above prepositions, and *C* above conjunctions. Label articles and possessive pronouns as adjectives.

Example:

PN V ADJ N ADJ ADJ ADJ N
She showed the crowd her dog's new trick.

6. Slowly, sadly, the woman behind the counter showed her driver's license to the police and admitted the truth.

7. That man in the sweat pants and Adidas shirt called me a liar.

8. I am not a liar, so I will steadily deny any accusations to the contrary.

9. The billowy white clouds floated gracefully across the deep-blue Kansas sky.

10. Across the shadows of the long auditorium aisle, came the limping janitor, yet his partner did not even notice him.

C. In the following sentences place brackets around all subordinate clauses and underline all verbal phrases. Indicate whether subordinate clauses are noun, adjective, or adverb by writing *N, ADJ,* or *ADV* in the space above the clause. Similarly, indicate whether the verbal phrases are participial, gerund, infinitive, or absolute by writing *P, G, I,* or *A* above each phrase. Finally, in the space at the right, indicate whether the sentence is simple, compound, complex, or compound-complex.

Example:

AV   AV   I
[When you get right down to it,]college is extremely difficult[if you hope to do well].   *complex*

11. Melinda didn't care about college very much.   _____

12. Although Melinda didn't care much about college, she cared deeply about how she was going to explain to her father her grades for last semester.   _____

13. Traveling around the city by subway to do research for her sociology paper, Melinda soon discovered that learning about the city was exciting, while writing research papers was drudgery.

14. In one sense she wasted her time, yet in another sense she learned a great deal. _____

15. Understanding the complexity of the city was not something that she could learn in books. _____

16. So she called her father, her hands trembling, to tell him about the two F's. _____

17. She wanted to tell her mother mainly, but it was her father who paid her college tuition. _____

18. After her parents' divorce, Melinda felt closer to her mother than to her father, but her father's business success made him the family's main source of money. _____

19. Her father was surprisingly understanding; it turned out later that her mother was most upset about the grades. _____

20. What her father had never told her was that he had flunked out of college twenty years earlier. _____

4
Correcting Run-ons and Comma Splices

Writers make comma splices and run-on errors whenever they fail to show that one sentence is ending and another is beginning. These errors can lead to considerable confusion for readers.

A *comma splice* occurs when a writer marks the end of a sentence with a comma instead of a period.

> The weather is beautiful, my neighbor is washing her car. [The two independent sentences "The weather is beautiful" and "My neighbor is washing her car" are spliced together with a comma. The writer has failed to show readers that one sentence is ending and another beginning.]

A *run-on error* occurs when two sentences are run together without any punctuation.

> The weather is beautiful my neighbor is washing her car. [Here there is no punctuation at all between the sentences.]

METHODS OF CORRECTION

Run-ons and comma splices can be corrected in a variety of ways depending on the context of surrounding sentences and the meaning you wish to convey. Sometimes you may choose to separate the ideas by placing them in two separate sentences. At other times you may wish to join the ideas into a single sentence using one of several options, again depending on the meaning you intend. What follows is an explanation of the different ways you can correct a comma splice or run-on. Any of these methods will be grammatically correct. You should choose, however, the method that best fits the rhetorical context of the passage you are writing.

4A Separate sentences with a period and a capital letter.

> The weather is beautiful. My neighbor is washing her car. [Here the writer shows that the ideas are not closely related and hence belong in two separate sentences.]

4B Join sentences with a comma and a coordinating conjunction.

> This method creates a compound sentence with two independent clauses. You should memorize the coordinating conjunctions *(and, or, nor, but, for, so, yet)*. When

using *so, yet,* or *for,* you may need to change the order of the sentences to create the intended logic.

> The weather is beautiful, and my neighbor is washing her car.

> My neighbor is washing her car, for the weather is beautiful.

> The weather is beautiful, so my neighbor is washing her car. [In these versions the writer has decided not to separate the sentences but to join them in order to show that the ideas are closely related. The *and* in the first example shows that the writer considers the two ideas as a single unit with equal emphasis on each part. The examples using *for* and *so* highlight a cause-and-effect relationship between the ideas.]

4C Join sentences with a semicolon.

This method also creates a compound sentence with two independent clauses. If you wish to indicate a logical relationship between the two clauses, you can add a *conjunctive adverb* (words like *therefore* or *nevertheless*) somewhere in the second clause.

> The weather is beautiful; my neighbor is washing her car.

> The weather is beautiful; therefore my neighbor is washing her car. [The semicolon places distinct emphasis on each of the clauses as separate units and yet indicates a close relationship between them.]

4D Join sentences with a subordinating conjunction or a relative pronoun.

This method creates a complex sentence with an independent clause and a subordinate clause. Or turn one of the sentences into a phrase, thereby creating a simple sentence with an added or embedded phrase.

Subordinating Conjunction

> Because the weather is beautiful, my neighbor is washing her car.

> My neighbor is washing her car because the weather is beautiful. [In these examples the main focus of the sentence is on the neighbor washing the car. The beautiful weather is cited as the cause of the neighbor's action but is not important for its own sake.]

PUNCTUATION POINTER: If the sentence begins with a subordinate clause, the subordinate clause should be followed by a comma; if the subordinate clause comes at the end of the sentence, do not use a comma unless the subordinating conjunction expresses a contradiction or change in the direction of thought (for example, the subordinating conjunction *although*).

Relative Pronoun

Comma splice:

> My neighbor is washing her car, she just returned from a mountain camping trip.

Correction:

> My neighbor, who just returned from a mountain camping trip, is washing her car. [The pronoun *she* has been replaced with the relative pronoun *who*; the

relative clause is then inserted after *neighbor*. In this sentence the fact that the neighbor just returned from a camping trip is treated as extra information that is secondary to the main point that she is washing her car.]

Conversion into a Phrase

Because of this beautiful weather, my neighbor is washing her car. [The independent sentence "The weather is beautiful" is changed to a prepositional phrase *because of this beautiful weather.* The emphasis is on the neighbor washing her car, with the beautiful weather treated as a reason.]

Having just returned from a mountain camping trip, my neighbor is washing her car. [The independent sentence "She just returned from a mountain camping trip" is changed to a participial phrase *having just returned from a mountain camping trip.* The writer implies that the mountain camping trip is a cause for washing the car—perhaps the car got dirty during the camping trip.]

GRAMMATICAL CORRECTNESS VERSUS MEANING

Although each of the above methods will produce a grammatically correct solution, your actual choice will depend on the meaning and emphasis you intend. Note in the following passages the ways the writer has chosen to join or separate the two ideas used in our examples—the beautiful weather and the neighbor washing her car.

It is a great day. The weather is beautiful. My neighbor is washing her car. Kids are playing in the street. The dog is sleeping in the sun. [Here the focus is on the writer's sense of a great day. The beautiful weather and the neighbor washing her car are only two of four separate pieces of evidence the writer uses to support the feeling. By putting them all in separate sentences the writer emphasizes each one.]

I open my front door and walk out onto the lawn, stretching and blinking in the morning sun. A little girl bounces her ball on the sidewalk, happy for the summer. Across the street my neighbor is washing the car, for the weather is beautiful. It is good to be alive. [Here the beautiful weather is seen as a cause for the neighbor's washing her car because the word *for* indicates a cause-and-effect relationship. But because *for* is a coordinating conjunction, the whole clause *the weather is beautiful* receives emphasis as a main point in the sentence. The writer feels and appreciates the beautiful weather just as the neighbor does.]

I was hoping to invite my neighbor over to watch the football game with me this afternoon. But because the weather is beautiful, she is washing her car. [Here the main point is the writer's disappointment that the neighbor isn't coming over to watch football. Once again the beautiful weather is the cause of her washing the car, but the subordinating conjunction *because* makes that information secondary. The writer isn't interested in the beautiful weather for its own sake, and hence the coordinating conjunction *for* would be less appropriate.]

My neighbor told me that she wanted to wash her car but that if it rained she planned to go shopping. Well, this morning the weather is beautiful; therefore, she is washing her car. [The conjunctive adverb *therefore,* like the coordinating conjunction *for* or the subordinating conjunction *because,* shows a cause-and-effect relationship. But the strongly emphatic word *therefore* calls attention to the logical link between the clauses. The writer isn't savoring the weather, but emphasizing a logical argument.]

These differences may seem subtle, yet they illustrate the extent to which writers have options. Punctuation is primarily a way of controlling and signaling meaning for readers. As you learn ways of correcting comma splices and run-ons, you will also become aware of the wide variety of signals that writers actually have available. Although the rest of this chapter will focus mainly on grammatical ways of correcting comma splices and run-ons, Chapter 13, "Coordinating and Subordinating Ideas," focuses on the different meanings that occur as a result of your choices. You might therefore choose to study this chapter and Chapter 13 at the same time.

Exercise 4-1 Self-study: Correcting run-ons and comma splices

In this exercise you will be practicing different methods for correcting comma splices and run-ons. As you make each of the following sentences *grammatically* correct, think also about the meaning each correction conveys.

A. In the first set of exercises correct the comma splice or run-on by creating two independent sentences. This method indicates that in the context of the writer's larger passage the writer wants to emphasize the independence of each idea.

Answer column

1. The train rumbled past my window, it was loaded with coal.

    1. The train rumbled past my window. It was loaded with coal.

2. The children were throwing Frisbees in the park suddenly one of them began to scream.

    2. The children were throwing Frisbees in the park. Suddenly one of them began to scream.

3. José hasn't yet changed the oil in his car therefore he doesn't want us to to take it to the game.

    3. José hasn't yet changed the oil in his car. Therefore he doesn't want us take it to the game. [*Therefore* is a conjunctive *adverb* and can't by itself join two sentences—see 4E following.]

B. In the next exercises correct the run-on or comma splice by creating one sentence with two independent clauses joined by a semicolon. Through this method, the writer indicates that the ideas are closely connected. The writer wants the reader to consider the sentence as one unit with two balanced parts.

4. The antique table lamp was covered with so much dust that we couldn't read the price marked on the tape, I blew off the dust and read $500.

    4. The antique table lamp was covered with so much dust that we couldn't read the price marked on the tape; I blew off the dust and read $500.

5. The children were throwing Frisbees in the park, suddenly one of them began to scream.

    5. The children were throwing Frisbees in the park; suddenly one of them began to scream.

C. In the next exercises, correct the run-on or comma splice by creating one sentence with two main clauses joined by a comma and a coordinating conjunction. Use the coordinating conjunction indicated. With this method the writer again considers the two sentences to be closely related. However, by choosing one of several coordinating conjunctions, the writer can signal the logical relationships between the parts.

6. I am going to study punctuation rules for another half hour then I am going to go to lunch. (and)

    6. I am going to study punctuation rules for another half hour, and then I am going to go to lunch.

7. I explained to the police officer that my speedometer was broken, she still gave me a ticket. (but)

    7. I explained to the police officer that my speedometer was broken, but she still gave me a ticket.

8. José hasn't yet changed the oil in his car, he doesn't want us to take it to the game. (so)

    8. José hasn't yet changed the oil in his car, so he doesn't want us to take it to the game.

9. My sister would especially like this salad, she loves mushrooms and lots of alfalfa sprouts. (for)

    9. My sister would especially like this salad, for she loves mushrooms and lots of alfalfa sprouts.

D. In the following sentences correct the run-on or comma splice by creating one sentence with a main clause and a subordinate clause. Use the subordinating conjunction indicated. Construct two versions of each sentence by locating the subordinate clause first at the beginning of the sentence and then at the end of the sentence. Note how a subordinating conjunction places primary emphasis on the main clause and secondary emphasis on the subordinate clause.

10. The carpenter will do no further work on our house we must pay him immediately. *(unless)*

10. Unless we pay him immediately, the carpenter will do no further work on our house.
    The carpenter will do no further work on our house unless we pay him immediately. [Note that if the sentence *begins* with a subordinate clause, there is a comma after the clause; there is no comma, however, if the sentence ends with the subordinate clause.]

11. José hasn't yet changed the oil in his car, he doesn't want us to take it to the game. *(because)*

11. Because José hasn't yet changed the oil in his car, he doesn't want us to take it to the game.
    José doesn't want us to take his car to the game because he hasn't yet changed the oil in it.

12. The wind was blowing quite hard, Lucy and Jim were still able to finish their tennis match. *(although)*

12. Although the wind was blowing quite hard, Lucy and Jim were still able to finish their tennis match.
    Lucy and Jim were still able to finish their tennis match, although the wind was blowing quite hard. [A comma occurs in the second sentence here — even though the subordinate clause comes last — because *although* indicates a change in direction of thought.]

13. The thunderclap struck the child began to cry. *(when)*

13. When the thunderclap struck, the child began to cry.
    The child began to cry when the thunderclap struck.

14. My wife and I are going to begin backpacking with our children, the snow melts in the spring. *(as soon as)*

14. As soon as the snow melts in the spring, my wife and I are going to begin backpacking with our children.
    My wife and I are going to begin backpacking with our children as soon as the snow melts in the spring.

E. In the next sentences correct the run-on or comma splice by changing one of the sentences to a relative clause. Use the relative pronoun indicated. Note how the relative clause adds extra information to the main clause.

15. José hasn't yet changed the oil in his car, he doesn't want us to take it to the game. *(who)*

15. José, who hasn't yet changed the oil in his car, doesn't want us to take it to the game.

16. The Victorians would have approved of my Aunt Ruth, she denies having any sexual feelings. *(of whom)*

16. My Aunt Ruth, of whom the Victorians would have approved, denies having any sexual feelings.

17. Mercury has an average temperature of 350°F, it is the closest planet to the sun. *(which)*

17. The closest planet to the sun is Mercury, which has an average temperature of 350°F.
    OR
    Mercury, which has an average temperature of 350°F, is the closest planet to the sun.

18. Neils Bohr spent his Nobel prize money to buy a home in the country, he had a taste for contemplation and leisure. *(who)*

18. Neils Bohr, who had a taste for contemplation and leisure, spent his Nobel prize money to buy a home in the country.

F. In the next exercises correct the run-on or comma splice by changing one of the sentences to a prepositional or participial phrase. Use the clues indicated. Note the various kinds of meanings that can be signaled in this compact, flexible way to correct a comma splice or run-on.

19. Paul tried dozens of diets then he decided just to quit eating for three straight days. (Begin with *having tried*.)

19. Having tried dozens of diets, Paul decided just to quit eating for three straight days.

20. My father was paralyzed from polio when he was a child, he has become a successful businessperson. (Begin with *despite his paralysis*.)

20. Despite his paralysis from polio when he was a child, my father has become a successful businessperson.

21. The red-faced golfer lost five golf balls in the lake on five consecutive shots, he threw his golf clubs in the water and stomped back to his car. (Begin with *after losing*.)

21. After losing five golf balls in the lake on five consecutive shots, the red-faced golfer threw his clubs in the water and stomped back to his car.

4E Recognize words, phrases, and mechanical elements that often cause run-ons or comma splices.

Comma splices and run-on errors are apt to occur when writers are using conjunctive adverbs, transitional expressions, personal pronouns as sentence subjects, or sentences with quoted dialogue. Be especially careful in these instances.

Conjunctive Adverbs

Conjunctive adverbs (words like *therefore, however*) are not grammatically equivalent to subordinating conjunctions (words like *because, although*) or to coordinating conjunctions (words like *and, but*)—see page 114. When using a conjunctive adverb between independent clauses, punctuate your sentence as if the conjunctive adverb weren't there.

Comma splice:

I like pickles, therefore, I bought ten bushels of cucumbers.

Corrected:

I like pickles; therefore, I bought ten bushels of cucumbers. [COMPARE: I like pickles; I bought ten bushels of cucumbers.]

Transitional Expressions

Transitional expressions (phrases like *in fact, as a result, on the other* hand—see page 114) also can lead a writer into making a comma splice or run-on. Again, punctuate your sentence as if the transitional expression weren't there.

Comma splice:

I bought ten bushels of cucumbers, as a result, I spent months enduring pickle jokes from my friends.

Corrected:

> I bought ten bushels of cucumbers; as a result, I spent months enduring pickle jokes from my friends.

Personal Pronouns

Personal pronouns as subjects (such as *I, we, she, he,* or *they*) can also lead writers into making a comma splice or run-on error.

Run-on:

> My neighbor in the next apartment is the most obnoxious he can tell fifty pickle jokes in a row.

Corrected:

> My neighbor in the next apartment is the most obnoxious. He can tell fifty pickle jokes in a row.

Quotations

Quotations within sentences can be confusing because quotations are usually introduced with such phrases as *"he says," "Polly shouted,"* and so forth. These phrases are set off from the quotation with commas. You can be misled into making a comma splice if you join the same "speaker-identifying phrase" to two different sentences.

Comma splice:

> "What is long and green and lives in the ocean?" my neighbor said, "I'll bet that one will stump you."

Corrected:

> "What is long and green and lives in the ocean?" my neighbor said. "I'll bet that one will stump you."

NOTE: You can put commas on both sides of a speaker-identifying phrase if the phrase occurs in the middle of a single sentence.

Correct:

> "What is long and green," my neighbor said, "and lives in the ocean?"

AN OVERVIEW OF PRINCIPLES

The following chart summarizes the methods used in standard written English to join two sentences.

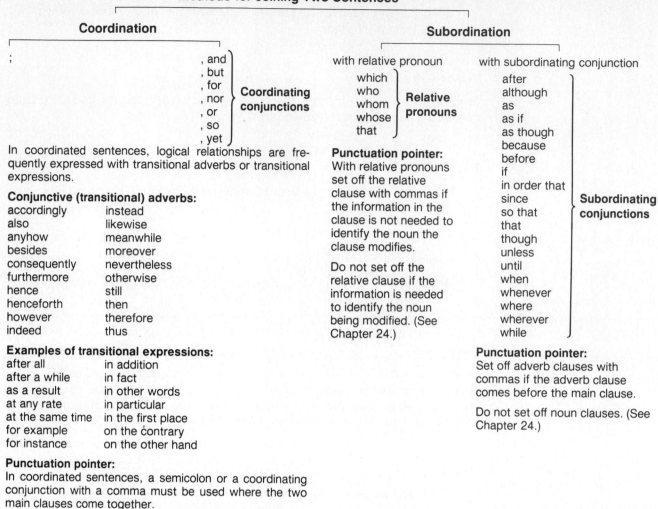

Coordination

;

, and
, but
, for
, nor
, or
, so
, yet
} **Coordinating conjunctions**

In coordinated sentences, logical relationships are frequently expressed with transitional adverbs or transitional expressions.

Conjunctive (transitional) adverbs:

accordingly	instead
also	likewise
anyhow	meanwhile
besides	moreover
consequently	nevertheless
furthermore	otherwise
hence	still
henceforth	then
however	therefore
indeed	thus

Examples of transitional expressions:

after all	in addition
after a while	in fact
as a result	in other words
at any rate	in particular
at the same time	in the first place
for example	on the contrary
for instance	on the other hand

Punctuation pointer:
In coordinated sentences, a semicolon or a coordinating conjunction with a comma must be used where the two main clauses come together.
Set off transitional adverbs or expressions with commas if your voice pauses around them.

Subordination

with relative pronoun

which
who
whom
whose
that
} **Relative pronouns**

Punctuation pointer:
With relative pronouns set off the relative clause with commas if the information in the clause is not needed to identify the noun the clause modifies.

Do not set off the relative clause if the information is needed to identify the noun being modified. (See Chapter 24.)

with subordinating conjunction

after
although
as
as if
as though
because
before
if
in order that
since
so that
that
though
unless
until
when
whenever
where
wherever
while
} **Subordinating conjunctions**

Punctuation pointer:
Set off adverb clauses with commas if the adverb clause comes before the main clause.

Do not set off noun clauses. (See Chapter 24.)

Exercise 4-2   Self-study: Understanding the difference between two kinds of connectives — subordinating conjunctions and conjunctive adverbs

In the preceding explanations you may have had trouble appreciating the difference between words like *however, therefore, in fact,* or *on the other hand* (which are conjunctive adverbs or transitional expressions) and words like *because* and *although* (which are subordinating conjunctions). Beginning writers sometimes mistakenly punctuate sentences as if these two kinds of connectives were grammatically equivalent. But with a little training, your ear can show you the difference between conjunctive adverbs (or transitional expressions) and subordinating conjunctions; then you will see why they require different methods of punctuation. Examine the following two sentences. Both of them are correctly punctuated.

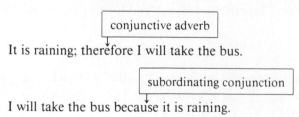

conjunctive adverb

It is raining; therefore I will take the bus.

subordinating conjunction

I will take the bus because it is raining.

Now note the differences in the kinds of variations possible with each sentence.

1. Conjunctive adverbs can move around within their clause.

It is raining; therefore I will take the bus.
It is raining: I will therefore take the bus.
It is raining; I will take the bus therefore.

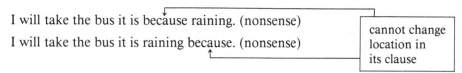

can change location in its clause

However, a subordinate conjunction must come only at the beginning of its clause. Note how it doesn't make sense to move it around in the same way you can move *therefore*.

I will take the bus it is because raining. (nonsense)
I will take the bus it is raining because. (nonsense)

cannot change location in its clause

2. On the other hand, clauses introduced by subordinating conjunctions can come before or after the main clauses to which they are linked.

Because it is raining, I will take the bus.
I will take the bus because it is raining.

However, a clause with a conjunctive adverb makes logical sense only if it comes after the clause to which it is linked.

Therefore I will take the bus; it is raining. (illogical)

The above examples suggest the logic behind the punctuation rules governing the use of subordinating conjunctions and conjunctive adverbs or transitional expressions. The subordinating conjunction *subordinates* a sentence (that is, it turns the sentence into a fragment that cannot stand alone). Thus, *because it is raining* is a sentence fragment by itself, but when joined to a main clause, *because it is raining* becomes a subordinate clause. Because the subordinating conjunction subordinates its whole clause, it is fixed to the head of the clause and cannot move around within the clause itself.

A conjunctive adverb or transitional expression, on the other hand, does not subordinate a clause, and it therefore has no effect on the grammar of the sentence or clause it occurs in. For this reason, conjunctive adverbs or transitional expressions can move around within their clauses. You are free to place them anywhere that sounds graceful to your ear. In fact, when punctuating sentences that contain conjunctive adverbs or transitional expressions, you can first decide on the correct sentence boundaries by omitting these connectives altogether.

It is raining; I will take the bus.

Then insert the conjunctive adverb or transitional expression at the most pleasing spot in the second clause. (Usually you set these expressions off with commas, but whether you do so is frequently optional. Trust your ear. If you pause noticeably when you say the conjunctive adverb or transitional expression, then put commas around it.)

It is raining; therefore I will take the bus.
It is raining; therefore, I will take the bus.
It is raining; I will therefore take the bus.
It is raining; I will, therefore, take the bus.

All these versions are correct. If the connective occurs in the middle of its clause and you choose to set it off with commas, be sure to put commas on both sides of it.

It is raining; I will, as a result, take the bus.
It is raining; I will, therefore, take the bus

commas both
sides

Once you know how to punctuate sentences containing subordinating conjunctions and conjunctive adverbs or transitional expressions, you are still left with the problem of recognizing them. One solution is to memorize them (a list of both is included in the chart on page 114). But a better way is to learn a simple technique. To begin, try out your ear on the following exercises.

In the space below, write a short sentence beginning with the word *when.*

When _____ .

Then write another short sentence beginning with the word *if.*

If _____ .

Finally, write a short sentence beginning with the word *moreover.*

Moreover _____ .

If you trusted your ear, the chances are that for both *when* and *if* you wrote a sentence with two clauses. You probably wrote one short clause, paused, and then felt the need to write another clause before the sentence felt completed. Perhaps your sentences went something like this:

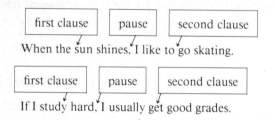

When the sun shines, I like to go skating.

If I study hard, I usually get good grades.

Chances are, however, that when you began with *moreover,* you felt slightly uneasy because your sentence by itself didn't seem to make much sense. It seemed to need another thought in front of it. Moreover, your sentence probably had only one clause instead of two, and if you paused at all, you probably paused after the word *moreover.*

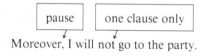

Moreover, I will not go to the party.

The two-clause sentences that you produced using *when* and *if* demonstrate that these words are subordinating conjunctions. The one-clause sentence produced with *moreover* demonstrates that *moreover* is a conjunctive adverb. You would also produce a one-clause sentence if you started with a transitional expression:

On the other hand _____ .
On the other hand, I enjoy watching television.

Now use this method to determine whether the following terms are subordinating conjunctions or conjunctive adverbs (or transitional expressions). Write a short sentence beginning with each word or phrase. If your sentence has two clauses, the term is a subordinating conjunction; if it has one clause, it is a conjunctive adverb or transitional expression. Check your answers by finding each word on the chart on page 114. Two examples are provided.

	One clause	Two clauses	Conjunctive adverb or transitional expression	Subordinating conjunction
As soon as *I got home, I fixed dinner*.		X		X
Also *I swept the floor*.	X		X	
Although				
Unless				
Until				
Then				
Henceforth				
Whenever				
Nevertheless				
For example				
Because				
In the first place				

The next exercise will help you apply this technique.

Exercise 4-3   Self-study: Distinguishing between subordinating conjunctions and conjunctive adverbs (or transitional expressions)

Combine the following pairs of sentences into one sentence using the word indicated in parentheses. Write two versions of each sentence. If the word indicated is a subordinating conjunction, first put the subordinate clause at the front of the sentence and then at the end of the sentence. If the word indicated is a conjunctive adverb or a transitional expression, locate it in two different positions in the second clause.

1. I will finish this assignment. I will watch TV. *(after)*

   1. After I finish this assignment, I will watch TV.
   I will watch TV after I finish this assignment. (*After* is a subordinating conjunction.)

2. I will finish this assignment. I will watch TV. *(later)*

   2. I will finish this assignment; later I will watch TV.
   I will finish this assignment; I will watch TV later. (*Later* is a conjunctive adverb.)

3. I like to study foreign languages. I have trouble with pronunciation. *(however)*

   3. I like to study foreign languages; however, I have trouble with pronunciation.
   I like to study foreign languages; I have trouble, however, with pronunciation.

4. I like to study foreign languages. I have trouble with pronunciation. *(although)*

   4. Although I have trouble with pronunciation, I like to study foreign languages.
   I like to study foreign languages, although I have trouble with pronunciation.

5. She had trouble learning punctuation. She never studied grammar in high school. *(because)*

   5. She had trouble learning punctuation because she never studied grammar in high school.
   Because she never studied grammar in high school, she had trouble learning punctuation.

6. She had trouble learning punctuation. She never studied grammar in high school. *(therefore)*

   6. She never studied grammar in high school; therefore, she had trouble learning punctuation.
   She never studied grammar in high school; she had trouble, therefore, learning punctuation.

7. Judy practiced the piano. Pete dusted the furniture. *(while)*

   7. Judy practiced the piano while Pete dusted the furniture.
   While Pete dusted the furniture, Judy practiced the piano.

8. Judy practiced the piano. Pete dusted the furniture. *(at the same time)*

8. Judy practiced the piano; at the same time Pete dusted the furniture.
Judy practiced the piano; Pete dusted the furniture at the same time.

9. The band blared its music across the dance floor. Ruth and Jacob began to push their way toward a rear exit. *(while)*

9. While the band blared its music across the dance floor, Ruth and Jacob began to push their way toward a rear exit.
Ruth and Jacob began to push their way toward a rear exit while the band blared its music across the dance floor.

10. The impact of the new computer technology is already being felt in our daily lives. Citizens of the future will need to be far better trained in computer science than most persons are today. *(consequently)*

10. The impact of new computer technology is already being felt in our daily lives; consequently, citizens of the future will need to be far better trained in computer science than most persons are today.
The impact of new computer technology is already being felt in our daily lives; citizens of the future, consequently, will need to be far better trained in computer science than most persons are today.

Exercise 4-4   Self-study: Using different categories of connectives

In the following exercise place the word or phrase in parentheses in the blank using correct punctuation. Your method of correction may differ from that shown in the answer column.

<u>Answer column</u>

1. I ate dinner at eight o'clock _____ I settled in for a movie on TV. *(then)*

1. . Then
OR
; then

2. I like cats _____ they are so unpredictable. *(because)*

2. because

3. Whenever I wash my hair in the evening _____ always asks me out for a Coke. *(someone)*

3. , someone

4. Educational TV is probably good for children _____ it may tend to make them bored with regular classrooms. *(however)*

4. ; however,

5. At present in America, we have a shortage of dialysis machines for people with malfunctioning kidneys _____ kind of problem raises serious ethical concerns for our citizens. *(this)*

5. . This

6. Teaching students to conduct moral arguments is an important function of philosophy departments _____ very few students take any philosophy in college. *(yet)*

    6. , yet

7. Writing courses sometimes focus on strategies of argumentation _____ there isn't enough time in a writing course to study the intricacies of moral reasoning. *(nevertheless)*

    7. ; nevertheless,

8. It is important _____ to keep in mind that students in our technological society are being asked to make complex decisions without being given the necessary skills. *(therefore)*

    8. , therefore,

9. Physics is the study of the material world _____ is a search for explanations for the way any physical object behaves. *(it)*

    9. . It

10. This search includes explanations for the behavior of the smallest imaginable objects such as protons _____ the largest imaginable objects such as exploding suns. *(as well as)*

    10. as well as

11. Physics _____ does not lead to the knowledge of absolute truth _____ it is the attempt to develop and support a consistent world view. *(however, rather)*

    11. , however,
    ; rather,

12. Some years ago scientists tried to visualize the structure of an atom as a miniature solar system _____ now they have abandoned that model and try to rely on mathematical descriptions that can't be visualized. *(but)*

    12. , but

13. "What causes a book to fall off a table?" asks Professor Lee, peering from behind the thick lens of his horn-rimmed glasses _____ can explain it?" *(who)*

    13. . "Who

14. "You said 'gravity'!" snorts Professor Lee. " 'Gravity' doesn't explain anything _____ is just a word for something we don't understand." *(it)*

    14. . It

15. The goal of a physics course is to help you view your world differently _____ you just listen passively and take notes _____ you will not learn the wonder of discovering your own questions. *(if, therefore)*

    15. . If
    , therefore,

16. When I took physics _____ I didn't have a good teacher _____ I really didn't learn much. *(however, as a result)*

    16. , however,
    . As a result,

17. _____ I plan to major in physics _____ I want to become an astronomer. *(nevertheless, because)*

    17. Nevertheless,
    because

18. I want to become an astronomer _____ I plan to major in physics _____ think I will transfer to another school. *(because, I)*

    18. . Because
    , I

Exercise 4-5   Self-study: Punctuating sentences with quotations

In the following exercises, eliminate comma splices or run-on errors by turning improperly joined sentences into two separate sentences. Some sentences may already be correct.

1. " 'To be or not to be,' " said Sarah, quoting Hamlet, "I wonder if he knew what he was talking about?"

2. "The hipbone is connected to the thighbone," drolled Professor Jones, "and the thighbone is connected to the knee."

3. The hipbone is connected to the thighbone," drolled Professor Jones, "moreover, the thighbone is connected to the knee."

4. "Whoever made up these sentences," said the annoyed student, "is a nerd."

5. "Whoever made up these sentences is a nerd," said Pete in a sneering voice, "I can't stand any more of them."

6. "Although the hipbone is connected to the thighbone," drolled Professor Jones, "the connective tissue isn't identified in the song."

7. "The hipbone is connected to the thighbone," drolled Professor Jones, "nevertheless, the connective tissue isn't identified in the song."

8. "He just did it again!" Pete exclaimed. "That guy just made up another hipbone sentence he should be strung up by his thumbs."

9. "I don't think he will make up any more now," said Pete, "at any rate, he had better not."

10. "The neck bone is connected to the head bone, Pete," drolled Professor Jones. "You'll need to know that for the test."

---

1. " 'To be or not to be,' " said Sarah, quoting Hamlet. "I wonder if he knew what he was talking about?"

2. Correct. [The quotation itself is one sentence: "The hipbone is connected to the thighbone, and the thighbone is connected to the knee."]

3. "The hipbone is connected to the thighbone," drolled Professor Jones. "Moreover, the thighbone is connected to the knee." [Here the quotation itself would need a semicolon since *moreover* is a conjunctive adverb. "The hipbone is connected to the thighbone; moreover, the thighbone is connected to the knee." When the speaker-identifying phrase *drolled Professor Jones* is added, it works best to divide the quotation into two sentences.]

4. Correct.

5. "Whoever made up these sentences is a nerd," said Pete in a sneering voice. "I can't stand any more of them."

6. Correct.

7. "The hipbone is connected to the thighbone," drolled Professor Jones. "Nevertheless, the connective tissue isn't identified in the song."

8. "He just did it again!" Pete exclaimed. "That guy just made up another hipbone sentence. He should be strung up by his thumbs."

9. "I don't think he will make up any more now," said Pete. "At any rate he had better not."

10. Correct.

Exercise 4-6   Self-study: Run-ons and comma splices in extended passages

In the following student paragraph look for comma splices and run-ons. Correct errors by crossing out and writing in the spaces above the lines. Use any of the correction methods you prefer. A corrected version of the passage follows the exercises; of course your corrections may differ from those in the sample answer.

If you have trouble with this exercise, try the following method of proofreading:

1. Read the passage aloud slowly, listening for when your voice pauses and drops (a fairly reliable indicator that you need a period or a semicolon) or for when your voice pauses and rises slightly (a fairly reliable indicator that you need a comma).

2. Count the sentences, thereby forcing yourself to look carefully for independent clauses.

3. Check for trouble words such as transition expressions or conjunctive adverbs.

Not many people have had the chance to drive a taxi, however, I consider myself to be one of the lucky few. You may be shocked you may even laugh at me for calling myself lucky to have driven a taxi. Before you laugh, however, let me explain why. There are only eight thousand taxi drivers in the United States this means there are fewer taxi drivers than waiters, bus drivers, police officers, fire fighters, bartenders, or people in any other service occupation, however, that isn't the only reason I consider myself lucky. Taxi driving is one of the few service occupations that people really respect. If a passenger gets on the wrong side of a driver, the driver may decide to pick up other passengers and take them to their destinations first. People don't tell you how to drive, they know you drive for a living. They don't tell you which way to go they know you know the city better than they do. It is a good feeling to know that all the passengers, who range from eminent businesspeople to town drunks, are dependent upon the taxi driver they don't want to do anything wrong to destroy their privilege of being driven to their desired destination.

Possible corrections

Not many people have had the chance to drive a taxi. However, I consider myself to be one of the lucky few. You may be shocked, or you may even laugh at me for calling myself lucky to have driven a taxi. Before you laugh, however, let me explain why. There are only eight thousand taxi drivers in the United States. This means there are fewer taxi drivers than there are waiters, bus drivers, police officers, fire fighters, bartenders, or people in any other service occupation. However, that isn't the only reason I consider myself lucky. Taxi driving is one of the few service occupations that people really respect. If a passenger gets on the wrong side of a driver, the driver may decide to pick up other passengers and take them to their destinations first. People don't tell you how to drive; they know you drive for a living. They don't tell you which way to go; they know you know the city better than they do. It is a good feeling to know that all the passengers, who range from eminent businesspeople to town drunks, are dependent upon the taxi driver. They don't want to do anything wrong to destroy their privilege of being driven to their desired destination.

Exercise 4-7 Mastery exercise: Run-ons and comma splices

Indicate in the blank at the right whether the passage contains a comma splice *(CS)* or a run-on *(RO)*; if the passage is correct, write *C*. Then correct the comma splices or run-ons using any correction method that seems appropriate.

Example:
In 1818, Shelley wrote "Ode to the West Wind," ⊙ *Its* its subject is the power of the west wind to create new life.   *CS*

1. I love to hear coffee perking in the pot on lazy Saturday mornings another of my favorite sounds is rain on a tin roof. _____

2. When the ice cream wagon begins playing its song in our neighborhood, the children run to greet it, clasping their dimes and quarters in grubby little hands. _____

3. Freud assumed that the unconscious was the basis for human behavior, therefore, he believed that the pleasure audiences receive from art comes from art's embodiment of unconscious material. _____

4. Because St. Augustine's conception of God was neo-Platonic, Augustine believed that existence in itself is good. He believed, therefore, that it is better to exist in misery than not to exist at all. _____

5. Although scientists don't know for sure how much dinosaurs actually ate, they know that the food intake of the great reptiles must have been enormous, a question they ask themselves, therefore, is what the dinosaurs actually ate. _____

6. The doctor told me that my x-ray revealed nothing to be alarmed about, nevertheless, she wants me to come back in six months for another checkup. _____

7. Juan and Jacob began taking the engine apart they worked diligently for four hours and then discovered that they didn't have the right tools to continue. _____

8. I should apologize for the snide letter I wrote you last week, although I must admit that I am still angry. _____

9. In a home aquarium fish will sometimes die from overeating the instructions on fish food boxes, therefore, stress that you feed fish a specified amount on a strict schedule. _____

10. "At its best liberal education develops thought and aesthetic appreciation," the speaker continued in the same monotonous voice, "it proceeds by imparting knowledge of the masterpieces of thought, of imagination, and of art." _____

5
Correcting Sentence Fragments

A *sentence fragment* occurs whenever a writer makes a part of a sentence look like a complete sentence by beginning with a capital letter and ending with a period, question mark, or exclamation point. A fragment also occurs if a phrase or subordinate clause is punctuated as a main clause through the use of a semicolon. Look carefully at the following examples, all of which are punctuated as sentences (that is, they begin with a capital letter and end with a period). The sentence fragments are marked with an *X*.

1. The fox scrambles rapidly through the dense underbrush. [A complete sentence with a subject—*fox*—and a complete verb—*scrambles.*]

X 2. Rapidly through the dense underbrush. [A phrase only. There is no subject or complete verb.]

X 3. The fox scrambling rapidly through the dense underbrush. [A phrase only. *Scrambling* is a present participle, not a complete verb.]

4. The fox is scrambling rapidly through the dense underbrush. [A complete sentence. The addition of the helping verb *is* turns *scrambling* into a complete verb. Compare with example 3.]

5. The fox scrambling rapidly through the dense underbrush is trying to escape the baying hounds. [A complete sentence. *Scrambling* remains as a present participle modifying *fox;* a new complete verb *is trying* is added to complete the sentence. Compare with examples 3 and 4.]

X 6. As the fox scrambles rapidly through the dense underbrush. [A subordinate clause only. The addition of the subordinating conjunction *as* turns the sentence into a fragment. Compare with example 1.]

7. As the fox scrambles rapidly through the dense underbrush, the baying hounds rush forward in excited pursuit. [A complete sentence; subordinate clause remains, and a new main clause is added to complete the sentence. Compare with example 6.]

X. 8. The fox that scrambles rapidly through the dense underbrush. [A noun with an attached subordinate clause. The addition of the relative pronoun *that* creates the relative clause *that scrambles rapidly through the dense underbrush,* leaving the original subject *fox* to dangle without a verb. Compare with example 1.]

9. The fox that scrambles rapidly through the dense underbrush will outlive the fox that runs across an open field. [A complete sentence. The relative clause remains, and a new complete verb is added — *will outlive* — so that *fox* no longer dangles by itself. Compare with example 8.]

These examples reveal that there are two kinds of sentence fragments: phrase fragments and subordinate clause fragments.

    a. *Phrase fragments* lack either a subject or a complete verb and are therefore phrases only.

Examples of phrase fragments:

Paul and Sarah love living in the mountains. *Going fishing in the morning. Watching the deer graze in the meadows.* [verbal phrases punctuated as sentences]

The bears rumble down to the stream; *to drink in the early morning sunlight.* [infinitive phrase punctuated as a main clause]

The chipmunks chattering in the tops of the pine trees. [noun and attached participial phrase punctuated as a sentence]

A pair of majestic eagles nest in the top of a lone pine; *with* only *the starry sky as a night roof.* [prepositional phrase punctuated as a main clause]

    b. *Subordinate clause fragments* have a subject and a complete verb, but the presence of a subordinator (either a subordinating conjunction or a relative pronoun) creates a subordinate clause, which cannot stand by itself as a sentence.

Examples of subordinate clause fragments:

Sarah and Paul often go for a hike. *As soon as the sun comes up.* [fragment created by subordinating conjunction *as soon as*]

At night they love to watch the eyes of owls. *Which blink at them from the branches of nearby trees.* [fragment created by relative pronoun *which*]

METHODS OF CORRECTION

When correcting fragments in your drafts, you must again make your decisions based on the meaning you intend, just as you do when correcting comma splices and run-ons. There are various ways of correcting a fragment, but each option produces a slightly different meaning.

5A Change the fragment to a complete sentence.

    1, 2 Correct the fragment by joining it to the sentence immediately before or after, whichever makes more sense.

This method, of course, is not possible in every case. When correcting a fragment in this way, the writer shows that the meaning of the fragment is closely related to the meaning of the adjoining sentence.

Fragment:

The buffaloes began to stampede. *Their heads flailing wildly.* They rushed away from the braves shaking wolfskins and headed toward the cliff.

Complete sentence:

The buffaloes began to stampede. Their heads flailing wildly, they rushed away from the braves shaking wolfskins and headed for the cliff. [absolute phrase joined to following sentence to indicate that the writer sees this phrase as part of the action within that sentence]

Fragment:

The buffaloes crashed to their deaths. Although braves killed the animals that were still alive, the work of preparing the hides and meat was left to the squaws. *Who set about their work immediately with stone tools.*

Complete sentence:

The buffaloes crashed to their deaths. Although braves killed the animals that were still alive, the work of preparing the hides and meat was left to the squaws, who set about their work immediately with stone tools. [Relative clause attached to preceding sentence. This decision keeps the emphasis of the passage on the "woman's work"—preparing the hides and meat.]

3   Turn the fragment into a sentence either by removing a subordinator or by adding appropriate helping verbs, complete predicates, subjects, or main clauses so that the sentence is complete.

In using this method, the writer shows that the information within the fragment should be regarded as an independent unit distinct from surrounding sentences.

Isolated Example

Fragment:

The woman washing the car.

Complete sentence:

The woman is washing her car. [helping verb added]

The woman washing her car is my neighbor. [new predicate added]

Fragment:

When the woman washes her car.

Complete sentence:

The woman washes her car. [subordinating conjunction removed]

When the woman washes her car, she uses a special kind of soap. [new main clause added]

Fragments:

> *As soon as I stood in the deserted streets;* my imagination brought back the old frontier days. But my daydream vanished when I noticed the vandalism. Soon this old ghost town would be gone. *The old buildings being torn down and the old barn wood being sold for paneling in modern homes.*

Revised:

> I stood in the deserted streets, letting my imagination bring back the old frontier days. But my daydream vanished when I noticed the vandalism. Soon this old ghost town would be gone. People were tearing down the old buildings and selling the old barn wood for paneling in modern homes. [The writer decided to change the emphasis of the opening sentence by removing the subordinating conjunction *as soon as* to create the independent clause *I stood in the deserted streets.* The writer then converted the original main clause—*my imagination brought back the old frontier days*—into a phrase beginning *letting my imagination. . . .* Finally the writer decided to emphasize the ideas in the last fragment by turning the fragment into an independent sentence. The writer added a subject *people* and a helping verb *were* to make a complete predicate *were tearing . . .* and *selling. . . .*]

5B   Recognize words and phrases that can trap writers into creating fragments.

- Participles, especially present participles (*ing* verb forms).

    Fragment:

    > I saw the dog. *Barking at the cat.*

    Corrected:

    > I saw the dog barking at the cat.

- Infinitives (verb forms introduced by *to*)

    Fragment:

    > My brother went back into the store. *To demand a refund.*

    Corrected:

    > My brother went back into the store to demand a refund.

- Subordinate conjunctions and transitional expressions (see list on chart, page 114)

    Fragment:

    > I dislike writing papers with a passion. *For example, freshman English essays.*

Corrected:

> I dislike writing papers with a passion, particularly freshman English essays.

OR

> I dislike writing papers with a passion. For example, freshman English essays give me the hives.

Fragment:

> However, my adviser made me take freshman English. *Because a student has to write a lot in college.*

Corrected:

> However, my adviser made me take freshman English because a student has to write a lot in college.

- Relative pronouns *(who, whom, whose, which, that)*

Fragment:

> Inez said to turn in the project to Ms. Rappoport. *Who will be in the library.*

Corrected:

> Inez said to turn in the project to Ms. Rappoport, who will be in the library.

Exercise 5-1   Self-study: Correcting sentence fragments

Identify the following passages as complete sentences *(S)* or fragments *(F)*. If a fragment, convert it into a complete sentence using two different methods. The provided answers may differ from your own. This exercise helps you see how to correct fragments *grammatically.* Although the exercise doesn't show you how to tell which methods would work the best in the context of a longer passage, it does show you different options.

Answer column

1. Although the sun shines for twenty-four straight hours at the North Pole on June 21. _____

1. *F.* The sun shines for twenty-four straight hours at the North Pole on June 21. [subordinator removed] Although the sun shines for twenty-four straight hours at the North Pole on June 21, the temperature seldom gets above freezing. [main clause added]

2. The cat scratching at the back door. _____

2. *F.* The cat is scratching at the back door. [helper added to turn verbal into a complete verb] The cat scratching at the back door is driving me crazy. [new predicate added]

3. My father will be coming home next week after he finishes talking to the negotiators. _____

3. *S*

4. The television which we can hear clear out in the street. _____

4. *F.* We can hear the television clear out in the street. [subordinator removed] The television which we can hear clear out in the street is being played by an elderly couple who are hard of hearing. [new predicate added]

5. As the bug crawls slowly around the lip of the lemonade pitcher. _____

6. Inside the eye of the hurricane. _____

7. Running at breakneck speed across our backyard. _____

5. *F.* The bug crawls slowly around the lip of the lemonade pitcher. [subordinator removed]
As the bug crawls slowly around the lip of the lemonade pitcher, the little girl tries to catch it in her hand. [new main clause added]

6. *F.* The plane flies inside the eye of the hurricane. [subject and predicate added]
Inside the eye of a hurricane, the weather is surprisingly calm. [subject and predicate added]

7. *F.* The man is running at breakneck speed across our backyard. [subject and helper added to turn verbal into complete verb]
Running at breakneck speed across our backyard, the man yells something at my mother, who is watering her flowers. [main clause added]

Exercise 5-2 Self-study: Fragments in an extended passage

Proofread the following passage adapted from a paper written by a student. Find all sentence fragments and correct them by one of the two main correction methods (turning the fragment into a complete sentence or connecting the fragment to a neighboring sentence). Choose a correction method which seems to fit best into the context of the passage. The corrected passage following the exercise may differ from your own.

Another difference between a taxi driver and other occupations being the way that taxi drivers interact with people. Driving a taxi is one of the few jobs where you really get to "know the customer." In other service jobs, you rarely get to know the customer's name. Such as waiter or bartender. In those jobs it is quite possible to wait on one hundred people in a night or mix drinks for two hundred. Without personally talking to five of them. In a taxi, however, each customer spends at least ten to fifteen minutes in a quiet car. Having nothing else to do but talk with the driver.

The job of driving a taxi is also interesting; because of the amount of variation the job itself contains. You probably picture a taxi driver buzzing through traffic. Or cursing at passing cars and impatiently waiting for a light to change. Of course, city driving is a large part of the job. But a cabby also has many opportunities to get out of the city. Taking someone to his rural home. Or picking up someone at an airport miles out of town. Also taking eccentric people on long trips.

The variety of people a taxi driver serves also adds spice to the job; such as doctors, lawyers, morticians, dentists, engineers, mechanics, housewives, preachers, and prostitutes. The job constantly changes with each person that steps into the cab. Because once in a while you will have a five-gallon container of rare human blood or a prizewinning Pomeranian sitting next to you. Once when I was called to a bar; a person asked me to take two Tanqueray tonics to his old football coach. Also to sing to the coach an old chant. Which was only used by the fellows on that football team. The man in the bar gave me a five-dollar tip. Besides paying for the taxi fare. His coach got such a kick out of it that he gave me a ten-dollar tip.

Possible corrections

Another difference between a taxi driver and other occupations is the way that taxi drivers interact with people. Driving a taxi is one of the few jobs where you really get to "know the customer." In other service jobs, such as waiter or bartender, you rarely get to know the customer's name. In those jobs it is quite possible to wait on one hundred people in a night or mix drinks for two hundred without personally talking to five of them. In a taxi, however, each customer spends at least ten to fifteen minutes in a quiet car, having nothing else to do but talk with the driver.

The job of driving a taxi is also interesting because of the amount of variation the job itself contains. You probably picture a taxi driver buzzing through traffic or cursing at passing cars and impatiently waiting for a light to change. Of course, city driving is a large part of the job. But a cabby also has many opportunities to get out of the city by taking someone to his rural home, picking up someone at an airport miles out of town, or taking eccentric people on long trips.

The variety of people a taxi driver serves also adds spice to the job. My riders have included doctors, lawyers, morticians, dentists, engineers, mechanics, housewives, preachers, and prostitutes. The job constantly changes with each person that steps into the cab. Once in a while you will have a five-gallon container of rare human blood or a prizewinning Pomeranian sitting next to you. Once when I was called to a bar, a person asked me to take two Tanqueray tonics to his old football coach and also to sing to the coach an old chant which was only used by the fellows on that football team. The man in the bar gave me a five-dollar tip besides paying for the taxi fare. His coach got such a kick out of it that he gave me a ten-dollar tip.

Exercise 5-3   Self-study: Fragments, comma splices, and run-ons — Putting it all together

Indicate whether each of the following word groups contains a sentence fragment *(F)*, a comma splice *(CS)*, or a run-on *(RO)*. If the word group is a complete sentence, mark it *S*. Correct all errors by whatever method seems appropriate. The provided answers may differ from your own. If your answer is different, try to see how it might convey a slightly different meaning or emphasis.

Answer column

1. Plato valued most those things that never change these he called the *ideas.* _____

1. *RO.* Plato valued most those things that never change. These he called the *ideas.* [Remember that a run-on occurs if two separate sentences are joined together without any punctuation.]

2. Aristotle, on the other hand, understood that the most striking aspect of nature was change, although he was a student of Plato, he nevertheless broke from the master and became, in effect, the father of scientific inquiry. _____

2. *CS.* Aristotle, on the other hand, understood that the most striking aspect of nature was change. Although he was a student of Plato, he nevertheless broke from the master and became, in effect, the father of scientific inquiry.

3. Even today scientists are always open to the notion of change, ready to throw away old theories if they no longer adequately explain the reality they observe and ready to test new theories even if they contradict a scientist's previous work. _____

3. *S*

4. It is hard to predict how science is going to turn out, if it is really good science, it is impossible to predict.

_____

4. *CS.* It is hard to predict how science is going to turn out, and if it is really good science, it is impossible to predict.

5. If the things to be found are actually new; they are by definition unknown in advance, and there is no way of telling in advance where a new line of inquiry will lead. _____

6. You cannot make choices in this matter; selecting things you think you're going to like and shutting off the lines that make for discomfort. _____

7. Either you have science or you don't if you have it, you are obliged to accept the surprising and disturbing pieces of information. Even the overwhelming and upheaving ones. _____

5. *F.* If the things to be found are actually new, they are by definition unknown in advance, and there is no way of telling in advance where a new line of inquiry will lead.

6. *F.* You cannot make choices in this matter, selecting things you think you're going to like and shutting off the lines that make for discomfort.

7. *RO, F.* Either you have science or you don't, and if you have it, you are obliged to accept the surprising and disturbing pieces of information, even the overwhelming and upheaving ones.

(Sentences 4 to 7 are based on Lewis Thomas, *Medusa and the Snail: More Notes of a Biology Watcher* (New York: Viking, 1974), p. 73.

Exercise 5-4   Mastery exercise: Sentence fragments, comma splices, and run-ons

Identify each of the following word groups as either a complete sentence *(S)*, a comma splice *(CS)*, a run-on *(RO)*, or a fragment *(F)*. Correct comma splices, run-ons, and fragments by whatever method seems appropriate.

Example:

A curious trait of Mark Twain was his hatred of the French people; however, his Francophobia was apparently unknown to the French government, which awarded him the Legion of Honor.   *C S*

1. Because of improvements in health care in the last two decades, many of us can now expect to live well into our seventies and eighties. Especially if we watch our diets and exercise carefully.   _____

2. Jones sensed that the storm had gathered strength since midnight when he had gone off watch, indeed, he felt that a major blow was soon coming.   _____

3. Suddenly the ship began to lurch, before Jones could grab something to hold on to, he was knocked across the floor of the cabin.   _____

4. In the process he scraped his foot against something sharp. Creating a gash that later required a dozen stitches.   _____

5. Even without sails the ship was scudding along at eight to nine knots, yawing dangerously in the churning sea with waves reaching heights of 30 or more feet.   _____

6. Because the pale golden glow of this fragile white table wine is an indication of its taste. _____

7. Large lumber mills use woodchips left over from the sawing and planing process to make a number of other useful products. Such as particleboard for furniture and chunk bark for gardens and playgrounds. _____

8. In 1947 a major breakthrough occurred in electronics technology with the development of the transistor at the Bell Telephone Laboratories. Because the transistor is very small and does not require large amounts of power for filament heating; it soon became an ideal component for digital computers. _____

9. The most recent explosive growth in electronics technology being the development of the integrated circuit at Fairchild Semiconductor and Texas Instruments in 1959. _____

10. An integrated circuit is made up of hundreds or even thousands of transistors organized on a single chip of silicon; which is typically less than a quarter-inch square. _____

6
Subject and Verb Agreement

In some tenses a verb changes its form to agree in person and number with its subject. These tenses are the simple present and all the tenses that use either a simple present helping verb *(has, have; does, do; am, is, are)* or the simple *past* of *to be (was, were).*

Singular	Plural
The <u>bird</u> <u>sings</u> in the tree.	The <u>birds</u> <u>sing</u> in the tree.
The <u>bird</u> <u>was singing</u> in the tree.	The <u>birds</u> <u>were singing</u> in the tree.
<u>Does</u> the <u>boy</u> <u>practice</u> basketball?	<u>Do</u> the <u>boys</u> <u>practice</u> basketball?

Note: Unlike nouns, which add an *s* sound to become plural, present tense verbs add an *s* sound to become singular.

Singular subject	Singular verb	Plural subject	Plural verb
(no *s*)	(adds an *s*)	(adds an *s*)	(no *s*)
The dog	barks.	The dogs	bark.

Some teachers call this the "rule of one *s*"; that is, if the subject ends in *s*, then the verb doesn't or if the verb ends in *s*, then the subject doesn't.

To create agreement in subject and verb, the writer must first locate the true subject of a verb and then decide whether that subject is singular or plural. If you have trouble locating subjects, refer to the explanations and exercises in Chapter 3, "Sentence Grammar."

Exercise 6-1   Self-study: Agreement

A. To understand agreement, you should begin by seeing how agreement works in relatively simple sentences. In the following sentences choose the verb that agrees with the subject. In the first group of sentences, the subject is identified for you.

Answer Column

1. The <u>boy</u> (is playing, are playing) in the alley.

2. The <u>trees</u> (sways, sway) in the breeze.

3. Before lunch, the two <u>men</u> (was splitting, were splitting) wood.

1. is playing [*Boy* is singular.]

2. sway [*Trees* is plural.]

3. were splitting [*Men* is plural.]

135

4. Before lunch, <u>Sarah</u> (was splitting, were splitting) wood.

    4. was splitting [*Sarah* is singular.]

5. After much consideration and planning, my <u>mother</u> (has decided, have decided) to accept the promotion.

    5. has decided [*Mother* is singular.]

B. In the next sentences locate the subject yourself and then make a decision about agreement.

6. After much consideration and planning, the two women (has decided, have decided) not to continue.

    6. have decided [The subject is *women.*]

7. Rural death rates among infants (has been dropping, have been dropping), but not as rapidly as urban death rates.

    7. have been dropping [The subject is *rates.*]

8. The infant death rate for both whites and blacks (has been dropping, have been dropping).

    8. has been dropping [The subject is *rate.*]

9. All my friends just (loves, love) pizza.

    9. love [The subject is *friends.*]

10. My friend Sally just (loves, love) pizza.

    10. loves [The subject is *Sally.*]

Once you understand agreement in simple sentences, most of your agreement problems will be solved. Your only remaining problems will occur in those occasional sentences where it is difficult to find the subject or to determine whether the subject is singular or plural. The remaining rules in this chapter all deal with these tricky cases.

6A   Singular nouns ending in *s*

Not all nouns ending in *s* are plural since some nouns, such as *moss, boss,* and *pass,* have singular stems ending in *s.*

Her ski pass is out of date.

My boss is not here.

6B   Nouns with irregular plurals

Although English nouns normally add an *s* to become plural, there are some nouns with irregular plural forms (*tooth/teeth, child/children, woman/women,* and so forth).

The <u>child</u> <u>is</u> <u>playing</u>.   The <u>children</u> <u>are</u> <u>playing</u>.

The <u>goose</u> <u>is</u> <u>cooked</u>.   The <u>geese</u> <u>are</u> <u>cooked</u>.

6C, D, E, G   Personal pronouns

If the subject of a sentence is a personal pronoun, use a singular verb when the pronoun is third person singular *(he, she, it)* and a plural verb with all other personal pronoun forms.

EXCEPTION: If the verb includes some form of the verb *to be,* it must agree with the subject in person as well as number (see Chapter 7).

<u>I</u> <u>am</u> <u>running</u>.   <u>He</u> (she, it) <u>is</u> <u>running</u>.   <u>We</u> (you, they) <u>are</u> <u>running</u>.

<u>I</u> <u>was</u> <u>running</u>.   <u>He</u> (she, it) <u>was</u> <u>running</u>.   <u>We</u> (you, they) <u>were</u> <u>running</u>.

6F Compound subjects joined by *and*

Use a plural verb for singular or plural subjects joined by *and*.

Paul <u>runs</u>. Mary <u>runs</u>. Paul and Mary <u>run</u>.

The <u>soup</u> and <u>salad</u> <u>were</u> excellent.

EXCEPTION: If the nouns joined by *and* are thought of as one unit, the verb is singular. Notice the different meaning in these two sentences.

My <u>brother</u> and my best <u>friend</u> <u>is</u> with me now. [This sentence means that my brother is with me now and that my brother is my best friend.]

My <u>brother</u> and my best <u>friend</u> <u>are</u> with me now. [This sentence means that two people are with me — my brother and my best friend.]

6H Intervening words

Be careful to discover the true subject when it is separated from the verb by intervening words, phrases, or embedded clauses.

The <u>desk</u> <u>needs</u> sanding.

The <u>desk</u> with the broken oak drawers and wobbly legs <u>needs</u> sanding.

The <u>desk</u> that my father bought at the auction more than seven years ago — the one with the wobbly legs, the broken oak drawers, and the mismatched accompanying chair — <u>needs</u> sanding.

Be especially careful when an indefinite word such as *one, each,* or *kind* is followed by a prepositional phrase beginning with *of.*

<u>One</u> of the girls in my class <u>is</u> from Korea. [Subject is *one,* not *girls.*]

<u>Each</u> of the students in my group <u>is</u> <u>going</u> <u>to</u> <u>interview</u> her about Korean life. [Subject is *each,* not *students.*]

Other intervening expressions causing difficulty are prepositional phrases beginning with *as well as, in addition to, along with,* and *including.* These prepositions are not equivalent to the coordinating conjunction *and* and can trick you into thinking that your subject is grammatically plural.

My <u>mother</u>, along with several of her coworkers, <u>is</u> <u>getting</u> a special award for excellence in customer relations.

BUT

My <u>mother</u> and <u>several</u> of her coworkers <u>are</u> <u>getting</u> a special award for excellence in customer relations.

<u>Joe</u> as well as Manuel <u>is</u> <u>applying</u> for the science scholarship.

BUT

<u>Joe</u> and <u>Manuel</u> <u>are</u> <u>applying</u> for the science scholarship.

6I Or, nor, either . . . or, neither . . . nor

The coordinating conjunctions *or, either . . . or, nor,* and *neither . . . nor* take singular verbs if they join singular subjects, and they take plural verbs if they join plural subjects. If they join a singular subject to a plural subject, the verb agrees with the nearer subject.

Either a coyote or a dog is getting into the chicken coop. [Both subjects are singular.]

Either coyotes or dogs are getting into the chicken coop. [Both subjects are plural.]

Either a coyote or some dogs are getting into the chicken coop. [Subject closest to the verb is plural.]

Either some coyotes or a dog is getting into the chicken coop. [Subject closest to the verb is singular.]

6J Indefinite pronouns

The indefinite pronouns *anybody, anyone, anything, each, either, everybody, neither,* and *nobody* are always singular.

The indefinite pronouns *all, any,* and *some* can use singular or plural verbs depending on their meaning. Since these words are generally followed by a prepositional phrase beginning with *of,* the intended number of the pronoun is usually determined by the number of the object of the preposition.

Some of the table is sanded. [This sentence indicates some part of one table is sanded.]

Some of the tables are sanded. [This sentence means that we have more than one table; several of the tables are completely sanded.]

The indefinite pronoun *none* requires a singular verb in strictly formal writing. However, when writing informally, some writers will consider *none* to be plural if the object of the preposition *of* following *none* is plural.

Formal:

None of the cakes is eaten yet. [Formal writers place *none* in the same category as *anybody, anyone, each,* and so forth.]

Informal:

None of the cakes are eaten yet. [When writing informally, some writers place *none* in the same category as *all, any,* and *some.*]

6K Inverted sentences

Be careful to locate the true subject of the verb in inverted sentences, in which the subject comes after the verb.

Hurtling through the far reaches of space, emitting radio pulses from beyond the stars, is a tiny space capsule.

Just beyond the fenceline on the other side of the road are some pheasants.

6L Inverted sentences beginning with *there* or *here* or *where*

Be especially careful with inverted sentences beginning with *here, there,* or *where.* Look for the subject after the verb and then decide upon agreement. Errors occur most frequently when a writer uses these words in contractions or in questions.

Here are the belt and the sweater that I lost. [When speaking informally, many persons tend to say "Here's the belt and sweater I lost," or "Where's my belt and sweater?" The careful writer, however, will note that the true subject is plural.]

There's one glass of lemonade left. [Singular subject demands that contraction be formed with *is.*]

Are there any more cups left in the cupboard?

6M Relative pronouns used as subjects

Relative pronouns used as subjects *(who, that, which)* are singular or plural depending on their antecedents. In a carefully made sentence, the antecedent will normally be the noun immediately in front of the relative pronoun.

A person who builds glass houses shouldn't throw stones. [*Who* is singular because its antecedent, *person,* is singular.]

People who build glass houses shouldn't throw stones. [*Who* is plural because its antecedent, *people,* is plural.]

Be especially careful when the antecedent is the object of the preposition *of.*

Helen is one of those persons who never keep their rooms clean. [The antecedent of *who* is the plural *persons,* not the singular *one.*]

One of the reasons which are frequently given is inflation. [Study the grammatical construction of this sentence. The verb of the main clause is singular because its subject is the singular *one*— "One of the reasons is inflation." But the verb in the relative clause is plural because its subject, *which,* has for its antecedent the plural *reasons.*]

EXCEPTION: If the words *the only* are placed before *one,* then the verb in the relative clause should be singular even though its apparent antecedent is plural.

Pete is the only one of Sam's children who wants to become a plumber.

BUT

Pete is only one of Sam's children who want to become plumbers.

6N Linking verbs

Linking verbs should agree with the subject of the sentence, not with the subjective complement. In cases where formal correctness sounds awkward, rewrite the sentence to avoid the problem.

Sleeping, eating, and drinking are his whole life. [Verb agrees with plural subject, not singular subjective complement.]

BUT

His whole life is sleeping, eating, and drinking. [Verb agrees with singular subject, not plural subjective complement.]

6O   Collective nouns

With collective nouns, such as *group, committee, crew, crowd, faculty, majority,* and *audience,* use a singular verb if you regard the collective group as one unit; use a plural verb if you wish to emphasize the members of the group acting individually.

The faculty at Hogwash College is divided on that issue. [Here *faculty* is regarded as a single unit.]

The faculty at Hogwash College are arguing at this very moment. [Here *faculty* refers to individual members.]

Some plural nouns that name quantities require singular verbs when the nouns suggest a single unit.

Fifteen hours is a long time to work without sleeping.

Ten yards was the longest rush of the afternoon for the Cougars.

6P   Nouns with plural form but singular meaning

The following nouns are generally considered singular: *news, gallows, mumps, measles, shambles,* and *whereabouts.*

The gallows stands high on the hill outside of town.

On the other hand, these words are generally considered plural: *trousers, scissors, riches, barracks.*

The soldier's barracks are ugly.

When in doubt whether a noun is singular or plural, consult a good dictionary.

Words Ending in *ics*

If a word ending in *ics* refers to a science, art, or body of knowledge, it is generally considered singular; if it refers to an activity or a quality, it is generally considered plural.

Physics (economics, and so forth) is my major field in school. [refers to a body of knowledge and is hence singular]

BUT

Athletics (gymnastics, acrobatics) are what I love most. [refers to an activity and is hence plural]

Some words ending in *ics* can be either singular or plural depending upon intended meaning.

Ethics (politics) is an important field of study. [refers here to a body of knowledge and is hence singular]

John Smith's ethics (politics) seem to me deplorable. [refers here to principles or qualities and is hence plural]

A Number/the Number

A number of (X) refers to a collection of individual items and takes a plural verb. *The number of (X)* refers to a unit and takes a singular verb.

A number of students are studying grammar this semester.

BUT

The number of students studying grammar is declining every year.

6Q Titles and words used as words

Titles or words referred to as words use singular verbs.

Snow White and the Seven Dwarfs is a famous Disney movie. [a title]

BUT

Snow White and the Seven Dwarfs are my favorite Disney characters. [refers to separate individuals]

Toenails is an ugly word. [refers to *toenails* as a word]

BUT

Toenails are ugly. [uses *toenails* in the ordinary manner, referring to the plural concept]

NOTE: Titles and words used as words are normally italicized, underlined, or placed in quotation marks. See Chapters 27 and 32.

Exercise 6-2 Self-study: Problems of Agreement

In the following exercises underline the true subject or subjects of the verb in parentheses; then choose the correct verb form.

	Answer column
1. We know how to build a bicycle that (lasts/last).	1. *that* lasts [Antecedent *bicycle* is singular.]
2. We know how to build bicycles that (lasts/last).	2. *that* last [Antecedent *bicycles* is plural.]
3. Everyone in both of my French classes (is/are) having trouble learning how to make the French *r* sound.	3. *everyone* is having [Subject is singular.]
4. Some of the students, however, (is/are) better than others.	4. *some* are [In this sentence *some* is plural; see 6J.]
5. Some of our time spent in class on pronunciation (is/are) wasted.	5. *some* is [Here *some* is singular; see 6J.]
6. There (is/are) some reasons that are better than others in this case.	6. are *reasons* [True subject is this inverted sentence is *reasons*.]

7. Where (is/are) the bag of golf clubs that I asked you to bring?

8. The armadillo's shell, which is made up of numerous bony plates, (is/are) jointed across the animal's back.

9. Named in Revelation 16 as the place where the rulers of the world will fight the last great battle between good and evil (is/are) Armageddon, located in the mountains of central Palestine.

10. My two best friends, along with Pablo Garcia, (is/are) going to climb Mt. Hood.

11. Pablo Garcia and my two best friends (is/are) going to climb Mt. Hood.

12. Pablo Garcia as well as my two best friends (is/are) going to climb Mt. Hood.

13. Either Pablo Garcia or my two best friends (is/are) going to climb Mt. Hood.

14. Neither my two best friends nor Pablo Garcia (is/are) going to climb Mt. Hood.

15. Some of the snow (has/have) melted.

16. Some of the snowflakes (has/have) melted.

17. Janice is one of those writers who never (composes/compose) on a typewriter.

18. A number of my friends (hates/hate) freshman English.

19. Each of the persons who (is/are) going on this trip (plans/plan) to take traveler's checks.

20. I don't think that Joe or Jim can do the job, but either of them (is/are) better than Louis.

21. Neither of the students (wants/want) to write the paper.

22. The scissors (needs/need) sharpening.

23. The number of my friends who (swims/swim) everyday (increases/increase) each year.

24. The young woman's gymnastics (thrills/thrill) the crowd.

25. The committee (is/are) sending individual letters to congress.

---

7. is *bag* [Subject is *bag.*]

8. *shell* is jointed [Intervening words don't affect the number of the verb; subject is shell.]

9. is *Armageddon* [In this inverted sentence, subject follows the verb.]

10. *friends* are going to climb [*Along with Pablo Garcia* is a prepositional phrase.]

11. *Pablo Garcia* and *friends* are going to climb

12. *Pablo Garcia* is going to climb [*As well as my two best friends* is a prepositional phrase and doesn't affect the subject.]

13. *Garcia* or *friends* are going to climb [Verb agrees with nearer subject, *friends,* since subjects are joined by *or.*]

14. *friends* nor *Pablo Garcia* is going to climb [Verb agrees with nearer subject, *Pablo Garcia.*]

15. *some* has melted [See 6J.]

16. *some* have melted [See 6J.]

17. *who* compose [Antecedent is the plural *writers;* therefore *who* is plural.]

18. *number* hate [*A number* is plural; *the number* is singular; see 6P.]

19. *who* are going [*Who* is plural because its antecedent is the plural *persons.*]
each plans [Intervening words don't affect true subject, which is the singular *each.*]

20. *either* is [*Either* is singular.]

21. *neither* wants [*Neither* is singular.]

22. *scissors* need [*Scissors* is considered plural; see 6P.]

23. *who* swim [Antecedent *friends* is plural.]
number increases [*A number* is plural; *the number* is singular.]

24. *gymnastics* thrill [See 6P.]

25. *committee* are sending [Group is thought of as acting individually.]

Exercise 6-3   Mastery exercise: Subject-verb agreement

In the following exercises underline the true subject or subjects of the verb in parentheses; then choose the correct verb form and write your answer in the space at the right.

Example:

<u>Some</u> of the sugar in this bowl (has/have) gotten wet.   *has*

1. Under a pile of old rags in the corner of the basement (is/are) a mother mouse and a squirming family of little baby mice.

    1. _____

2. The funnel cloud, looking like a classic photograph of a cyclone, (snake/snakes) down from the ink-black sky.

    2. _____

3. Hard work, together with intelligence, initiative, and a bit of good luck, (explains/ explain) the success of many wealthy businesspeople.

    3. _____

4. Far beyond the power of speech (is/are) a lover's touch.

    4. _____

5. The first thing she emphasized (was/were) the differences between Pacific and Atlantic breeding patterns of these fish.

    5. _____

6. The myth, legend, prayer, and ritual of primitive religions (contains/contain) many common themes.

    6. _____

7. The distinguished literary critic and author of numerous articles (appears/appear) tonight at 8:30 on local TV.

    7. _____

8. Unfortunately, neither of the interviewers for the local TV station (has/have) read any of her works.

    8. _____

9. There (is/are) a number of students who (is/are) waiting to see the teacher.

    9. _____

    _____

10. (Does/do) one of the students still have my notebook?

    10. _____

11. Either Sam or one of his friends (has/have) it.

    11. _____

12. One of the students who (is/are) trying out for the play (wants/want) to become a professional actor.

    12. _____

    _____

13. He is the only one of all the students in the theater arts class who really (has/have) professional ambitions.

    13. _____

14. Why (isn't/aren't) there any more crackers in this dish?

    14. _____

15. The committee (is/are) each writing individual letters to the judge.

    15. _____

16. Fifteen gallons (is/are) all my gas tank holds.

    16. _____

17. For young adult males, mumps (is/are) a dreaded disease.

17. _____

18. Among preteen girls in many parts of the United States, there (is/are) a new
fascination for gymnastics.

18. _____

7
The Forms of Verbs

7A, B **To understand how verbs work, you should learn the principal parts of verbs and their uses in forming verb tenses.**

As explained in Chapter 3 on grammar, verbs are used in two ways: as complete verbs, in which case they make assertions about subjects and thus serve as predicates in a sentence, and as incomplete verbs (verbals), in which case they operate as nouns, adjectives, or adverbs in the sentence. To gain control over verbs, you should be able to form their three principal parts — the present stem, past stem, and past participle — and also the infinitive and present participle, which are formed the same way for all verbs. Most verbs form their principal parts according to regular rules and are therefore called **regular.** Some verbs, however, are **irregular** because their past stems and past participles don't follow the regular pattern. These irregular parts must simply be memorized in order to write (or speak) the standard edited English dialect.

Principal part	Regular verb examples	Irregular verb examples	Special irregular case
Infinitive (begins with *to*; the word following the *to* is called the **infinitive stem**)	to love to borrow	to begin to get	to be
present stem (same as infinitive stem except for verb *to be*)	love borrow	begin get	am, is, are
past stem (regular verbs add an *ed* to present stem; irregular verbs have different form)	loved borrowed	began got	was, were
past participle (same as past stem for regular verbs; usually a different form for irregular verbs)	loved borrowed	begun gotten	been
present participle (for all verbs, adds an *ing* to the stem of the infinitive)	loving borrowing	beginning getting	being

Verbs often change their forms in sentences in order to show different senses of time. Grammarians call a verb's "time" its *tense.* For two of the tenses — the simple present and the simple past — a complete verb is formed by using one word only. For all the other tenses it takes two or more words to form a complete verb. The extra words are called helping, or auxiliary, verbs. In some tenses the main verb itself or one of the helping verbs will change form in order to agree with its subject in person and number (see Chapter 6 on subject-verb agreement).

There are six main tenses, each with two forms—simple and progressive.

Simple present (uses the present stem; adds an *s* or *es* to the third person singular)

I love, you love, he *loves,* we love, you love, they love

I go, you go, she *goes,* we go, you go, they go

The simple present is used for actions happening at the moment ("Sally eats a sandwich"). It can also be used to express habitual, continuous, or characteristic action ("We pay our bills on the fifth of the month"; "Steve Trout pitches for the Cubs").

Simple past (uses the past stem)

I loved, you loved, she loved, we loved, you loved, they loved

I went, you went, he went, we went, you went, they went

The simple past describes an action completed at a definite time in the past ("Sally ate her sandwich and left the house").

Simple future [uses the present stem with *will* (or sometimes *shall*) as a helping verb]

I will love, you will love, she will love, we will love, you will love, they will love

I will go, you will go, he will go, we will go, you will go, they will go

The simple future describes an action that will happen at a future time ("Sally will eat a sandwich for lunch tomorrow").

Present perfect (uses the past participle with the present stem of *to have* as a helping verb: subject + have or has + past participle)

I have loved, you have loved, he *has* loved, we have loved, you have loved, they have loved

I have gone, you have gone, she *has* gone, we have gone, you have gone, they have gone

The present perfect tense usually implies an action begun in the past and completed close to the time the sentence is spoken ("Sally *has eaten* her sandwich, so we can leave now"). It can also be used to express continuous or habitual action in the past with the implication that the action still continues in the present ("Sally *has eaten* sandwiches for lunch ever since she was a child").

Past perfect (uses the past participle with the past stem of *to have:* subject + had + past participle)

I had loved, you had loved, she had loved, we had loved, you had loved, they had loved

I had gone, you had gone, he had gone, we had gone, you had gone, they had gone

The past perfect is always used in conjunction with another verb in the past time. The past perfect indicates that a past action was completed before another past action was completed ("Sally had already eaten her sandwich when I remembered the leftover chili"). The time sequence can be displayed on the following time line, in which earlier actions occur to the left of later actions.

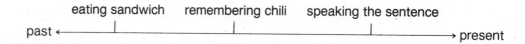

Future perfect (use the past participle with the future tense of *to have*: subject + will have + past participle)

I will have loved, you will have loved, she will have loved, we will have loved, you will have loved, they will have loved

I will have gone, you will have gone, he will have gone, we will have gone, you will have gone, they will have gone

The future perfect is always used in conjunction with another verb expressing future time. It specified a future action that will be completed before another future action ("By the time Pete finishes making the milkshake, Sally will have eaten her sandwich.")

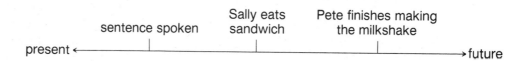

Each of the tenses also has a *progressive* form to indicate actions that are ongoing or in process.

Present progressive:

Sally *is eating* her sandwich at this moment.

Past progressive:

Sally *was eating* her sandwich when the phone rang.

Future progressive:

Sally *will be eating* her sandwich when you arrive.

Present perfect progressive:

Sally *has been eating* her sandwich for twenty minutes but still hasn't finished it.

Past perfect progressive:

Sally *had been eating* her sandwich for twenty minutes when suddenly her friends lost their patience and left.

The Forms of Verbs **147**

Future perfect progressive:

> I predict that by the time you finish making the milkshake, Sally *will have been eating* that sandwich for twenty minutes.

> Several of these tenses also have an *emphatic* form, which uses the helping verb *to do* combined with the infinitive stem. The emphatic form is used for giving special stress, for asking questions, and for making negations.

> I *did go. Did* the dog *bark? Do* you *like* peanuts? The child *does* not *sit* still.

> Additionally, a variety of other helping verbs and helping verb clusters can be used to form complete verbs with different senses of time and attitude: *can, must, would, could, used to, going to, is about to, should, might, may,* and so forth.

> I *can run.* We *used to run.* Pete *should run.* Sally *is about to run.*

Exercise 7-1 Self-study: Tenses of verbs

In the following sentences decide on the correct form of the verb *to feed.* This exercise should help you appreciate how verbs change their form to signal different senses of time.

Answer column

1. Jim (feed) the dog at two o'clock yesterday.
   1. fed [Past tense shows completed action.]

2. At the time you called, Jim (feed) the dog.
   2. was feeding [Progressive form shows that the action was occurring at the specified moment.]

3. Jim (feed) the dog at two o'clock tomorrow afternoon.
   3. will feed [This form (simple future) shows future time.]

4. Jim is trustworthy. I'll bet that if you check at three o'clock tomorrow afternoon, Jim (feed) the dog.
   4. will have fed [Future perfect indicates that the action of feeding will occur before the action of checking.]

5. Jim (feed) the dog at two o'clock every afternoon for the past ten years.
   5. has fed [Present perfect indicates habitual action begun in the past and touching the present.]

6. Jim (feed) the dog at two o'clock every afternoon.
   6. feeds [Simple present indicates ongoing habitual action.]

7. When you called at three o'clock yesterday afternoon, Jim (feed) the dog already.
   7. had fed [Past perfect indicates that the action of feeding occurred before the action of calling.]

8. If you call at exactly two o'clock tomorrow, Jim (feed) the dog.
   8. will be feeding [Progressive form indicates an action that is in the process of occurring at a specified moment.]

9. When I called at two o'clock yesterday afternoon, Jim didn't answer because he (feed) the dog.
   9. was feeding [Again, progressive form indicates ongoing action.]

10. Since it takes Jim ten minutes to feed the dog, if you call tomorrow at 2:05 in the afternoon, Jim (feed) the dog for five minutes.
    10. Will have been feeding [Future perfect progressive combines progressive form to show ongoing action with the future perfect to show that the act of feeding began before the act of calling.]

7C When joining clauses or when joining verbal phrases to clauses, be sure that you maintain a logical sequence of tenses.

> When two or more verbs or verbals occur together in the same sentence, it is sometimes tricky to keep the sequences of tenses logical.

Illogical:

When the engine ran out of gas, the helicopter slowly drifts to the ground.

Logical:

When the engine ran out of gas, the helicopter slowly drifted to the ground.

Illogical:

We should have bought the car when they drop prices in August.

Logical:

We should buy the car when they drop prices in August.

We should have bought the car when they dropped prices in August.

Although it is difficult to formulate rules for sequencing tenses, native speakers of English have a natural "feel" for ways of putting the tenses together. Here, though, are several principles:

- When the verb in the main clause is in any present tense, any future tense, or the present perfect tense, then the verb in a subordinate clause can be in any tense that your meaning requires.

I think that I will go to the ball game tomorrow. [present followed by future]

I think that Paul went to the ball game yesterday. [present followed by past]

All day long I have been thinking that Paul will go to the game tomorrow. [present perfect progressive followed by future]

- When the verb in the main clause is in the past tense or the past perfect tense, the verb in a subordinate clause must also be in a past or past perfect tense.

Yesterday I thought that I would go to the game today. [*Would* expresses a future time imagined in the past. COMPARE: "I think that I will go tomorrow."]

Yesterday I thought that Paul had gone to the game on Wednesday.

All day yesterday I thought that I would have seen the Red Sox play by this time today. [Again, *would* substitutes for *will* to show a future time imagined in the past. COMPARE: "I think that I will have seen the Red Sox play by this time tomorrow."]

- If you want to express action using an infinitive, choose a present infinitive to show action occurring at the same time as or later than the main verb and use a past infinitive to show action that happens earlier than the main verb.

I want to play basketball at three o'clock today.

I am mad at the coach's schedule. I want to have played basketball already.

7D Learn to form the moods of verbs.

The three moods—indicative, subjunctive, and imperative—state the attitude of the writer toward the statement the verb makes.

Indicative

The indicative mood is the most common and is used for statements or questions about facts.

> She is riding in the car. Joe pays the bill. Where is Sally?

Subjunctive

The subjunctive is formed in the present tense by using the infinitive stem. In the past tense, only the verb *to be* has a distinctive subjective form, which is always *were*.

Although the subjunctive mood is becoming extinct, some uses of it still remain because it expresses subtle distinctions in meaning not otherwise possible. The following sentences, for example, have different meanings.

> If she is here, she is having fun. [indicative mood]
>
> If she were here, she would be having fun. [subjunctive mood]

In the first sentence the speaker doesn't know whether she is here or not, but if she *is* here, then she is having fun. In the second sentence the speaker knows that she is *not* here, because the *were* in the second sentence (the subjunctive mood) indicates a condition contrary to fact. Other uses of the subjunctive include expressions of desire, request, or command in certain clauses beginning with *that*.

> If she *were* riding in the car, she would now be carsick. [Condition contrary to fact—she is *not* riding in the car.]
>
> I request that Joe *pay* the bill. [Clause beginning with *that* conveying request.]

Imperative

Finally, the imperative mood conveys a command or request. It is the same as the second person present tense, except for the verb *to be,* which uses *be.*

> Be here.
>
> Pay the bill immediately.

Exercise 7-2   Self-study: Sequencing verb tenses

A. In the following sentences, insert a form of the verb that fits logically. Some sentences may have more than one appropriate answer.

	Answer column
1. When I get up each morning, I (walk) the dog.	1. walk
2. She (be) in Utah many times in the past.	2. has been
3. George (swim) in the state meet next weekend.	3. will swim
4. By three o'clock tomorrow, I want to (finish) this essay.	4. have finished
5. Before he broke the vase, he (juggle) three tennis balls.	5. had been juggling

6. We (watch) the game on television when the lightning (strike).

7. She asked that Ralph (submit) his paper by nine o'clock.

8. She drank a quart of ice tea after she (finish) her tennis match.

9. The runners have passed Milton's store and (a progressive form of head) down Clearwater Road.

10. After the doctors (finish) suturing the incision, a nurse noticed a missing sponge.

11. My ears (stop) hurting by the time I got to the doctor's office.

12. I (realize) for some time now that Jack will be resigning in August.

13. (Participle of finish) the assignment, he was surprised to realize how much he (learn).

14. If Spot (be) my dog, I (teach) him not to chase cars.

15. He wanted (infinitive of finish) the pizza completely by the time the group arrived for the meeting.

6. were watching
   struck

7. submit

8. had finished

9. are heading

10. had finished

11. had stopped

12. have realized

13. Having finished
    had learned

14. were
    would teach

15. to have finished

B. In the following exercise convert direct quotations into indirect quotations as follows:

Direct quotation:

"I don't know where Mom went," he said.

Indirect quotation:

He said that he didn't know where his mom had gone.

This exercise will give you further practice in tense sequencing.

16. "I will spend more time on my assignments," Tom told me.
    Convert to: Tom told me that _____
    _____

16. he would spend more time on his assignments.

17. "I will have examined the IRS statement by noon tomorrow," my accountant told me.
    My accountant told me that she _____
    _____

17. would have examined the IRS statement by noon the next day.

18. "You're making fine progress," the teacher told me.

The teacher told me that I _____

_____

18. was making fine progress.

19. "I will never forget all that Father Joseph has done for me," he said.

He said that he _____

_____

19. would never forget all that Father Joseph had done for him.

20. "Where have you been?" he asked me.

He asked me where _____

20. I had been.

7E   Learn to form the active and passive voices.

Use the active voice to emphasize the agent doing or performing an action; use the passive voice to emphasize the receiver receiving the action or to show that the actor is unimportant or unknown, as in scientific reports.

The voice of a verb tells us whether the subject of the verb acts upon something else or has something else act upon it. Active and passive voices occur only with transitive verbs, which transfer action from an actor to a receiver. In active voice verbs the subject is the actor and the direct object is the receiver.

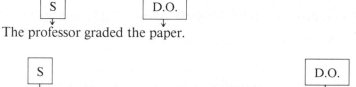

In the passive voice the subject is the receiver of the action and the actor is either omitted from the sentence or made the object of the preposition *by*. The passive voice verb is formed with the past participle and the helping verb *to be*.

> The paper was graded (by the professor).
>
> The parking meters were robbed (by the man in the blue trench coat).

In general, experienced writers prefer active voice verbs because they are stronger and more economical than passive voice verbs.

Weak:

> The cake and ice cream were eaten, and then games were played.

Stronger:

> The children ate the cake and ice cream and then played games.

Additionally, because passive voice verbs can omit the actor, persons sometimes use them to evade responsibility.

Evasive:

A decision has been made to raise the dues.

Braver:

The president and the treasurer have decided to raise the dues.

NOTE: The passive voice occurs frequently in scientific writing where the objects being observed are frequently more important than the observer.

The distillate is then removed from the liquid.

Exercise 7-3   Self-study: Active-passive transformations

In the following exercises convert all transitive passive sentences to transitive active and all transitive active sentences to transitive passive. Leave intransitive sentences unchanged. In converting some transitive passive sentences to transitive active, you may have to add an actor or agent. For each sentence, try to determine in which rhetorical situations the active voice version would be better and in which situations the passive would be better.

Answer column

1. The wind blowing from the north rattled the windows in our bedroom.

2. It has been decided that the game will be canceled.

3. The squirrel fled to the highest branches of the tree.

4. The little girl in the green sunsuit slowly covered her sleeping father with piles of sand.

5. Some of the most important scientific principles have been discovered accidently.

6. Many western forests are being severely damaged by the mountain pine beetle.

7. Aunt Molly, wearing an old nightgown and rubber boots, had already tracked the criminal into the toolshed when the police arrived.

8. The shadow of the moon crossed the earth's surface near Portland, Oregon.

9. Three hundred dozen potatoes were peeled by Sgt. Williams' platoon during the rainy season at Fort McCloud.

10. The motor was probably ruined by the turbine bearing's being rusted out.

1. The windows in our bedroom were rattled by the wind blowing from the north.

2. (The coaches) decided to cancel the game.

3. Intransitive.

4. The sleeping father was slowly covered with piles of sand by the little girl in the green sunsuit.

5. (Investigators) have discovered some of the most important scientific principles accidently.

6. The mountain pine beetle is severely damaging many western forests.

7. When the police arrived, the criminal had already been tracked into the toolshed by Aunt Molly, wearing an old nightgown and rubber boots.

8. The earth's surface was crossed by the shadow of the moon near Portland, Oregon.

9. During the rainy season at Fort McCloud, Sgt. Williams' platoon peeled three hundred dozen potatoes.

10. The turbine bearing's being rusted out probably ruined the motor.

7F   Use the infinitive form of the verb to complete the sense of other verbs, to serve as nouns, and to form the basis of some phrases.

Infinitives have present and perfect tenses and can show active and passive voice.

I want *to love.* [present infinitive]

To have loved and lost is better than not *to have loved* at all. [present perfect infinitive]

I want *to be loved* [present infinitive, passive voice]

Oh, *to have been loved* by the crowd would have made my performance complete. [present perfect infinitive, passive voice]

Infinitives can serve a variety of purposes in a sentence.

I want *to love.* [used as noun in direct object slot]

She is not a woman *to be loved lightly.* [used as adjective modifying *woman*]

He stood up *to announce his love for her.* [used as adverb because it answers *why* and thus modifies the verb]

Sometimes the infinitive marker *to* is omitted in infinitives following verbs like *hear, help, let, see,* and *watch.*

Let me *go* to the dance. [Let me (to) go to the dance.]

Should I help you finish the dishes? [Should I help you (to) finish the dishes?]

Split Infinitives

Writers who are conservative in their use of language avoid splitting infinitives. (A split infinitive occurs when an adverb or other phrase comes between the *to* and the infinitive stem.)

Split infinitive:

I wish *to* solemnly *swear* to you that I am innocent.

Connected infinitive:

I wish *to swear* to you solemnly that I am innocent.

Other writers, however, disregard this "rule" the way they disregard older distinctions between *shall* and *will.* In general, you should probably avoid splitting infinitives in formal essays if relocating the adverb or other phrase is equally graceful. Always avoid splitting infinitives if the resulting sentence sounds awkward.

7G Be watchful for the most common errors in the use of verbs.

1 Avoid confusing the simple past and past participle in irregular verbs. The past participle in predicates always needs a helping verb.

Faulty:

I begun the test late. [past participle confused with past stem]

Correct:

I began the test late.

Faulty:

I should have began the test at nine o'clock. [past stem confused with past participle]

Correct:

> I should have begun the test at nine o'clock.

2 Avoid trying to regularize irregular verbs.

Faulty:

> Joe throwed the ball at Pete.

Correct:

> Joe threw the ball at Pete.

3 Keep the distinction between *lie* and *lay*.

To lie means "to recline" and is intransitive. Its principal parts are *lie, lay,* and *lain.*
To lay means "to put down" or "to place" and is transitive. Its principal parts are *lay, laid, laid*

Confusion probably occurs because the past tense of *to lie* is *lay.*

Faulty:

> I am laying on my bed.

Correct:

> I am lying on my bed. [COMPARE: I am reclining on my bed.]
>
> BUT
>
> I am laying my suitcase on the bed. [COMPARE: I am placing my suitcase on the bed.]

4 Keep the distinction between *sit* and *set*.

Sit, like *lie,* is an intransitive verb and can't take a direct object. Its principal parts are *sit, sat, sat.*
Set, like *lay,* is a transitive verb that takes a direct object. Its principal parts are *set, set, set.*

Faulty:

> Please set in the chair.

Correct:

> Please sit in the chair.

Faulty:

> He sat the vase on the table.

Correct:

> He set the vase on the table.

5 Avoid illogical shifts in tense.

Illogical:

> The computer blinks at me confusingly, and I was getting mad.

Correct:

> The computer blinks at me confusingly, and I am getting mad.
> The computer blinked at me confusingly, and I was getting mad.

Exercise 7-4   Self-study: Special verb problems

	Answer column
A. In sentences 1 to 9, choose the correct option in parentheses.	
1. I (lie/lay) the book on the bed.	lay
2. He (lies/lays) on the bed.	lies
3. I (have lain/have laid) on the bed all morning	have lain
4. (Lying/laying) on the kitchen table is a book of matches.	lying
5. (Lying/laying) the matches on the table, I begin searching for a knife.	laying
6. (Sit/set) down, please.	sit
7. (Sit/set) your suitcase in the corner, please.	set
8. I like (to cautiously sneak up/to sneak up cautiously)	to sneak up cautiously
9. After you (sit/set) your briefcase on the desk, feel free (to lie/to lay) down for an hour.	set to lie
B. In sentences 10 to 14 choose the correct form of the verb in parentheses.	
10. The dog barked at the cat and then *(to run)* around the yard.	ran
11. Yesterday he *(to hit)* the ball, *(to run)* into the alley, *(to do)* a cartwheel, *(to throw)* a rock at the garbage can, and then suddenly *(to see)* the police officer.	hit; ran; did; threw; saw
12. I *(to swim)* across the river early this morning.	swam
13. I have *(to swim)* across the river many times.	swum
14. This essay is *(to write)* well.	written

NAME _____ DATE _____

Exercise 7-5   Mastery exercise: Verbs

A. For sentences 1 to 9, write the appropriate form of the verb in the space at the right.

1. They (a form of *lie* or *lay*) Six Gun Sam's body in the casket yesterday.   1. _____

2. By now, DeWitt and Paula *(choose)* the name for their new baby.   2. _____

3. At this moment he (a form of *lie* or *lay*) on the bed watching television for forty-eight straight hours.   3. _____

4. By noon tomorrow he (a progressive form of *watch*) television for sixty straight hours.   4. _____

5. I insist that this car (a form of *be*) repaired by five o'clock tonight, or I will begin a lawsuit.   5. _____

6. She (a past form of *begin*) to cry after the butterfly (a form of *fly*) away.   6. _____ _____

7. When I get some extra money, I (a form of *buy*) some new sandals.   7. _____

8. (A participle of *enjoy*) the cool of the evening, we (a past form of *drink*) mint juleps on the front porch.   8. _____ _____

9. (A participle of *finish*) the mint juleps, we (a past form of *go*) into the house to escape the mosquitoes.   9. _____ _____

B. In the following passage examine each underlined construction. If it is correct, place a *C* in the appropriate space at the right. If it is incorrect, place a corrected version in the space at the right.

(10)
It was hot in the room that evening after we <u>have come</u> back from the park.   10. _____

(11)
<u>Deciding</u> to spend the evening quietly at home, we were annoyed when the   11. _____
        12. _____
(12)   (13)
phone <u>has been ringing</u>. "If I <u>was</u> you," said the voice on the other end of the   13. _____
        14. _____
(14)
line," I <u>would not stay</u> in that room this evening." Of course, being detectives,   15. _____

(15)
we <u>were use</u> to mysterious calls, but this one especially troubled us.

C. Convert the following sentences from transitive active to transitive passive or from transitive passive to transitive active. If the verb is intransitive, write *I* in the right hand margin. For some transformations from passive to active voice, you may have to add an actor or agent.

16. Postindustrial people are rediscovering the pleasures of primitive life.

_____
_____
_____

The Forms of Verbs   **157**

17. The present reasoning crisis in our schools results from our emphasis on "right answer" teaching instead of on "right question" teaching.

_____

_____

18. A new sense of purpose is being regained by educators in the light of new discoveries about the nature of thinking.

_____

_____

19. The murder weapon was carefully selected from a drawerful of death-wielding implements.

_____

_____

8

Pronoun Problems

Pronouns, which take the place of nouns, allow us to avoid awkward repetitions when we speak and write. The noun that a pronoun stands for is called the antecedent of the pronoun. Writers can confuse their readers if they use pronouns without a clear antecedent, and they can annoy their readers if they use pronoun forms that violate the usage rules of edited American English.

8A Make clear connections between pronouns and their antecedents by avoiding confusing references and by keeping pronouns as close as possible to their antecedents.

Confusing:

Jim explained to his son the reasons he couldn't go to the meeting.

Clear:

Jim explained the reasons why his son couldn't go to the meeting.

"I'll explain why I can't go to the meeting," Jim told his son.

8B Make your pronouns agree in number with their antecedents.

This rule presents difficulties mainly in those instances when it is not clear whether the antecedent is singular or plural. The problem of pronoun-antecedent agreement is thus similar to the problem of subject-verb agreement (see Chapter 6). The following rules cover most cases:

- *Compound constructions.* Use a plural pronoun to refer to a compound antecedent joined by *and;* use a singular pronoun if the compound antecedent is joined by *or.* (If a compound antecedent is joined by *or* and one antecedent is singular while the other is plural, the pronoun agrees with the nearer antecedent.)

Rebecca and Paul invited us to *their* party.

Either Jim or Pete will bring *his* volleyball to the party.

Either Jim or his sisters will bring *their* volleyball.

Either the sisters or Jim will bring *his* volleyball.

- *Collective nouns (team, committee, audience,* and so forth). Use a singular pronoun to refer to a collective noun acting as a group; use a plural pronoun to refer to a collective noun acting as individuals.

The committee reported *its* opinion.

The committee began arguing among *themselves.*

- *Indefinite pronouns (each, either, neither, everyone, everybody, someone, somebody, anyone, anybody).* Edited American English usually requires a singular pronoun when its antecedent is an indefinite pronoun.

Everybody coming to the party should bring *his* own drinks.

NOTE ON SEXIST LANGUAGE: (see also Chapter 21.) In the past, one regularly chose the masculine pronoun to refer to indefinite antecedents, but today many persons regard this usage as sexist. No solution is universally agreed upon, but most writers try to avoid the problem by recasting the sentence using plural forms where possible (since plural pronouns don't have gender). Other solutions are to alternate periodically between masculine and feminine pronouns or occasionally to say "his or her."

Everybody coming to the party should bring *her* own drinks.

Everybody coming to the party should bring *his or her* own drinks. [cumbersome]

Everybody coming to the party should bring his/her own drinks. [cumbersome and inelegant — unacceptable in formal prose]

Everybody coming to the party should bring *their* own drinks. [because of lack of agreement in number, not yet widely accepted in formal usage]

All people coming to the party should bring *their* own drinks. [best solution]

8C   Avoid making broad references with the pronouns *this, that, it, which,* and *such.*

A broad reference occurs whenever a pronoun stands for an idea or a whole group of words rather than for a single noun.

Confusing:

Harold Krebs in Hemingway's "Soldiers Home" rebels against his parents. He does *this* by refusing to accept their values, and *this* is why his parents are so upset by *it.* [Pronouns refer not to specific nouns but to ideas; in this case the ideas shift with each pronoun, confusing the reader.]

Revised:

Harold Krebs in Hemingway's "Soldiers Home" rebels against his parents by refusing to accept their values. This rejection explains why his parents are so upset by his later actions.

8D   Do not use *it* as an expletive (as in "It is raining") in the same sentence that *it* is used as a pronoun.

Awkward:

Watch out for our driveway. When *it* rains, *it* always gets slippery.

Revised:

Watch out. When it rains, our driveway always gets slippery.

8E   Use the second person *you* as a general reference to your readers in informal prose; use *one* in formal usage.

> If you start thinking about the riddle, you will be puzzled for days. [informal]
>
> If one starts thinking about the riddle, one will be puzzled for days. [formal]

8F   Use the first person pronouns *I, me, my, mine* when writing about personal experience or when letting readers know your own opinion on a controversial issue; avoid intrusion of the first person into contexts where it distracts readers from your main topic.

> *Intrusive:*
>
> I think that indoor track meets are jammed with excitement because I like the circus atmosphere. I remember one time when I saw massive shot-putters, graceful high jumpers, and wiry mile runners all compete simultaneously out of different corners of my vision. [puts emphasis on the writer rather than on the track meet]

> *Better:*
>
> Indoor track meets are jammed with excitement because of the circus-like atmosphere. Out of different corners of your vision you can watch massive shot-putters, graceful high jumpers, and wiry mile runners all competing simultaneously.

8G   Avoid unnecessary pronouns immediately following their antecedents.

> *Redundant:*
>
> My mother *she* is going door to door asking for votes.

> *Revised:*
>
> My mother is going door to door asking for votes.

8H   Use the proper cases for pronouns.

> Many pronouns change their form depending on the grammatical slot they fill in a sentence.

Name of case	Used for these slots	Personal pronouns					Relative pronouns
subjective	subject, subject complement	I	we	he	she	they	who whoever
objective	direct object, indirect object, object of preposition, subject of infinitive	me	us	him	her	them	whom whomever
possessive	adjective showing possession	my mine	our ours	his	her hers	their theirs	whose

She and I are good friends. [subjects]

Paul likes *her and me.* [direct objects]

George wants to give *her and me* a present. [indirect objects]

This secret is just between *her and me.* [objects of preposition]

The persons chosen for the executive committee were *she and I.* [subject complements]

Patricia asked *her and me* to write the final report. [subjects of infinitive]

The report represents *their* thinking but *my* writing. [possessive adjectives]

Writers generally handle pronoun cases accurately. However, the following instances give special trouble:

1 In dependent clauses, a pronoun takes its case from the way it is used in its own clause, not from the way the dependent clause is used in the rest of the sentence.

Give the prize to *whoever* says the secret word. [At first it may seem that the pronoun is the object of the preposition *to* and should therefore be *whomever.* But the object of the preposition is actually the whole noun clause *whoever says the secret word. Whoever* is the subject of *says.*]

2 Pronouns that serve as objects (direct objects, indirect objects, and objects of prepositions) must be in the objective case: Be especially careful in compound constructions.

Correct:

Martha gave *him and me* the job. [indirect object]

Incorrect:

Martha gave *he and I* the job.

This error is readily avoided if you choose in a compound construction the same case you would choose if you used each pronoun separately.

Martha gave *him* the job. Martha gave *me* the job.

3 In appositive constructions in which a noun follows a pronoun, use the case that would be proper for the pronoun if the noun were not there.

The principal told *us* boys to go home. [told *us* to go home]

We boys hid around the corner until the principal went back to her office. [*We* hid around the corner.]

4 When pronouns occur after *than* or *as* introducing implied clauses, choose pronoun cases according to the pronoun's use in the implied clause.

Both of the following sentences are correct, but their meanings are different:

I like Paul better than he. [I like Paul better than he likes Paul.]

I like Paul better than him. [I like Paul better than I like him.]

5   Use the objective case for pronouns that are subjects or objects of infinitives.

I asked *him* to type the letter.

Sally wants *him and me* to run the errand. [not *he and I*]

Be especially careful with pronouns in front of occasional infinitives that omit the *to* (see page 154).

Let's you and *me* go to the show this evening. [Let us, you and me, (to) go to the show this evening (not *you and I*.) COMPARE: Let me go to the show this evening.

6   Use the possessive case before gerunds (*ing* verbals used as nouns) and the subjective or objective case before present participles (*ing* verbals used as adjectives).

I saw *him* running away from the police. [*Running* is a participle modifying the direct object *him*.]

I think *his* running away from the police was his biggest mistake. [*Running* is a gerund, the subject of *was*.]

7   In appositive constructions, use pronouns that agree in case with the nouns or pronouns with which they are paired.

The students elected to the council, *she* and *I*, will be going to the state capitol in a month. [Subjective case; the noun with which pronouns are in apposition — *students* — is the subject of *will be going*.]

James gave the award to the students elected to the council, *her* and *me*. [Objective case; here, *students* is the object of the preposition *to*.]

Exercise 8-1   Self-study: General pronoun usage

In the following sentences, revise any constructions that use pronouns incorrectly. There may be more than one possible solution, so the answers at the right are guides only.

Answer column

1. John told Keith that he was afraid he drank too much.

   1. "I'm afraid I drink too much," John told Keith.
      OR
      John confided to Keith his fear that he drank too much. [ambiguous antecedent]

2. A person who wants to get ahead in life should practice improving his skills at public relations.

   2. . . . should practice improving his or her skills at public relations
      OR
      People who want to get ahead in life should practice improving their skills. . . . [avoiding sexist language]

3. Look at this flower bed! It makes me furious to find it torn up by the neighbor's dog.

   3. Look at this flower bed! I am furious that the neighbor's dog tore it up. [expletive *it* close to pronoun *it*]

4. She had wished for new ice skates for Christmas, but it did not come true.

   4. . . . , but her wish did not come true. [unclear antecedent]

5. In Dr. Jones' lecture, she said that esters, which are formed from combinations of acid and alcohol, have a sweet smell.

5. In her lecture, Dr. Jones said that. . . . [Unclear antecedent: Dr. Jones' is a possessive adjective, not a noun.]

6. I appreciate him watching the kids for me.

6. . . . his watching the kids for me. [*Watching* is a gerund.]

7. I like our new car better than him.

7. . . . better than he. [Writer probably means "I like our new car better than he likes it," rather than "I like our new car better than I like him."]

8. Let's you and I work on the project together.

8. Let's you and me work on the project together. [Let us (you and me) (to) work on the project together—subject of infinitive.]

9. Please give the flowers to Brian and I.

9. . . . to Brian and me. [Object of preposition. COMPARE: Give the flowers to me.]

10. Just between we boys, I think that each girl should bring their own money for the tickets.

10. Just between us boys, I think that each girl should bring her own money for the tickets. [Object of preposition *between; her* agrees with singular *each girl.*]

11. The professor wants either Marla or I to turn in the assignment by noon tomorrow.

11. . . . Marla or me. . . . [Subject of infinitive. COMPARE: The professor wants me to turn in my assignment.]

12. Either the older women or thirteen-year-old Joanne will be at the county fair selling their paintings.

12. . . . will be at the county fair selling her paintings. [With *either. . . or,* pronoun agrees with nearer antecedent.]

13. Give the magazine to whomever wants it.

13. . . . to whoever wants it. (*Whoever* is the subject of *wants.*)

14. I want Sally and she to finish the repairs on the transmission.

14. . . . Sally and her. . . . [Subject of infinitive. COMPARE: I want her to finish the repairs.]

15. She doesn't want Paul and I in the play.

15. . . . Paul and me. . . . [Direct object. COMPARE: She doesn't want me in the play.]

Exercise 8-2   Self-study: Using sentence-combining to understand *who/whom/whose*

A. Understanding when to use *who* (same case as *I, we, he, she, they*), *whom* (same case as *me, us, him, her, them*), and *whose* (same case as *my, our, his, her, their*) is an easy matter if you understand how adjective clauses are formed. Observe the following sequence of transformations as two sentences are gradually converted into a single sentence with an adjective clause.

1. The *man* will be our new neighbor. I just met the *man.*
2.   I just met *him.*
3.   I just met *whom.*
4.   *whom* I just met.
5. The man whom I just met will be our new neighbor.

In sentence 2 the pronoun *him* replaces *man* (*him* is used rather than *he* because the objective case is needed—*man* is a direct object). At this point we still have two distinct sentences.

The man will be our new neighbor. I just met him.

However, if you wanted to use the information "I just met him" to identify which man will be the new neighbor, you could convert the second sentence into an adjective clause. In this case you put a *relative* pronoun (*who, whom, whose*) into the slot rather than a personal pronoun (*he, him, his*). Choose the relative pronoun that matches the case of the personal pronoun — in this case *whom* to match *him* (sentence 3 above). Next, move the relative pronoun to the head of the clause (sentence 4 above). Finally, insert the whole clause into the first sentence after *man* (sentence 5 above). Thus one can tell whether to use *who, whom,* or *whose* simply by seeing what personal pronoun would be used in the same slot. Here is another example:

1. She is the *person*. The *person* will be elected governor.
2.   *She* will be elected governor.
3.   *who* will be elected governor. [*Who* is same case as *she.*]
4.   She is the person who will be elected governor.

Sometimes a third clause (called a **parenthetical clause**) can be inserted into the adjective clause, but it doesn't affect the case of the relative pronoun.

1. She is the person. The person will be elected governor. I think this.
2. She is the person. She will be elected governor. I think this.
3. She is the person who will be elected governor. I think this.
4. She is the person who I think will be elected governor.

Remember two things: (1) The case of the relative pronoun is the same as the case of a personal pronoun inserted in the same slot. (2) The word order of the clause is frequently different from that of an ordinary sentence because the relative pronoun is moved as close as possible to the head of its clause.

Here are two more examples:

1. The *teacher* is sick. I gave the manuscript to the *teacher.*
2.   I gave the manuscript to *him.* [objective case]
3.   I gave the manuscript to *whom.* [same case as *him*]
4.   To *whom* I gave the manuscript.
5. The teacher to whom I gave the manuscript is sick.

1. The girl is my friend. The girl's car was stolen.
2.   *Her* car was stolen. [possessive case]
3.   *whose* car was stolen [*Whose* matches *her*—possessive case.]
4. The girl whose car was stolen is my friend.

In the following problems, combine the sentences into a single sentence either with an adjective clause or with an adjective clause and parenthetical clause. Test the case of the relative pronoun by first inserting a personal pronoun in the appropriate slot.

Answer column

1. The woman will be here in the morning. I love the woman.

1. I love *her.* [Choose *whom*—direct object.] The woman whom I love will be here in the morning.

2. I heard that Mrs. Posey just won a fellowship at the Institute of Music. I took violin lessons from Mrs. Posey.

2. I took violin lessons from *her.* [Choose *whom*—object of preposition.] I heard that Mrs. Posey, from whom I took violin lessons, just won a fellowship at the Institute of Music.

3. The professor gave me an A on the paper. I borrowed the professor's book.

3. I borrowed *his* book. [Choose *whose*—possessive.] The professor whose book I borrowed gave me an A on the paper.

4. They are the kind of students. The students would make good doctors. I think this.

5. They are the kind of students. I expect the students to be great doctors.

6. Rembrandt is the painter. She most admired the painter. I suppose this.

7. The letters on water control legislation were written by Walter Schmoe. I expect Walter Schmoe to be the next Democratic candidate for state legislature.

8. The letters on water control legislation were written by Walter Schmoe. Walter Schmoe will be the next Democratic candidate for state legislature. I expect this.

9. I don't like Polly Larson. He is taking Polly Larson to the prom.

10. Pete acts in real life like a fussy old man. Pete was chosen to play Polonius in *Hamlet.*

4. *They* would make good doctors. [Choose *who*—subject.] They are the kind of students who I think would make good doctors.

5. I expect *them* to be great doctors. [Choose *whom*—subject of infinitive.] They are the kind of students whom I expect to be great doctors.

6. She most admired *him.* [Choose *whom*—direct object.] Rembrandt is the painter whom I suppose she most admired.

7. I expect *him* to be the next Democratic candidate for state legislature. [Choose *whom*—subject of infinitive.] The letters on water control legislation were written by Walter Schmoe, whom I expect to be the next Democratic candidate for state legislature.

8. *He* will be the next Democratic candidate. [Choose *who*—subject.] The letters on water control legislation were written by Walter Schmoe, who I expect will be the next Democratic candidate for state legislature.

9. He is taking *her* to the prom. [Choose *whom*—direct object.] I don't like Polly Larson, whom he is taking to the prom.

10. *He* was chosen to play Polonius. [Choose *who*—subject.] Pete, who was chosen to play Polonius in *Hamlet,* acts in real life like a fussy old man.

B. Now that you see how adjective clauses are formed, you can decide whether to use *who, whom,* or *whose* in your own sentences by "disassembling" the clause back into a simple sentence and testing the case by inserting a personal pronoun. For example, suppose you are confronted with the following decision:

I voted for Ralph Winkley, (who/whom) I think will win the election by a landslide.

In your mind you can disassemble this sentence into three simple ones.

I voted for Ralph Winkley.
Ralph Winkley will win the election by a landslide.
I think this.

Since you would say, "*He* will win the election by a landslide," you can see that *who* is the correct choice. It operates as the subject of *will win.*

I voted for Ralph Winkley, who I think will win the election by a landslide.

In the following sentences, choose the correct case by disassembling the adjective clause back into a simple sentence and testing the case with a personal pronoun.

Answer column

11. I am going on a vacation with Sam Smith, (who/whom) owns a ski cabin near McCall, Idaho.

11. *who. He* owns a ski cabin near McCall, Idaho. [subjective case]

12. The bushmen, (who/whom) live on the edge of the Kalahari Desert in southwest Africa, are experts in tracking and stalking game.

13. The little girl (who/whom) the dog scratched is no longer crying.

14. The teacher for (who/whom) I wrote this paper is incapable of understanding it.

15. My friend Hisako, to (who/whom) the letter is addressed, is excited by the chance to visit Japan again.

16. My aunt is the woman (who/whom) I think is most likely to win the blue ribbon at the fair.

17. The girl for (who/whom) he baked the cake turned out to be allergic to chocolate.

18. (Who/whom) did you see jogging down the street this morning?

19. The boy (who/whom) delivers the papers is always late.

20. The person (who/whom) my wife is tutoring is a Korean.

12. *who. They* live on the edge of. . . . [subjective case]

13. *whom.* The dog scratched *her.* [objective case]

14. *whom.* I wrote this paper for *him.* [objective case]

15. *whom.* The letter is addressed to *her.*

16. *who. She* is most likely to win the blue ribbon at the fair. I think this.

17. *whom.* He baked the cake for *her.*

18. *whom.* You did see *her* jogging down the street. [objective case: Here a decision about *who/whom* occurs in a question rather than a relative clause, but the same strategy still works.]

19. *who. He* delivers the papers.

20. *whom.* My wife is tutoring *her.*

Exercise 8-3   Broad reference

In the following passages, circle all "broad reference" pronouns. Then revise the passage to eliminate broad reference. (Broad reference generally occurs because the writer uses *this* or *which* to stand for a whole idea that is clear to the writer but often puzzling to the reader.) You may frequently have to restructure the passage, sometimes adding material for clarity. If you have to add ideas, invent your own, making them as plausible as you can.

NOTE: Your task here is similar to the kind of revision most writers have to do on their own rough drafts midway through the composing process. Such revision takes time and craftsmanship.

Example:

The raccoon always washes his food as he eats. No one knows exactly why he does (this.) Nevertheless, (it) must be an old habit because he gets his Latin name from (this,) which is *lotor,* or "the washer." The raccoon's long, nimble fingers make it easy for him to do (this.) He especially likes creatures that live in and out of shallow pools. Easily opening the shells of snails or mussels without even looking, he sits at the edge of the pool and carefully does (this) as he dines. However, raccoons sometimes live in dry regions, (which) means they don't have to do (this.) When hungry, a raccoon will gobble down his meal without (this) and not seem to mind a bit.

One possible revision
No one knows exactly why the raccoon always washes his food as he eats. Nevertheless, his odd habit must be an old one because his name in Latin is *lotor,* or "the washer." The raccoon's long, nimble fingers make it easy for him to hold his food while he washes it. The raccoon especially likes small creatures that live in and out of shallow pools. Easily opening the shells of snails or mussels without even looking, he sits at the edge of the pool and carefully dips his food in and out as he dines. However, raccoons don't have to wash their food. They sometimes live in dry regions, and when hungry, they will gobble down an unrinsed meal without seeming to mind it one bit.

1. Circle all the broad reference pronouns. Then try your hand at revising this passage. Use your own paper for the revision.

   As a female engineer, I have experienced discrimination firsthand, which gives me a personal expertise on the topic. This hasn't always been the case. As a child I liked to play with mechanical games and toys, which was encouraged by my parents. Although some of my teachers didn't like this and tried to get me to play with dollhouses, my grade school teachers generally supported this, for which I am thankful. One of my high school teachers, a mathematician, was especially good about this. He helped me get a grant to study computers one summer, which increased my interest in electrical engineering. But when I applied for college, this seemed more difficult than I had expected. I was the only woman majoring in electrical engineering. This made it hard for me to find people to study with. This also made me seem an oddball in class. But this wasn't as bad as the way I was treated when I began interviewing for jobs after graduating near the top of my class. A lady electrical engineer working for our company? They didn't like this. This would mean I would quit work to get married or to have children. This would be expensive to the companies. This gave them an excuse not to hire me, which is strong evidence that woman engineers have to overcome this.

2. Circle all the broad reference pronouns, and then revise this passage to avoid broad reference. Use your own paper for the revision.

For as long as I can remember, I have done mischievous things. This always gets me in trouble, which isn't too bad, however, because I remember the fun more than the punishment. An example of this was when I was a child and I used to slide across our smooth lineoleum floor on a cushion of talcum powder. I did this by taking the baby's talcum off the shelf and sprinkling it on the floor like powdered sugar on french toast, which allowed me to glide across the floor like a graceful ice skater. (To do this I wore just my socks.) But this was mere child's play compared to the kind of mischief I like to do now that I am in college. My best trick is the old "Ajax bomb." I do this by filling a paper sack with powdered cleanser soap, after which I put a big firecracker or cherry bomb inside the sack. Then I sneak into someone's dorm room and light it. This causes an incredible explosion which blows fine white powder like a dust storm into every nook and cranny of the room. This drives the victim crazy. This settles on everything, which makes it almost impossible to clean up. If you sweep this, the broom goes right over it. If you vacuum it, the exhaust actually blows more powder into the air. If you mop it, this makes suds everywhere. This lasts sometimes for more than a week. Of course, some people think I am a jerk for doing this—especially the victims!—but some people like me for this too. At any rate, this is me, the mischievous troublemaker.

Exercise 8-4   Mastery exercise: Pronoun case and agreement

In the following sentences, cross out the incorrect choices in parentheses and write the correct choices in the blank.

Example:
Sam gave the ball to (~~she and I~~, her and me).

her and me

1. He is the one (who, whom) I think won the race.

1. _____

2. Martha told (he and I, him and me) to do the work.

2. _____

3. Neither the pneumonia nor the broken ankle left (its, their) mark on Pedro's decision to keep lifting weights.

3. _____

4. After examining the maps you drew of the new trail network, I don't find (it, them) sufficiently detailed.

4. _____

5. Please let (we, us) boys ride our bikes to the store.

5. _____

6. I was surprised to hear of (him, his) being selected for the award.

6. _____

7. Just between you and (I, me), I think Smith's lectures are as dull as dirt.

7. _____

8. An individual should always fulfill (their, her) responsibilities.

8. _____

9. Out of all the students who took creative writing this year, Martha is the poet (who, whom) I believe has the greatest chance for success.

9. _____

10. The dean chose two students, Sandra and (I, me), to represent the math department on the committee for student evaluations.

10. _____

11. I did not see Sonia and (he, him) until after the movie.

11. _____

12. Jack Benny and Bob Hope will always be remembered for (his, their) contributions to an American form of comedy.

12. _____

13. Anyone who buys groceries regularly knows that (they, he or she, him or her) can't escape inflation.

13. _____

14. The lawyer (who, whom) we hired for the contract negotiations has just been indicted for fraud.

14. _____

15. People who take portable stereos to the beach often bother (their, his or her) neighbors who want to escape the noise of the city.

15. _____

16. Neither Paul nor his girlfriends will bring (his, her, their) cassette tapes.

16. _____

17. I saw (him, his) walking his dog.

17. _____

18. Show the encyclopedias to (whoever, whomever) will let you in the door.

18. _____

19. I told George that (he, him, his) mowing the lawn every Saturday morning at six o'clock was making me a nervous wreck.

19. _____

20. Give the award to (whoever, whomever) the committee chooses.

20. _____

9
Adjective and Adverb Modifiers

Adjectives and adverbs are modifiers; that is, they add information to other words in order to describe them more fully or to identify them more precisely.

Adjectives modify nouns or pronouns. They usually come just before or just after the words they modify, but they also occur frequently as subjective complements after linking verbs (see page 88).

> The *sleek, muscular* horse leaped the fence. [adjectives precede noun]
>
> The horse, *sleek* and *muscular,* stood by the barn. [adjectives follow noun.]
>
> The horse was *sleek* and *muscular.* [adjectives used as subjective complements]

Present and past participles of verbs often function as adjectives.

> *Sipping* on a straw, the *tired* old man watched the *ticking* clock. [*Sipping* and *tired* are participles modifying *man; ticking* is a participle modifying *clock.*]

Adverbs modify verbs, adjectives, other adverbs, and sometimes whole phrases, clauses, or sentences. Adverbs usually answer the questions "when?" "where?" "how?" "how often?" "how much?" "to what degree?" or "why?" Adverbs modifying verbs can usually be placed in various positions within a sentence; adverbs modifying adjectives or other adverbs are usually located in front of the words they modify.

> *Quickly* the firefighters unrolled the hose. The firefighters *quickly* unrolled the hose. The firefighters unrolled the hose *quickly.* [*Quickly* modifies the verb *unrolled;* its position in the sentence is not fixed.]
>
> They had a *reasonably* good chance of putting out the fire. [Adverb modifies the adjective *good* and is located immediately in front of the adjective.]
>
> The wind came up *unexpectedly* fast. [Adverb modifies another adverb *fast* and is located in front of the adverb.]
>
> The wind came up *just* when the firefighter had hopes of success. [Adverb modifies whole clause beginning with *when;* it is located immediately in front of clause.]

Some adverbs, such as *therefore, however, thus, consequently,* and *furthermore,* modify whole sentences and serve as transitions. As transitions, they show logical relationships between adjoining sentences and can usually be located in various positions.

PUNCTUATION POINTER: Do not punctuate these adverbs as if they were conjunctions, or you will create a comma splice. (See Chapter 4.)

Comma splice:

I love Italian food, nevertheless, I can't go to Mamma Leone's tonight.

Correct:

I love Italian food; nevertheless, I can't go to Mamma Leone's tonight.

9A (section 2)   Avoid overuse of nouns as adjectives.

Although nouns frequently can act as adjectives (a *chocolate* cake, a *history* book, a *television* repairperson), overuse of this procedure can lead to a pileup of nouns typical of bureaucratic jargon.

Noun pileup:

Consideration of an applicant physical disability access plan by the student services reform committee will occur forthwith.

Better:

The committee for reforming student services will soon consider a plan for giving physically disabled applicants easier access to the building.

9C   Be cautious when you use adverbs to modify whole sentences.

Normally, an adverb modifies a single word or a group of words in a sentence. Sometimes, however, writers use an adverb to modify a whole sentence.

Unluckily, the wide receiver dropped the pass.

While this sentence seems clear enough, this usage can sometimes lead to ambiguity.

Ambiguous:

Sadly, the bank officers decided not to cover my check. [Who is sad here? The bank officers or the writer of the sentence? Probably the writer of the sentence is intended, but grammatically the word *sadly* modifies *decided.*]
Hopefully, the teacher will read my next essay by Monday. [Is the writer hopeful or is the teacher expected to read with hope?]

Clear:

I am sad that the bank officers did not cover my check.

I hope the teacher will read my next essay by Monday.

9D Do not use adjectives where adverbs are called for.

>*Nonstandard:*
>
>>I did real bad on that test.
>
>*Better:*
>
>>I did really badly on that test.

9E Choose carefully the appropriate modifier after verbs that can be either linking verbs or action verbs.

>Linking verbs are used in sentences with subjective complements (see page 88). The subjective complement following the linking verb is frequently an adjective modifying the subject. Certain linking verbs, especially the sense verbs *feel, look, taste, smell,* and *sound,* as well as a few others, can also be action verbs. After such verbs, choose an adjective if the word modifies the subject and an adverb if it modifies the verb.
>
>>The captain looked *angry.* [Adjective; COMPARE: "the angry captain. . . ."]
>>
>>The captain looked *angrily* at the crew. [Adverb; *angrily* tells how the captain did the looking.]
>>
>>The teacher remained *calm* as the students began throwing spitwads. [Adjective; COMPARE: "the calm teacher. . . ."]
>>
>>The teacher remained *calmly* in his seat as the students began throwing spitwads. [Adverb; *calmly* tells how the teacher remained in his seat.]

9G Learn the correct use of positive, comparative, and superlative forms for adjectives and adverbs.

>Short adjectives (and a few short adverbs) form their comparative and superlative degrees by adding *er* and *est* to the positive (or simple) form. Adjectives and adverbs with more than one syllable generally use *more (less)* for the comparative and *most (least)* for the superlative. A few modifiers are irregular.

Positive	Comparative	Superlative
happy (adjective) happily (adverb)	happier, more happy less happily	happiest, most happy least happily
good (adjective), well (adverb)	better (both adjective and adverb)	best (adjective and adverb)
bad (adjective), badly (adverb)	worse (both adjective and adverb)	worst (adjective and adverb)

>**1 Use the comparative degree for two persons or things and the superlative for three or more.**
>
>>Of the two players, Mary is the *better.* [not the *best*]
>>
>>Of the whole team, Mary is the *best.*

3 Do not use comparative and superlative degrees with absolute adjectives such as *unique* or *impossible*.

Nonstandard:

Her dress was the *most unique* one I had ever seen.

Standard:

Her dress was *unique.*

Her dress was the *most unusual* one I had ever seen.

4 Avoid the superlative when you are not making actual comparisons.

Colloquial:

John has the *cutest* puppy!

Formal:

John has a *cute* puppy.

John's puppy is the *cutest one I have ever seen.*

5 Avoid double comparatives or superlatives.

Nonstandard:

Raphael is *more smarter* than George.

Standard:

Raphael is *smarter* than George.

6 Avoid making illogical comparisons between items not actually comparable.

In making comparisons, check your sentence structure to be sure that you haven't omitted necessary words.

Illogical:

Our Volvo is better than any car on the road. [The statement inadvertently implies that this Volvo isn't on the road.]

Revised:

Our Volvo is better than any *other* car on the road.

Illogical:

Handwritten papers are harder to read than typing. [Papers cannot be compared with typing.]

Revised:

Handwritten papers are harder to read than *typed papers.*

Exercise 9-1   Self-study: Adjectives and adverbs

A. In the following sentences, choose the correct form in parentheses.

1. Of all my friends, Ralph is the (angrier/angriest) about the slashed tires.

    1. *angriest* [Superlative degree is used because more than two things are being compared.]

2. Between the two of us, Ralph is the (angrier/angriest) about the slashed tires.

    2. *angrier* [Comparative degree is used because only two things are compared.]

3. Jane is (the smartest/a very smart) person.

    3. *a very smart* [Sentence does not make a comparison.]

4. Antonio is (the most fastest/the fastest) person on the team.

    4. *fastest* [The use of *most* would make a double comparison.]

5. Randy performed (bad/badly) on the test.

    5. *badly* [modifies the verb *performed*]

6. I feel (bad/badly) about forgetting to return your book.

    6. *bad* [adjective modifying *I* (subjective complement)]

7. Since I can't distinguish braille letters with my fingers, I must feel (bad/badly).

    7. *badly* [adverb modifying *feel*]

8. Pauline views traveling by motorcycle (different/differently) from the other women in the group.

    8. *differently* [adverb modifying *views*]

9. I did (good/well) on this test.

    9. *well* [adverb]

10. I feel (good/well) about this test.

    10. *good* [adjective (subjective complement)]

B. Revise the following sentences for greater clarity.

11. The Lake Area rapid transit emergency evacuation procedures planning report has been completed.

    11. The planning report for emergency evacuation on the Lake Area rapid transit has been completed. [buildup of nouns used as adjectives]

12. I like marshmallows better than you.

    12. I like marshmallows better than you do. [incomplete comparison without the *do*]

13. He does as well, if not better than, many professional actors.

    13. He does as well as, if not better than, many professional actors. [Omission of the second *as* left the comparison grammatically incomplete.]

14. The success was caused more by Anita's hard work than by Paul.

    14. The success was caused more by Anita's hard work than by Paul's. [Original sentence compared *work* to Paul.]

15. I love poached eggs on toast more than any food.

    15. I love poached eggs on toast more than any other food. [Since poached eggs are food, the *other* keeps the comparison clear.]

16. How does Pete Rose's slugging percentage compare with other famous batters?

    16. How does Pete Rose's slugging percentage compare with that of other famous batters? [*That* is a pronoun standing for *slugging percentage* and keeps the comparison clear.]

17. Unhappily, the police officer gave my brother a ticket for speeding.

    17. I'm unhappy that the police officer gave my brother a ticket for speeding. [The original sentence seems to say that the police officer was unhappy.]

18. Hopefully, the sun will be shining for tomorrow's game.

    18. I hope that the sun will be shining for tomorrow's game.

19. Eating at Whacko Burgers is a lot different from Thanksgiving at our house.

20. Regretfully, this class will have to be cancelled because of the blizzard.

19. Eating dinner at Whacko Burgers is a lot different from eating Thanksgiving dinner at our house. [Added words make the items to be compared more clearly parallel.]

20. We regret that this class will have to be cancelled because of the blizzard.

Exercise 9-2   Generating sentences with adjectives and adverbs

A. In the following sentences, circle all adjectives and adverbs including nouns used as adjectives. Then change the sentence by replacing the circled words with new modifiers of your own.

Example:
The (curious) visitors could (barely) see the (gray) building through the (dense) fog.

The disappointed visitors could hardly see the famous building through the pea-soup fog.

1. The moose, stately and proud, stood like an iron statue at the edge of the rippling water.

2. Grasping frantically for the narrow ledge, Jack felt the rubber soles of his hiking boots slide slowly down the steep-faced rock.

3. Her green eyes flashing angrily at her astonished boss, Maureen walked silently toward the file cabinet, removed a steel drawer, and dumped the contents on the plush executive carpet.

4. He seemed more nervous than I had originally expected, especially after his expensive training in relaxation techniques.

5. The big, fat, juicy angleworm crawled slowly away from the spot of light.

B. In each of the following exercises write a sentence of your own according to the instructions provided.

6. A sentence containing the words *looked fierce*

7. A sentence containing the words *looked fiercely*

8. A sentence containing the words *tasted bitter*

9. A sentence containing the words *tasted bitterly*

10. A sentence containing *however* punctuated as follows: ; however,

11. A sentence containing the word *however* punctuated as follows: , however,

12. A sentence containing the words *less successful than*

13. A sentence containing the words *less successfully than*

14. A sentence that compares your skill at some activity (playing tennis, writing papers, sleeping in the morning) with that of one other person

15. A sentence using the superlative degree in which you speak of the same skill mentioned in sentence 14 above

16. A sentence using *clear* to modify a noun

17. A sentence using *clearly* to modify a verb

18. A sentence using *clearly* to modify an adjective

C. In each of the following exercises write three sentences using the adjectives indicated. In the first sentence make the adjectives precede the noun they modify; in the second make them follow the noun; and in the third make them follow a linking verb in the subjective complement slot.

19. *jagged and torn*

20. *soft, warm, and radiant*

Exercise 9-3   Mastery exercise: Adjectives and adverbs

A. In the following sentences, choose the correct form in parentheses and write it in the space provided at the right.

1. Of all the great tenors I have ever heard, I liked Richard Tucker (well/the better/ the best).

   1. _____

2. His arm was so (severe/severely) injured that we had to rush him (quick/quickly) to the hospital.

   2. _____

   _____

3. I liked this book (real/really) well.

   3. _____

4. He can write poetry (as well/as well as), if not better than, she can.

   4. _____

5. Roman always seems to do this kind of work more (efficient/efficiently) than Albert.

   5. _____

6. At least Roman appears more (efficient/efficiently) than Albert.

   6. _____

7. Of the two, Roman is the (most/more) efficient.

   7. _____

8. That new cereal invented by the graduate student in food science has (the strangest/a very strange) taste.

   8. _____

9. Among all the people I know, Lucille is (unique/ the more unique/ the most unique).

   9. _____

10. This cereal tastes (weird/weirdly).

    10. _____

11. Does their music seem (unreasonable/unreasonably) loud to you?

    11. _____

12. Do you think I will look (unreasonable/unreasonably) if I walk into their house and pull the stereo's plug out of the wall?

    12. _____

13. Will they think I am acting (unreasonable/unreasonably) if I wait until they are asleep and then start blowing the new horn I got for my truck into their bedroom window?

    13. _____

14. Of the two kinds of pizza, this one is the (more bad/worse/worst).

    14. _____

15. This book (surely/sure) seems unusual to me.

    15. _____

B. Revise each of the following sentences for greater clarity.

16. Georgette claims that reading Shakespeare is quite different from other literature classes.

17. My dog can jump as high or higher than that mutt of yours.

18. The Great Flat Lake parent/teacher day-care discussion group summer reading list committee report will be read on Monday.

19. Doreen enjoys playing pool more than any game.

20. Did you say that your score on the endurance test was higher than an entrance-level astronaut?

10

Misplaced Sentence Parts

Because the meaning of English sentences depends heavily on word order, misplaced sentence elements can result in confusion and sometimes in unintentional humor. In general, adverb modifiers can be located in various positions in a sentence.

Along the way we saw lots of roses. We saw *along the way* lots of roses. We saw lots of roses *along the way.* [prepositional phrase used as an adverb: position not fixed]

Because the tire went flat, we were two hours late. We were two hours late *because the tire went flat.* [adverb clause: position not fixed]

Adjective phrases and clauses, however, cannot move around freely in a sentence without changing the sentence's meaning or causing confusion.

The young couple *with the tiny dog* watched the ducks *swimming in the pond.*

Swimming in the pond, the young couple watched the ducks *with the tiny dog.* [Here the repositioning of *swimming in the pond* (a participial phrase) and *with the tiny dog* (a prepositional phrase used as an adjective) greatly changes the meaning of the sentence.]

10A   Avoid dangling verbal phrases or elliptical clauses.

An important grammatical rule in English is that an introductory verbal phrase used as a modifier must modify the subject of the sentence (see section 3C for discussion of verbals). In other words, the subject of the sentence must also do the action specified by the introductory verbal.

Participial phrase:

Fishing downstream, my sister caught two rainbow trout. [Here *sister*, the subject of the sentence, does both the fishing downstream (the action of the participle) and the catching of the trout (the action of the main verb in the sentence.) Test by seeing if the subject really does the action of the verbal: My sister fishes downstream — OK.]

Prepositional phrase with gerund object:

> *In applying for the job,* Joe learned a lot about himself. [TEST: Joe applies for the job — OK.]

Infinitive phrase:

> *To learn French,* a student needs good study habits. [TEST: A student learns French — OK.]

The same rule applies for an elliptical clause. (An elliptical clause is an adverb clause with an omitted but implied subject and predicate.) When an elliptical clause begins a sentence, the implied subject of the elliptical clause must be the same as the subject of the sentence itself.

Elliptical clause:

> *When in the army,* my father won many medals. [TEST: When my father was in the army he . . . — OK.]

These introductory modifiers are said to "dangle" whenever the subject of the sentence obviously cannot do the action of the verbal phrase or the elliptical clause.

Examples of dangling modifiers:

> *Fishing downstream,* two trout were caught. [TEST: Two trout were fishing downstream — obviously not intended meaning. Dangles.]
>
> *In applying for a job,* much valuable information can be gained. [TEST: Valuable information applies for a job — no. Dangles.]
>
> *To learn French,* good study habits are essential. [TEST: Good study habits learn French — no. Dangles.]
>
> *When in the army,* winning medals was my father's main achievement. [TEST: Winning medals was in the army — no. Dangles.]

There are two methods of correcting dangling modifiers: (1) Rearrange or rewrite the main part of the sentence making the correctly intended word the subject; or (2) expand the introductory verbal phrase or elliptical clause into a complete clause with its own subject and predicate.

Dangling:

> Firing again and again, the elephant dropped to its knees.

Corrected:

> Firing again and again, the hunter watched the elephant drop to its knees. [method one — main part of sentence rewritten]
>
> After the hunter fired her rifle again and again, the elephant dropped to its knees. [method two — introductory phrase expanded to clause]

Dangling:

> In trying to uncover the dinosaur bones, curious visitors had to be kept away from the digging site.

Corrected:

> In trying to uncover the dinosaur bones, the scientists had to keep curious visitors away from the digging site. [method one]

> While the scientists tried to uncover the dinosaur bones, curious visitors had to be kept away from the digging site. [method two]

Dangling:

> When only a baby, my father taught me how to swim.

Corrected:

> When only a baby, I was taught how to swim by my father. [method one]

> When I was only a baby, my father taught me how to swim. [method two]

Additionally, verbal phrases coming at the end of a sentence and set off from the sentence by a comma follow the same rule. The subject of the sentence must be the same as the implied subject of the verbal phrase.

Dangling:

> It was quiet on the front porch, watching the sunset.

Corrected:

> We sat quietly on the front porch, watching the sunset. [method one]

> It was quiet on the front porch as we watched the sunset. [method two]

NOTE: A phrase that already contains the noun that the participle modifies, called an **absolute phrase,** does not dangle. (See page 98.)

> His teeth flashing in the sun, John waved at the crowd. [*Flashing* does not dangle because it modifies the noun *teeth* at the head of the phrase.]

10B,C Avoid misplaced verbal phrases, prepositional phrases, or clauses that seem to modify the wrong sentence elements.

Keep modifiers as close as possible to the words that they are intended to modify.

Misplaced:

> My brother smashed his car into a fence coming into town. [Misplaced participle *coming* seems to modify *fence.*]

Revised:

> Coming into town, my brother smashed his car into a fence.

Misplaced:

> A woman was riding a bicycle with a beautiful suntan. [Prepositional phrase *with a beautiful suntan* seems to modify *bicycle.*]

Revised:

A woman with a beautiful suntan was riding a bicycle.

Misplaced:

The movers brought the piano up the stairs, which weighed more than four hundred pounds. [Relative clause seems to modify *stairs.*]

Revised:

The movers brought the piano, which weighed more than four hundred pounds, up the stairs.

10D **Avoid placing certain adverbs or adverbial phrases where they seem to make sense both with what comes before them and with what comes after them.**

Confusing:

The woman who winked at Carl provocatively walked into the next room. [Did she wink provocatively or walk provocatively?]

The woman who winked provocatively at Carl walked into the next room.

OR

The woman who winked at Carl walked provocatively into the next room.

10E **Place adverbs defining degree, extent, or limitation, such as *merely, only, just, hardly, nearly,* and *scarcely,* immediately before the words they modify.**

Note the differences in meaning in the following sentences:

Just the cat ate the puppy's dinner.

The cat *just* ate the puppy's dinner.

The cat ate *just* the puppy's dinner.

Because slight differences in location of these words can signal an importnat difference in meaning, good writers are careful about positioning them correctly.

Loose:

The baby only slept three hours.

Better:

The baby slept only three hours.

Loose:

Sam nearly jumped three feet when he heard the rattlesnake.

Better:

Sam jumped nearly three feet when he heard the rattlesnake.

Exercise 10-1 Self-study: Using sentence-combining to form introductory verbal phrases and elliptical clauses

A good way to avoid dangling phrases and clauses is to understand how to combine short sentences to form longer sentences with introductory elements. In the following exercises, combine the short sentences to form a new sentence with the structure indicated. Make the first sentence the main clause and convert the remaining sentences to verbal phrases or elliptical clauses.

Answer column

1. He awoke with fright. He heard footsteps in the hall. (introductory participial phrase)

1. Hearing footsteps in the hall, he awoke with fright. [Notice that *he* is the subject of both short sentences and that *he* remains as the subject of the combined sentence.]

2. The kite looked like a gigantic hawk. The kite glided gracefully in the sky. (introductory participial phrase)

2. Gliding gracefully in the sky, the kite looked like a gigantic hawk. [Note again how the same word is subject of both short sentences.]

3. Most people can successfully learn a foreign language within two years. These people study regularly an hour each day. (introductory gerund phrase serving as object of preposition *by*)

3. By studying regularly an hour each day, most people can successfully learn a foreign language within two years.

4. Ricardo found a melted candy bar on the rug behind the dresser. Ricardo was searching for his missing wallet. (introductory elliptical clause beginning with *while*)

4. While searching for his missing wallet, Ricardo found a melted candy bar on the rug behind the dresser.

5. You need to keep an older car tuned up. You will get the best gas mileage from an older car this way. (introductory infinitive phrase)

5. To get the best gas mileage from an older car, you need to keep it tuned up.

6. One must first explain the concept of metaphysical analogy. Then one can describe the poetry of John Donne. (introductory infinitive phrase)

6. To describe the poetry of John Donne, one must first explain the concept of metaphysical analogy.

7. Be sure to visit the Charlie Russell Museum. Do this when you are in Great Falls, Montana. (introductory elliptical clause beginning with *when*)

7. When in Great Falls, Montana, be sure to visit the Charlie Russell Museum. [Note that *you* is the subject of both short sentences. *You* is implied in the initial imperative sentence.]

8. Betty Lou drove a taxi on weekends to help pay her expenses. Betty Lou did this while she was in college. (introductory elliptical clause)

8. While in college, Betty Lou drove a taxi on weekends to help pay her expenses.

9. The little boy glared at the bully. His hand clutched the candy bar tightly. (introductory absolute phrase)

9. His hand clutching the candy bar tightly, the little boy glared at the bully. [Note that the same word is *not* the subject of both short sentences. Note also that the subject of the second short sentence, *hand,* remains as the headword of the absolute phrase. Thus absolute phrases are self-contained and therefore do not dangle.]

10. The hummingbird hovered gracefully above the flower. Its wings beat too rapidly for human sight to detect. (introductory absolute phrase)

10. Its wings beating too rapidly for human sight to detect, the hummingbird hovered gracefully above the flower.

Exercise 10-2   Self-study: Avoiding misplaced sentence parts

In the following exercises, revise any sentences with misplaced sentence parts.

1. Walking down the street, a flowerpot fell on my head from an apartment window.

   1. While I was walking down the street, a flower-pot. . . .

      OR

      Walking down the street, I was struck on the head by a flowerpot that fell. . . .

2. Exhausted from the final sprint, the runner's face was red and flushed.

   2. His face red and flushed, the runner was exhausted from the final sprint. [This method uses an absolute phrase.]

      OR

      Exhausted from the final sprint, the runner smiled at the crowd with his face red and flushed.

3. This used stereo only cost seventy-five dollars.

   3. This used stereo cost only seventy-five dollars.

4. I know a man with a wooden leg named Joe.

   4. I know a man with a wooden leg; his name is Joe.

5. Hating himself for having signed up for this course in the first place, Joe's fist slammed into the desk in disgust.

   5. Hating himself for having signed up for this course in the first place, Joe slammed his fist into the desk in disgust.

6. I merely wanted to annoy him a little bit, not to infuriate him.

   6. I wanted merely to annoy him a little bit, not to infuriate him.

7. While we were sipping our coffee slowly we began to explore the hidden meanings in our small talk.

   7. While we were slowly sipping our coffee, we. . . .

      OR

      While we were sipping our coffee, we began slowly. . . .

8. The newlyweds watched Niagara Falls drunk with love in the moonlight.

   8. The newlyweds, drunk with love, watched Niagara Falls in the moonlight.

9. To find the sunken vessel, the ocean bottom was explored by the divers.

   9. To find the sunken vessel, divers explored the ocean bottom.

10. Its wings motionless against the blue sky, the hawk circled gracefully in search of prey.

    10. Okay—absolute phrase.

Exercise 10-3   Avoiding misplaced sentence parts

A. In sentences 1 to 5 insert the specified modifier into the sentence at whatever location or locations that make the sentence both clear and graceful. If the modifier can logically appear in several locations, write the sentence as many ways as possible.

Example:
The bird flapped its wings. *(rapidly)*

The bird rapidly flapped its wings.
The bird flapped its wings rapidly.

1. The man began writing down all the information in his notebook. *(who saw the accident)*

2. The man began writing down all the information in his notebook. *(whistling softly to himself)*

3. The man began writing down all the information in his notebook. *(after he had seen the accident)*

4. The man began writing down all the information in his notebook. *(about the accident)*

5. The man began writing down all the information in his notebook. *(having seen the accident)*

6. He said that he fed the dog. *(only*—note how different positions have different meanings)

7. He is able to finish successfully every task he undertakes. *(almost*—choose the most logical position)

8. The old sergeant stopped to chat with the soldier's mother. *(wearing combat boots and fatigues)*

9. The majority of students were unable to induce a satisfactory generalization from the provided data. *(tested in this study)*

10. The majority of students were unable to induce a satisfactory generalization from the data. *(provided by the telephone company)*

B. In sentences 6 to 9 insert the modifying element into the base sentence if doing so results in a clear, graceful, grammatically correct sentence. Otherwise either expand the modifying element into a complete clause or rephrase the base sentence so that the modifying element can be added.

Example:
The burglar's face was covered by a nylon stocking. *(entering the store at approximately 1:00 P.M.)*

His face covered by a nylon stocking, the burglar entered the store at approximately 1:00 p.m.

11. The movement of glaciers was finally proved by the Swiss zoologist, Louis Agassiz. *(studying glaciers high in the Alps)*

12. The cabin was discovered to have moved four thousand feet down the mountain. *(returning after twelve years to a priest's cabin on the Glacier of the Rhone)*

13. Twelve stakes were driven into the ice eighteen feet deep and checked each year for movement. *(in order to test his theory that glaciers move down mountains)*

14. The stakes became evidence not only that the glaciers had moved but also that the center of the glaciers had moved faster than the sides. *(having moved down the valley at different rates)*

C. In sentences 10 to 14, add a main clause to the provided introductory verbal phrase of elliptical clause.

Example:
In attempting to lift the box

In attempting to lift the box, I sprained my back.

15. While climbing Hardscrabble Mountain

16. In order to talk to Luigi the Enforcer

17. Seen from the top of the Empire State Building

18. Dumping the pitcher of ice tea on Jack's head

19. When playing craps in a back alley

D. In sentences 15 to 20, add specified elements according to the provided instructions.

Example:
The dog bit the mail carrier. (introductory infinitive phrase)

To show that he was boss of the yard, the dog bit the mail carrier.

20. Joan smashed the mugger in the nose with the side of her hand. (introductory participial phrase)

21. The man is the person I saw in the park. (participial phrase following *man*)

22. The university is providing seventy additional full-tuition scholarships for students. (participial phrase modifying *students*)

23. The conductor signaled for the tubas to begin the final cadence. (absolute phrase beginning with *his arm* . . .)

24. The chef's salad received rave reviews from members of the gourmet recipe club. (introductory participial phrase)

25. The plane descended rapidly through the turbulent air. (absolute phrase following *plane;* participial phrase following *air*)

Exercise 10-4   Mastery exercise: Misplaced sentence parts

Revise the following sentences to avoid misplaced sentence parts. If the sentence is correct as is, put a *C* in the right hand margin.

Example:
Looking through a microscope, the drop of pond water seemed alive with wiggling monsters.

Looking through a microscope, the child discovered that the drop of pond water seemed alive with wiggling monsters.

1. A batter who can miss a slowly pitched softball completely baffles me.   _____

2. Their heads tilted back in awe, the children on this summer's night began trying to count the stars.   _____

3. Seen through a telescope that magnifies things sixty times, Jupiter appears as big as the moon.   _____

4. By studying the light reflected by Jupiter, its clouds are a poisonous mixture of ammonia floating in hydrogen.   _____

5. Having long expected to return to Harlem after graduation, the young accountant was not prepared for the changes he saw on Lenox Avenue.   _____

6. While cruising at 10,000 feet 45 miles east of Albuquerque, New Mexico, on July 16, 1945, at approximately 5:30 A.M., a brilliant flash of light, brighter than the sun, blazed the horizon.   _____

7. We were absolutely startled, unable to explain the sun-like flash or to grasp the meaning of the huge mushroom cloud that soon appeared above the desert floor. _____

8. Reporting what we had seen by radio to ground authorities, no satisfactory explanation could be found. _____

9. The following morning, still plagued with curiosity about the event, the newspapers only reported that an ammunition dump had exploded in the approximate area where we had seen the flash. _____

10. Listening to radio on August 6, 1945, a similar flash of light occurred over Hiroshima, Japan; then we realized what we had seen several weeks earlier — the first explosion of an atomic bomb. _____

11
Confusing Shifts

As much as possible, you should maintain consistency in patterns of grammatical structure, tone, and point of view in your sentences and paragraphs. Readers appreciate consistency and are annoyed or confused by needless shifts.

11A   Avoid needless shifts in your verb tenses.

Shift:

> While attempting to ride his bicycle on the rear wheel only, the boy struck a bump and suddenly crashes into the curb. [shift from past to present tense]

Consistent:

> While attempting to ride his bicycle on the rear wheel only, the boy struck a bump and suddenly crashed into the curb.

11B   Avoid needless shifts in the mood of verbs.

Shift:

> Juanita requested that Jefferson be at the field by 7:30 and that he will bring his catcher's mitt. [shift from subjunctive mood to indicative mood]

Consistent:

> Juanita requested that Jefferson be at the field by 7:30 and that he bring his catcher's mitt.

11C   Avoid needless shifts in voice for verbs in closely related clauses and sentences.

Shift:

> The river washed out two bridges and more than a hundred homes were also destroyed by the flooding waters. [shift from active to passive voice]

Consistent:

> The river washed out two bridges and destroyed more than a hundred homes.

11D Avoid needless shifts in the person and number of your pronouns.

Shift in person:

> When one tries to be especially careful, you always make more mistakes. [shift from third person *one* to second person *you*]

Consistent:

> When you try to be especially careful, you always make more mistakes. [informal]

> When one tries to be especially careful, one always makes more mistakes. [formal]

Shift in number:

> If a person jogs three miles every morning, they always feel superior to everybody else. [shift from singular *person* to plural *they*]

Consistent:

> If a person jogs three miles every morning, he or she always feel superior to everybody else.

OR

> People who jog three miles every morning always feel superior to everybody else.

NOTE: This rule frequently places contemporary writers in the dilemma of choosing between bulky wording *(he or she)* and sexist language (*he* by itself or *she* by itself). (See Chapter 21.)

11E Avoid needless shifts in point of view.

Shift:

> I watched Juan turn toward the curb and wave for a taxi. How can I ever explain the hundred dollars to my wife, he thought to himself, as the taxi pulled beside him. [The passage begins in the first person with the use of *I*; this writer could not therefore be inside Juan's head knowing what Juan was thinking.]

Consistent:

> I watched Juan turn toward the curb and wave for a taxi. I'll bet he is wondering how to explain the hundred dollars to his wife, I thought to myself as the cab pulled beside him.

11F Avoid unnecessary shifts in the tone and purpose of your writing, especially sudden outbursts of emotion or sarcasm.

Because readers are generally influenced by logical, well-supported argument, they can be annoyed by shifts away from rational persuasion to emotionalism or sarcasm.

Ineffective:

> Ms. Peterson is probably the worst teacher in the universe. She drives me crazy! Actually, I just love the way she comes to class late and then fumbles through her well-organized (if you call a wastepaper basket organized!) briefcase made out of choice, ripped-apart leather. I praise my wonderful luck for this wasted time because it is so much better than her boring lectures. What a drag! [The writer's emotional language and sarcasm may well increase the reader's sympathy for Ms. Peterson.]

Better:

> Ms. Peterson is not an effective teacher. Last term she was late for class more than ten times, and even when arriving before the bell rang, she often appeared disorganized, unable to find her lecture notes in her messy briefcase. Her lectures were mainly restatements of the material already in the textbook; in fact, on many occasions she read directly from the text, several paragraphs at a time, in a monotonous voice. [This version is building a persuasive case against Ms. Peterson.]

Exercise 11-1 Self-study: Confusing shifts

In the following exercises, revise each sentence to eliminate confusing shifts. Some sentences may not need revision.

Answer column

1. After I saw the boy run into the store, I tell his brother to call Mr. Peterson.

   1. . . . I told his brother. . . . [consistency in tense]

2. Sam requested that I be at the meeting by eight o'clock sharp and would I bring my previous notes.

   2. . . . that I be at the meeting by eight o'clock sharp and that I bring my previous notes. [consistency in mood]

3. The mice gnawed holes in several boxes in our basement, and also three of my best sweaters were ruined by them.

   3. The mice gnawed holes in several boxes in our basement and also ruined three of my best sweaters. [consistency in voice: both active]

4. When one revises a rough draft, you should be especially careful to see that each paragraph is unified and coherent.

   4. When you revise a rough. . . .
   OR
   When one revises a rough draft, one should be. . . . [consistency of person: either both second person *(you)* or both third person *(one)*]

5. Each one of you should be sure they bring their bathing suits.

   5. . . . should be sure you bring your own bathing suit. [consistency in person]

6. Still recovering from the flu, I sat on the lawn chair and watched my dad broiling hamburgers on the barbecue. Down in the basement my little brother began smacking his lips in anticipation of dad's famous burgers.

   6. . . . on the lawn chair. In my mind's eye I could picture my little brother down in the basement smacking his lips in anticipation of dad's famous burgers. [Consistency in point of view; writer can't see "down in the basement" while sitting in the lawn chair.]

7. A good soccer goalie must decide when to rush the ball and when to sag back. Often you must make the decision in a split second.

   7. . . . to sag back. Often he or she must make the decision in a split second. [consistency in person]

8. King Lear, the hero of Shakespeare's most disturbing tragedy, banishes his good daughter and gives his kingdom to his two evil daughters. Midway through the play, the pitiful, old king went mad.

   8. . . . Midway through the play the pitiful, old king goes mad. [*went* changed to *goes* to maintain present tense started with *banishes* and *gives*]

9. According to my writing instructor, a common error among beginning writers is to have too many short, underdeveloped paragraphs, and we should also make sure each of our paragraphs supports the thesis statement.

10. Teachers insist that we follow directions exactly and also we should be creative at the same time.

9. According to my writing instructor, beginning writers should avoid too many short, underdeveloped paragraphs and should also make sure each of their paragraphs supports the thesis statement. [consistency of mood and person]

10. Teachers insist that we follow directions exactly and also that we be creative at the same time. [consistency of mood]

Exercise 11-2   Revision exercise on confusing shifts

Revise the following letter to help the author get a refund on his stereo system. Eliminate confusing shifts as well as inappropriate outbursts of emotion or sarcasm. Use your own paper.

Dear Director of the Complaint Bureau:

I would like to ask you to replace the idiotic piece of junk I just bought from your wonderful store. I refer of course to your stereo system #43871, which is actually one of the finest and most beautifully crafted stereo systems on the market if you like the smooth sound of static buzz in the left channel. I am so glad I bought it at your store because your salespeople can't tell static buzz from Z. Z. Topp.

If people listen to the right channel, you really wouldn't think anything was wrong. But when the left channel is listened to, I was annoyed by the buzz. Here I am in my room opening the stereo box in anticipation of getting my new system hooked up. I place my record on the turntable, turn on the amplifier, a hideous buzz comes out of the left speaker, and your salesperson is drinking coffee in the back room glad another sucker bought their stereo system.

I would be most grateful if you would either replace my system or repair it under warranty. Thank you very much.

Exercise 11-3   Mastery exercise: Confusing shifts

Revise each of the following sentences to avoid unnecessary shifts in tense, mood, or voice in verbs; unnecessary shifts in person or number in pronouns; or unnecessary shifts in point of view or tone. If revisions are lengthy, write out the corrected sentence completely in the provided space; make minor corrections by using crossouts and making neat revisions above the lines.

Example:

After you catch the subway to Jefferson Avenue, ~~a person~~ *you* should be able to relax.

1. To have your suit cleaned and pressed on the same day, customers should bring their suits in by 9:00 A.M. and also please remove all personal articles from the pockets.

2. After they washed the dishes, the floors were swept and mopped.

3. If anyone wants a free ticket to next Saturday's game, you should drop by the People's Bank before noon on Monday.

4. A person must have cranked many engines with an old pull rope before they will appreciate the virtues of the new electric-starting power mowers.

5. What Bob did next still terrifies me. He spun on his heels and walked out of the room angrily, his fists clenched, his eyes glaring at me sitting in the back of the room. He stormed down the hall and entered the elevator. Once inside, he began to laugh and his face broke out in a broad smile.

6. Discussions in my literature class are sometimes characterized by a heated excitement that carried over into hour-long discussions in the Student Union building.

7. Facing her husband after her long day at the office, Beatrice doesn't know whether to tell him to fix his own dinner or should she just continue to do all the cooking herself.

8. Mr. Hardnose told every student in the law class to study the next case entirely on their own.

9. When you read *The Red Badge of Courage,* one is always surprised to discover how nasty each soldier is to their fellow soldiers.

10. George insisted that Laura pay her own way for the dinner dance and that she should also chip in some gas money for his car.

12
Establishing
Sentence Logic

For readers to understand the meaning of a sentence easily and clearly, each part of the sentence must be related logically to other parts. When you revise your drafts, you can improve the logic of your sentences by eliminating irrelevant details, by arranging your wording so that the most important ideas are emphasized, by avoiding unsupported generalizations, and by avoiding mixed images or other illogically constructed sentence parts.

12A Revise sentences that contain irrelevant details.

Sentences that include too many ideas and details are in danger of losing their focus. Eliminate material that isn't clearly related to the main idea of the sentence. Of course, the material you eliminate can be developed elsewhere in the essay if you think it is important.

Irrelevant details:

> Writing persuasive essays, which are required in all the composition courses on our campus, a beautiful wooded area twenty miles outside of the city, requires special attention to opposing ideas.

Revised:

> Writing persuasive essays requires special attention to opposing ideas. Because argumentation helps develop students' thinking skills, persuasive essays are required in all the composition courses on our campus.

12B Arrange your sentences so that the most important ideas are emphasized.

The most emphatic positions in a sentence are the beginning and end. In order to emphasize important ideas, avoid burying them in the middle of the sentence.

Important ideas buried:

> Along with many other books accused of secular humanism, the school board burned copies of a recent biology textbook in a public bonfire as a sign that they didn't approve of these books.

Revised:

> The school board burned copies of a recent biology textbook, along with many other books accused of secular humanism, in a public bonfire.

12C Check sentences to see that you have signaled the intended logical relationship between parts. Make sure you don't imply cause and effect if you don't mean it.

English has a wealth of connecting words that signal various kinds of logical relationships (*because, after, therefore, but, however,* and so forth). You will confuse your readers if you use these words inaccurately.

Confusing:

> She showed me the broken vase; she didn't seem angry because it had cost a lot of money. [The word *because* is confusing. Since the vase was expensive, one would expect her to be angry. Instead of *because,* the writer needs a connecting word that expresses contrast.]

Clear:

> She showed me the broken vase; although it had cost a lot of money, she didn't seem angry.

Often two parts of a sentence linked by *and* will seem to have a cause-and-effect relationship even if you don't intend such a meaning. Revise any sentences that seem ambiguous in this way.

Unintended cause-and-effect connection:

> He bought a new stereo and flunked his biology test. [This sentence seems to imply that the new stereo caused him to flunk biology.]

Revised:

> John's day had its ups and downs: He bought a new stereo but flunked his biology test.

12D Avoid sweeping statements that assert too much or too little evidence.

Be cautious whenever you make blanket statements about all members of a class. Just one exception will destroy the truth of your generalization. Such generalizations can sometimes be qualified with such words as *most, some,* and *usually.*

Faulty generalization:

> Professors at this university are too concerned with research to care about the quality of undergraduate education.

Revised:

> Many professors at this university seem too concerned with research to care about the quality of undergraduate education.

12E   Avoid mixed images.

Whenever you use figurative language, be careful that you don't begin a sentence with one image and end it with a second, unrelated image. (See Chapter 18.)

Mixed image:

She danced her way into their hearts, like a spark on a dynamite fuse. [Sparks on dynamite fuses don't dance.]

Logical:

She burned her way into their hearts, like a spark on a dynamite fuse.

12F   When defining a word, do not use another form of the same word in your definition. Also avoid using the phrase *is where* or *is when,* since the resulting sentence is grammatically illogical.

Illogically constructed:

A coward is someone who acts cowardly.

A coward is when you don't have any courage.

Better:

A coward is a person who lacks courage.

Exercise 12-1   Self-study: Creating logical sentences

Revise the following sentences to make them more unified and logical. The provided answers are models only.

Answer column

1. After hundreds of formal scientific studies, which have taken place over the last twenty years and have been reported in both scientific journals and many popular magazines such as *The Reader's Digest* and *Parent Magazine,* reasonable people now must conclude that TV violence does indeed have harmful effects.

1. After hundreds of formal scientific studies, reasonable people now must conclude that TV violence does indeed have harmful effects. [Omitted material was irrelevant to the main idea of the sentence.]

2. TV watchers are regularly treated to a diet of brutal killings, rapes, robberies, and maimings, as anyone who owns a TV knows.

2. TV watchers are regularly treated to a diet of brutal killings, rapes, robberies, and maimings. [Omitted phrase was unneeded and created an unemphatic sentence.]

3. I am now going to go out on a limb and take the bull by the horns: The federal government must create regulations to stop excessive TV violence.

3. I am now going to take a a controversial stand: The federal government must create regulations to stop excessive TV violence. [The original opening is doubly flawed: It contains clichés, and the clichés create mixed images.]

4. Although my proposal will be controversial, TV violence will need to be defined carefully.

4. Because my proposal will be controversial, TV violence will need to be defined carefully. [*Although* signals an illogical connection between the two ideas.]

5. Excessive TV violence is when a TV show depicts a violent scene without reason.

6. One proof that TV violence is harmful occurred in a study I read last year. Heavy TV watchers tended to overestimate the frequency of muggings and other violence in our society. Thus TV violence is definitely harmful to people.

7. Many network producers now agree that TV violence is harmful, although Neilson Ratings continue to be the chief force in network decision-making.

5. Violence can be defined as the use of bodily force that brings physical harm to a victim. TV violence becomes excessive when it occurs frequently and pointlessly as a source of entertainment. [Original version uses an *is when* construction and uses the word *violent* in defining *violence.*]

6. One piece of evidence suggesting that TV violence is harmful is a study showing that heavy TV watchers tended to overestimate the frequency of muggings and other violence in our society. [Avoid sweeping generalizations.]

7. Many network producers now agree that TV violence is harmful, but they are reluctant to remove violent shows from the airwaves because viewers seem to enjoy watching them. As always, Neilson Ratings continue to be the chief force in network decision-making. [Original version omitted key connecting thoughts. Logical progression of thought demands development of each part of the argument.]

Exercise 12-2 Mastery exercise: Creating logical sentences

Revise each of the following passages for unity, clarity, and logical relationsips.

1. If you want to begin learning about computers, which are now so popular that many school districts are buying them by the dozens for elementary school classrooms, you will need to start with some definitions. Although "computer-talk" involves dozens of slang terms, find a "user-friendly" salesperson at one of your local computer stores, which have sprung up like fast-food chains across the country. Even a computer salesperson who speaks your language, therefore, will have to throw some specialized computer terms at you. You can digest most of these curve balls if you know a handful of terms. One important term is random access memory (RAM). RAM is when the computer has random access to all parts of the memory.

2. The first European seafarers, who must have been Vikings or other Northern Europeans who had developed the art of shipbuilding and who had the courage or imagination to sail into unknown territory, landed on Easter Island at the beginning of the eighteenth century. They must have been surprised. Moreover they saw hundreds of colossal statues lying scattered about all over the island. These gigantic statues, which are still visible today if you can afford to go to the Easter Island on vacation, stand like robots grown from the seed of a giant. These statues couldn't have been built by men because they are far too large. Therefore these statues prove that ancient civilizations were visited by intelligent beings from outer space. [Adapted from Erik Von Doniken, *Chariots of the Gods.*]

13
Coordinating and Subordinating Ideas

Experienced writers know how to manipulate the grammatical structures of their sentences to convey exactly the meaning they intend. If writers wish to give two or more elements in a sentence equal weight, they will use structures that grammarians call **coordination.**

> The writing center's word processor broke, so I finished my essay on a typewriter. [In this *coordinated* sentence both elements—the breaking of the word processor and the finishing of the essay—receive equal emphasis. The word *so* is one of the coordinating conjunctions.]

On the other hand, if writers wish to emphasize the importance of one element over another, they will use structures called **subordination.**

> Although the writing center's word processor broke, I finished my essay on a typewriter.

> Because the writing center's word processor broke, I finished my essay on a typewriter. [In these subordinated versions, "finishing the essay on a typewriter" is the emphasized element. The sentence beginning with *although* suggests that finishing on a typewriter was difficult, an accomplishment that someone wouldn't expect once the word processor broke down. The version beginning with *because* says simply that the breaking of the word processor was the cause of finishing on the typewriter. The words *although* and *because* are subordinating conjunctions.]

13A When you wish to give equal emphasis to elements of a sentence, use coordination.

Coordination occurs when you link sentence elements with the coordinating conjunctions *and, but, or, nor, for, so,* and *yet.* In addition, you can coordinate main clauses by joining them with a semicolon or with a semicolon and a conjunctive adverb such as *however* or *therefore.* By phrasing coordinated parts so that they follow the same grammatical structure, you create a pleasing grammatical effect called *parallelism* (see Chapter 14).

Nonparallel:

> He enjoyed swimming in the lake on a warm summer's evening and to play poker on Saturday nights with the boys. [The coordinating conjunction *and* gives equal emphasis to the swimming and the poker playing; however, *swimming* is an *ing* form (gerund) while *to play poker* is a *to* form (infinitive). The coordinated ideas are not expressed in equivalent grammatical structures.]

Parallel:

> He enjoyed swimming in the lake on a warm summer's evening and playing poker on Saturday nights with the boys. [Now there are two *ing* forms: *swimming* and *playing.*]

Coordination shows a relationship between ideas that cannot be expressed either by subordinating one of the ideas or by keeping the ideas in two separate sentences. In fact, if equal and closely related ideas are not expressed in coordinated structures, your meaning can become confused.

Related ideas not coordinated, and hence not clear:

> Bill spends his money strangely. He bought an expensive amplifier and turntable. For sound he uses two car speakers which he mounted in cigar boxes.

Coordination of related ideas:

> Bill spends his money strangely. He bought an expensive amplifier and turntable, but for sound he uses two car speakers which he mounted in cigar boxes. [Bill's strange spending habits are clear only if his buying the expensive equipment is contrasted with his using the cheap speakers. The original version places these two ideas in separate sentences and thus doesn't convey the ironic relationship expressed in the coordinated version.]

On the other hand, you will also confuse your readers if you coordinate ideas that in fact don't have a close relationship.

Confusing coordination:

> Bill spends his money wisely. He bought an expensive amplifier and turntable, and for sound he uses two car speakers which he mounted in cigar boxes.

Relationships clarified:

> Bill spends his money wisely. He bought an expensive amplifier and turntable and is now saving his money for good speakers. In the meantime he is using two car speakers which he mounted in cigar boxes. [Since the point now is that Bill spends his money wisely, not strangely, joining the elements about the expensive amplifier and the cheap speakers is confusing. The revised version shows the intended relationship of ideas.]

13B Highlight main ideas by subordinating minor ideas.

Since coordination places equal emphasis on each idea, excessive coordination can prevent writers from keeping their sentences focused on the central point of a passage. Subordination allows you to keep your prose focused on main ideas.

Excessive coordination:

It was cold for a March day, and I listened to the whir of the helicopter blades. We flew over the snow-laden peaks, and we searched the granite edges of cliffs below us. We were looking for bighorn sheep. We wanted to shoot them with tranquilizer darts. Our goal was to attach radio collars to them.

Focus improved through subordination:

It was cold for a March day. I listened to the whir of the helicopter blades as we flew over the snow-laden peaks, searching the granite edges of cliffs below us. We were looking for bighorn sheep to shoot with tranquilizer darts so that we could attach radio collars to them. [The revised version emphasizes first the cold, then the flying over the peaks, and then the looking for sheep. The original version emphasizes everything—the cold, the listening to the helicopter, the flying over the peaks, the searching of the cliff edges, and so forth.]

You can subordinate elements by using a subordinating conjunction, such as *although, because, when,* or *if,* or by using a relative pronoun, such as *who, whom, whose, that,* or *which.* You can also subordinate elements through *embedding,* a grammatical term which means simply that you condense a sentence-length idea into a word or phrase that you insert into another sentence.

Coordinated ideas:

Maria walked up the steps of the cathedral. She walked slowly and looked very sad. She walked toward the altar and then she knelt down. Earlier at this same altar she had vowed to resist the Fuehrer's order. She had knelt at that time too.

Various ways that some of these ideas could be subordinated:

After she had walked slowly up the steps of the cathedral, a look of sadness on her face, Maria knelt at the front altar because this was where she had first vowed to resist the Fuehrer's order. [Uses the subordinating conjunctions *after* and *because.* The original sentence "She walked slowly and looked very sad" is now "embedded" in the new passage as the adverb *slowly* and the phrase *a look of sadness on her face.*]

Maria, who many years before had knelt at the altar to vow resistance to the Fuehrer's order, walked slowly and sadly up the steps of the cathedral toward that same altar, where she now intended to kneel again. [uses the relative pronoun *who*]

Slowly, sadly, Maria walked up the steps of the cathedral toward the very altar where, solemnly kneeling, she first vowed to resist the Fuehrer's order. Now she knelt again. [Most highly embedded version; note special emphasis placed on *she knelt again* by the short, separate sentence.]

None of these sentences is necessarily better than the original coordinated version, but each has a different rhythm and feel and each conveys the event in a slightly different way. Because any passage can be rewritten in different ways, writers are always choosing from among various options.

Just as excessive coordination prevents a writer from achieving focus, excessive subordination can create a confusing maze of subordinate structures. Revise your rough drafts to make sure ideas are clear.

Excessive subordination:

> Because she said she was going to the movies because she hadn't yet seen *Porky's VII* because she had been out of town when it was here before, we decided not to invite her to the party.

Revised:

> Because she said she was going to the movies, we decided not to invite her to the party. We knew she wouldn't miss *Porky's VII* this time since she had been out of town when it was here before.

Exercise 13-1 Self-study: Coordination

Combine the following sentences into one or two sentences that use coordination to give equal emphasis to equally important ideas. Use appropriate coordinating conjunctions to signal the intended meaning *(and, but, or, either . . . or, nor, neither . . . nor, for, so,* and *yet).* The provided answers are models only.

Answer column

1. Sam hates peanuts. He likes peanut butter.

2. Everything was done by the members. We all put in hours of work. Nobody got any special benefits.

3. The new store emphasizes natural foods. It also emphasizes nutrition. It tries to stay away from foods with preservatives.

4. Some of the bulk foods have been packaged by the employees. Customers are welcome to package their own goods.

5. She has lost more than twenty pounds. She is buying herself an entirely new wardrobe.

6. She has lost more than twenty pounds. She still isn't satisfied with her weight.

7. She has lost more than twenty pounds. She has finally decided to change her self-image.

8. Sally's writing has its ups and downs. She is a highly creative thinker. Her ideas tend to be disorganized.

9. Sally's writing has its ups and downs. She is a highly creative thinker. She organizes her ideas well. She goes through all stages of the writing process. Her individual sentences tend to get grammatically tangled.

10. You can't ever predict what Sally's essays will be like. She will have a brilliant idea. The essay will be developed unclearly. She will have a well-organized essay. Its ideas will be dull. Its ideas will also be commonplace.

---

1. Sam hates peanuts, but he likes peanut butter.

2. Everything was done by the members. We all put in hours of work, and nobody got any special benefits.

3. The new store emphasizes natural foods and nutrition and tries to stay away from foods with preservatives. [Or you could have something like "Emphasizing natural foods and nutrition, the store tries to stay away from foods with preservatives."]

4. Some of the bulk foods have been packaged by the employees, but customers are welcome to package their own goods.

5. She has lost more than twenty pounds, so she is buying herself an entirely new wardrobe.

6. She has lost more than twnety pounds, yet she still isn't satisfied with her weight.

7. She has lost more than twenty pounds, for she has finally decided to change her self-image.

8. Sally's writing has its ups and downs. She is a highly creative thinker, but her ideas tend to be disorganized.

9. Sally's writing has its ups and downs. She is a highly creative thinker, she organizes her ideas well, she goes through all stages of the writing process, yet her individual sentences tend to get grammatically tangled.

10. You can't ever predict what Sally's essays will be like. Either she will have a brilliant idea but her essay will be unclearly developed, or she will have a well-organized essay but her ideas will be dull and commonplace.

Exercise 13-2   Self-study: Subordination

Combine the following sentences using subordination. If you wish to create subordinate clauses, consider subordinating conjunctions such as these:

For this relationship:	Use this subordinating conjunction:
cause	because, since, so that
contrast	although
condition	if, unless, as long as
time	when, before, after, while, whenever
place	where, wherever

You can also use relative pronouns *(who, whom, whose, which,* and *that),* or you can embed ideas into sentences by condensing ideas into words or phrases. Whatever method you choose, emphasize the most important thought, putting other ideas into the background. Once again, the "answer" sentences are models only.

Answer column

1. You could take integral calculus now. You would be better off to try it next winter.

    1. Although you could take integral calculus now, you would be better off to try it next winter.

2. Isn't there any advantage in taking it now? Then I will wait.

    2. If there is no advantage in taking it now, I will wait.

3. George will graduate on time. George transferred to Maple College as a junior. George's adviser went out of her way. She wanted to help George. He needed to plan his schedule.

    3. Although George transferred to Maple College as a junior, he will graduate on time because his adviser went out of her way to help him plan his schedule.

4. I notice that I am having more trouble with my ankle. Perhaps I need to see my doctor again.

    4. Since I am having more trouble with my ankle, perhaps I need to see my doctor again.

5. She saw that the horse was skittish. She decided not to go riding. This was wise.

    5. When she saw that the horse was skittish, she wisely decided not to go riding.

    OR

    Seeing that the horse was skittish, she wisely decided not to go riding.

6. You must decide this. I need to take this course. Otherwise I won't be able to graduate on time.

    6. Unless you decide that I can take this course, I won't be able to graduate on time.

7. My sister wants to take computer programming in grade school. She got a small computer for her birthday.

    7. My sister, who got a small computer for her birthday, wants to take computer programming in grade school. [Or to change the meaning slightly, "Because my sister got a small computer for her birthday, she. . . ."]

8. The runner was surprised. People were looking at him. They gave him odd looks. The runner was jogging through the main street. His pace was leisurely.

    8. Jogging leisurely through the main street, the runner was surprised to see people looking at him oddly.

9. Every year our university gives International Peace Scholarships. These are given to women. The women must be from foreign countries. The women must be doing graduate work in the United States. They must be working in just certain fields. These fields must be needed in their native countries.

    9. Every year our university gives International Peace Scholarships to women from foreign countries doing graduate work in the United States in fields needed in their native countries.

10. The women must promise the following: They will return to their native country. This is after they graduate. These are the recipients of the International Peace Awards.	**10.** The women who receive the International Peace Awards must promise that they will return to their native countries.

Exercise 13-3   Mastery exercise: Coordination and subordination

Revise the following passages using both coordination and subordination effectively. Use the structure of your sentences to show the intended relationships between ideas. Add any words or phrases you need to make your meanings clear. There are, of course, no single "right answers." Experiment with several different ways of combining the sentences. Use your own paper for this exercise.

1. Martha identified with Rapunzel. Rapunzel was the heroine of a fairy tale. She let her hair grow long. A prince climbed up her long hair. He rescued her from a castle. Martha began to identify with Rapunzel after a certain event. Her father divorced her mother. He then remarried. This girl went to live with her father and stepmother. She hated her stepmother. She wanted to let her hair grow long. Her stepmother made her cut it short. Long hair became a symbol for her. It symbolized freedom. It also symbolized happiness. The story became a dream of hope. The story convinced her of this. A prince would come some day. The prince would rescue her. This conviction sustained her. Sometimes life seemed too difficult. Then she would imagine this. Martha would be Rapunzel. Her hair would be long. A loving prince would come. [Based on a passage from Bruno Bettelheim, *The Uses of Enchantment: The Meaning and Importance of Fairy Tales.*]

2. We drove over the road. The road was in the backcountry. I heard the sound of drums. They sounded staccato. We approached the next village. People were packed alongside the road. The road was dusty. The people were waving. They were yelling noisily. The sound got louder and louder. I stood up in the Land Rover. I finally realized this. They were shouting: "Meester Kinte! Meester Kinte!" I was a symbol for something. This was in their eyes. I symbolized all black people in the United States. The forefathers of American black people had been torn out of Africa. These people's forefathers remained in Africa. [Based on a passage from Alex Haley, *Roots.*]

14

Parallelism

14A Use parallel constructions for grammatical clarity and for forceful style.

The need for parallelism occurs anytime a writer uses a coordinating conjunction *(and, or, nor, but, for, yet,* and *so)* for joining two or more items in series. By choosing a coordinating conjunction, the writer indicates that the elements being joined are equal in importance. English sentence structure requires that each of these elements be grammatically parallel, that is, that nouns be joined to nouns, verbs to verbs, prepositional phrases to prepositional phrases, clauses to clauses, and so forth. You will discover that parallelism increases the force and clarity of your sentences, making them easier for readers to comprehend and to remember. Parallel structure, then, is a matter of both grammar and style.

Each of the following sentences illustrates parallel construction:

The girl had long blond *hair,* a deep *tan,* flashing *eyes,* and a pleasant *smile.* [nouns in series]

With a loud "varoom" from the deep-throated muffler, the car *squealed* around the corner, *sped* through a red light, and *swerved* onto the gravel cutoff at the edge of town. [verbs in series]

He walked calmly *through the open doorway, down the stairs,* and *into the street.* [prepositional phrases in series]

Sharon, who just got her M.B.A., told me *that getting good undergraduate grades is not a sure sign of success in graduate school, that learning to think is more important than learning to memorize,* and *that doing what you enjoy is sometimes the best strategy for college life.* [noun clauses in series (note repetition of *that)*]

Be sure to make the elements of a parallel construction grammatically similar.

A nonparallel construction occurs anytime a writer fails to maintain the same grammatical structure for each item in a series.

Nonparallel:

Joan likes playing soccer and to roller-skate. [begins with gerund phrase *(playing soccer)* but switches to infinitive]

Parallel:

> Joan likes to play soccer and to roller-skate. [two infinitives]

Nonparallel:

> As a teacher, he was a courteous listener, helpful during office hours, and he lectured in an exciting way. [noun switches to adjective which switches to independent clause]

Parallel:

> As a teacher, he was a courteous listener, a good helper during office hours, and an exciting lecturer. [all nouns]

Nonparallel:

> This term paper is illogical, poorly documented, and should have been typed. [adjectives switch to verb]

Parallel:

> This term paper is illogical, poorly documented, and illegible. [all adjectives]
>
> This term paper, which should have been typed, is illogical and poorly documented. [original verb phrase removed from parallel series]

14B When using correlative conjunctions (such as *either . . . or, neither . . . nor, both . . . and, not only . . . but also*), make sure that each unit of the correlative precedes the same grammatical structure.

> Correlatives, which are coordinating conjunctions used in pairs, should join parallel structures. To keep your parallelism clear, place each unit of the correlative in front of equivalent grammatical units.

Confusing:

> I not only like ice cream but also root beer. [*Not only* precedes a verb; *but also* precedes a noun.]

Better:

> I like not only ice cream but also root beer.

Confusing:

> She expects either to take calculus or statistics.

Better:

> She expects to take either calculus or statistics.

14C Use parallelism in making lists and outlines

Nonparallel:

Here is what I especially like about this university:
a. Pretty.
b. Teachers take time to help you.
c. Good climate.
d. Sports.
e. Social life if you want it.
f. Getting from one place to another on bicycle.
[single nouns, adjectives, phrases, and sentences mixed together]

Parallel:

Here is what I especially like about this university:
a. The campus is spacious and beautiful.
b. Teachers take time to help you.
c. The climate is good.
d. There is a good intramural sports program.
e. Social life is available if you want it.
f. System of bike paths makes transportation easy.
[all sentences]

Here is what I like about this university:
a. Beautiful, spacious campus
b. Helpful teachers
c. Good climate
d. Large intramural sports programs
e. Available social life
f. Easy transportation about campus with bicycle
[all grammatically equal phrases]

14D For increased clarity, you may wish to repeat such function words as articles, prepositions, conjunctions, and the infinitive sign *(to)* at the beginning of each item in a parallel series.

Confusing:

In his pocket, Bobby had a broken pencil stub from a golf course, pocketknife, marble, and comb.

Clearer:

In his pocket Bobby had *a* broken pencil stub from a golf course, *a* pocketknife, *a* marble, and *a* comb.

Confusing:

The drill sergeant told the recruits that there would be no weekend passes and they would be on KP instead.

Clearer:

The drill sergeant told the recruits *that* there would be no weekend passes and *that* they would be on KP instead.

14E   Be sure that a clause beginning with *and which, and that, and who,* or *and whom* is preceded in an earlier part of your sentence with a parallel clause beginning with *which, that, who,* or *whom.*

Nonparallel:

Of all my friends, Paul is the one with the greatest sense of courage and who most believes in honesty.

Parallel:

Of all my friends, Paul is the one *who* has the greatest sense of courage and *who* most believes in honesty.

Of all my friends, Paul is the most courageous and the most honest.

Nonparallel:

Carla is a student with exceptional intelligence and who should have little trouble getting into medical school.

Parallel:

Carla is a student *who* has exceptional intelligence and *who* should have little trouble getting into medical school.

Sentence restructured to avoid parallelism:

Carla, an exceptionally intelligent student, should have little trouble getting into medical school.

Exercise 14-1   Self-study: Correcting nonparallel constructions

In the following sentences correct all nonparallel constructions by restructuring nonparallel elements or by recasting the sentence to avoid parallel structure. Because some sentences may have more than one solution, the answers at the right are not the only ones possible.

Answer column

1. I relax most whenever I go fishing or to a golf course.

2. Whenever I go to a show, I always end up sitting behind a person with a large hat and who is tall.

3. He learned that you need plenty of strength to be a lumberjack and your life is always in some danger.

4. The college catalog showed a beautiful, snow-covered campus, students skating on a pond, and explained how this quiet country setting contributed to academic excellence.

5. Creative problem-solving demands the ability to change perspectives on a problem, brainstorming rapidly, working backward from the goal to various potential solutions, and the patience to let ideas "cook" in the subconscious.

1. I relax most whenever I go fishing or golfing.

2. Whenever I go to a show, I always end up sitting behind a tall person with a large hat.

3. He learned that you need plenty of strength to be a lumberjack and that your life is always in some danger.

4. The college catalog showed a beautiful, snow-covered campus with students skating on a pond and explained how this quiet country setting contributed to academic excellence.

5. Creative problem-solving demands such skills as changing perspectives on a problem, brainstorming rapidly, working backward from the goal to various potential solutions, and having the patience to let ideas "cook" in the subconscious.

6. This airplane has unusual strength and that can land on a very short runway.

7. I not only enjoyed studying for this exam but also receiving the only A.

8. At the zoo we saw a tiger, monkey, wild coyote, and several lions.

9. I can fly to Las Vegas either by making connections at Denver or at Salt Lake City.

10. George was overjoyed and feeling exuberant when he heard the news.

6. This unusually strong airplane can land on a very short runway.

7. I enjoyed not only studying for this exam but also receiving the only A.

8. At the zoo we saw a tiger, a monkey, a wild coyote, and several lions.

9. I can fly to Las Vegas by making connections either at Denver or at Salt Lake City.

10. George was overjoyed and exuberant when he heard the news.

Exercise 14-2   Combining sentences to form parallel structures

In the following exercises combine the short sentences into one longer sentence with parallel structures. In many cases there are numerous possible solutions. Try for the most graceful and effective sentence that you can.

Example:
The car seemed to be impossible to control.
It shook violently.
It began to fishtail from side to side.

Shaking violently and fishtailing from side to side, the car seemed impossible to control.

1. Curious human beings need explanations.
    These explanations could come from mythology.
    Theology might provide explanations.
    Other explanations might be from science.

2. The dog wagged his tail.
    A happy bark came from the dog.
    The dog leaped into the wagon.

3. All languages are systems of human conventions.
    Languages are not systems of natural law.

4. The English language has changed rapidly in the last two generations.
This has been caused by extraordinary changes in transportation and communication.
Cultural and technological changes have also contributed.
Another cause is large movements of population.

5. The young man came back from the x-ray room.
He was wringing his hands.
His body also shook with fearful trembling.

6. I know this.
The report isn't ready to be sent out.
The boss will be furious if it isn't on his desk by five o'clock.

7. The corn looked sick.
   Its stalks were bare.
   Grasshoppers had eaten its leaves.
   The ears were gnawed.
   Earwigs had infested the ears.

8. I especially like children.
   These children love to play on swings.
   "Bake sales" in front of their houses feature mud pies.
   They bring bouquets of dandelions to their mothers.

9. Students frequently find "existentialism" confusing.
   These students have not had the opportunity to study the history of ideas from the Renaissance onward.
   Plato's ideas are unknown to them.
   They lack appreciation for the impact of World War I on the European intellectual.
   They have little personal sense of *angst*.

10. My English teacher said that grading stacks of student papers is a difficult task.
    She has to read everyone's essay charitably.
    Her own biases must be fought against.

Exercise 14-3   Creating your own parallel constructions

A. In sentences 1 to 5, fill in the blanks with parallel elements to create a graceful sentence.

Example:

I love Helen because she cares deeply for others and *because she is generous with her time* .

1. The tiny kitten, its eyes not yet open, its _____ ,
began nuzzling toward its mother.

2. Methods commonly used to correct dangling participles are to expand the participial phrase into a complete
clause or _____ .

3. Her constant complaining about her grades and _____
are driving me crazy.

4. I insist that my children clean up their rooms each morning, that _____
_____ ,
and _____ .

5. Creating a good thesis statement, _____ ,
and _____
are three important keys to effective organization.

B. In sentences 6 to 10 create each sentence according to the instructions provided.

6. Write a sentence about your favorite activities using three parallel gerund phrases for subjects.

7. Write a sentence about people who annoy you. Compose your sentence using three parallel relative clauses beginning with *who, whom,* or *whose.*

8. Write a sentence with an opinion in the main clause and with three reasons for holding that opinion in parallel subordinate clauses beginning with *because.*

9. Write a sentence about your attitude toward studying using the phrases *not only . . . but also.*

10. Write a sentence about two possible solutions to a problem you currently have. Use the words *either . . . or.*

Exercise 14-4   Using parallelism in formal outlines

What follows is an outline for a student paper on the "writing process." Revise the outline so that the entries are parallel. Use your own paper. Here is an example for another paper on "teaching methods" (only main topic headings are shown).

Example:
Kinds of teaching methods
a. Some teachers lecture.
b. Class discussion in which teacher asks the questions and leads discussion.
c. Break class down into small groups that work independently.
d. Computer-assisted instruction.
e. Students' studying independently.

Revised:

Kinds of teaching methods
a. *Lecture*
b. *Class discussion in which teacher asks the questions and leads discussion*
c. *Small-group discussions in which groups work independently*
d. *Computer-assisted instruction*
e. *Independent study*

Explanation

In the original version, A is a sentence, B is a noun with modifiers, C is an imperative sentence, D is a noun, and E is a gerund phrase. In the revised version, all entries are nouns or nouns with modifiers. (The addition of modifiers, even whole clause modifiers, doesn't destroy the parallelism as long as each entry begins with a noun.)

The Writing Process

I. Begin thinking of ideas during a prewriting stage.
   a. You can make lists.
   b. Brainstorming on paper.
   c. Brief nonstop writing.
   d. Learn to change perspectives.
II. Making a first draft.
   a. Many writers don't worry about organization or style yet.
   b. Get something down on paper.
III. Organization.
   a. Developing a thesis statement.
   b. Know your audience.
   c. Your purpose.
   d. Effective outline.
IV. Revising and editing.
   a. Each draft a "re-vision" or "re-seeing" of your topic.
   b. Improvement of organization.
      1. Develop your paragraphs.
      2. Relationship between paragraphs and thesis statement.
      3. Paragraph unity and coherence.
      4. Making sure you have good transitions between sentences and paragraphs.
   c. Improvement of sentence structure and style.
      1. Be clear.
      2. Graceful.
      3. Achieving variety and emphasis.

d. Usage and mechanics.
   1. Check grammar, spelling, and punctuation.
   2. Good manuscript form.
e. Be sure to proofread carefully.
   1. Some people check spelling by reading backward word by word.
   2. Omitted words are a frequent problem.

Exercise 14-5   Mastery exercise: Parallel construction

In the following sentences, alter the italicized element to create parallel structure or to eliminate parallelism. Write your corrected version in the space provided at the right. If the sentence is already correct, write a *C* in the provided space.

Example:
The homemade root beer had exactly the right color, smelled delicious, and *fizzing with just the right amount of carbonation.*

fizzed with just the right amount of carbonation.

1. We improved our car's acceleration by resetting the spark plug caps and *also we boiled out the carburetor.*

1. _____

2. Our writing teacher specifies a different audience for each paper so that we will learn to adjust our tone and strategy to reach various readers and *to give us practice in real-world situations.*

2. _____

3. Race car driving requires much practical experience, and *your reactions must be quick.*

3. _____

4. The eye is like a camera since both have *an opening for light to enter,* a lens or lens system, and a screen for registering an image.

4. _____

5. Rays of light coming from external objects enter each eye through a multilayered transparent dome called the cornea and *which begins refracting* the light rays.

5. _____

6. The light passes in sequence through the cornea, *pupil, crystalline lens,* and the vitreous humor until it finally reaches the retina.

6. _____

7. The most complex part of the system is the crystalline lens, which can be flattened or elongated by the encircling ciliary muscle *and which thus serves as a multipurpose lens, focusing both near and distant objects.*

7. _____

8. The retina, a transparent membrane *and which contains millions of tiny light-sensitive receptors,* serves like the film of a camera.

8. _____

9. It doesn't record the image, however, but instead *passing along to the brain through the optic nerve the many sensations it receives.*

9. _____

10. After studying the eye in my anatomy class and *after I was fitted for contact lenses,* I became convinced I wanted to be an optometrist.

10. _____

11. The girls *not only will play baseball this afternoon but also soccer.*

11. _____

12. *Either she will drive the car herself* or go by taxi.

12. _____

13. Every fall my father starts up the old pickup, loads the chainsaw, and *we head for the forest to get firewood.*

13. _____

14. The company president ordered all personnel to submit a new Form 105 and *that we must review our pay vouchers for the year.*

14. _____

15. We judge our teachers not by how they lecture but *what concern they have for students.*

15. _____

16. You can avoid a comma splice by joining main clauses with a comma and a coordinating conjunction, *with a semicolon,* or by changing one of the main clauses to a subordinate clause.

16. _____

17. The coach explained that the game would probably be delayed but *to be in the locker room by six o'clock.*

17. _____

18. Again and again psychologists explore the same questions: Are we shaped by our heredity, by our environment, or *do we have free will?*

18. _____

19. To make friends you must first be a friend and *then listening carefully.*

19. _____

20. This typewriter has two annoying features: The overstrike lock at the end of the line sometimes doesn't work and *an overly sensitive carriage return key.*

20. _____

15

Emphasis

Good writers pay attention to the effect of their prose upon readers. They know that effective writing involves not only good content and organization but also an efficient prose style that emphasizes the most important ideas.

15A **Occasionally write sentences that begin with less important details and end with the most important word or thought. Sentences constructed this way are called periodic sentences.**

Many sentences—probably most—begin with the most important ideas and then add less important details in subordinate clauses and phrases. Such sentences are sometimes called **loose.** Periodic sentences, on the other hand, build suspense by beginning with less important ideas and ending with the main thought. Occasional periodic sentences, especially those that reveal artistic planning and shaping, can be strongly emphatic.

Loose:

A snarling dog sprang at my throat just as I was entering the yard.

Periodic:

Just as I was entering the yard, a snarling dog sprang at my throat.

Loose:

We studied hard but failed the test even after drinking coffee until midnight and trying to memorize all the dates.

Periodic:

We studied hard, drinking coffee until midnight, trying to memorize all the dates, but we still failed the test.

15B **Because the end of a sentence calls for strength, avoid putting weak or parenthetical expressions there.**

Unemphatic:

> Shakespeare's major tragedies are marked throughout by despair and hopelessness, according to one group of modernist critics.

Emphatic:

> According to one group of modernist critics, Shakespeare's tragedies are marked throughout by despair and hopelessness.

OR

> Shakespeare's tragedies, according to one group of modernist critics, are marked throughout by despair and hopelessness.

15C **For a different kind of emphasis, write a sentence that begins with a short statement of the main idea, and then add a series of free modifying elements to the end of the sentence. Such sentences are called cumulative.**

A cumulative sentence adds modifying elements to the end so that ideas in the opening clause are described in increasing detail as the sentence progresses. Modifiers added to the ends of sentences are called **free** modifiers because they are not bound to a fixed position inside the core of the sentence.

Two kinds of free modifiers are particularly effective: participial phrases and absolute phrases (see section 3C).

Participial Phrases

Unemphatic:

> The man puffed up the hill on his bicycle. He was wheezing loudly. He was also wiping his head with his handkerchief.

Cumulative sentence:

> The man puffed up the hill on his bicycle, wheezing loudly, wiping his head with his handkerchief.

Absolute Phrases

Unemphatic:

> My brother raced toward the fly ball. His hat fell over his eyes. His arms waved frantically.

Emphatic:

> My brother raced toward the fly ball, his hat falling over his eyes, his arms waving frantically.

15D **When you wish to emphasize the actor or agent in your writing, use the active voice.**

As explained in Chapter 7, verbs that transfer action from an actor to a receiver are called transitive verbs and can have either active or passive voice. In general, use the active voice, thus emphasizing the actor, unless you have special reason to emphasize the receiver.

Unemphatic:

The bank was robbed by two teenage girls. [passive voice]

Emphatic:

Two teenage girls robbed the bank. [active voice]

15E Occasionally give emphasis by repeating key words or phrases over several clauses or sentences.

I *like* everything about my new car. I *like* the solid way the doors close. I *like* the smooth, rich leather seats. I *like* the feel of the steering wheel and the grip of the shift knob. I *like* the way the key turns precisely in the ignition and the way the engine purrs when it idles. I *like* pulling out into traffic, shifting through the gears, and heading for the winding country road. I *like* steering into the corners, braking on hills, and shifting down when I stop. Best of all, I *like* myself when I drive this car.

NOTE: Such repetition, if done too frequently or for too long, becomes distracting.

15F Occasionally give special emphasis to an idea by putting it in a very short sentence that follows longer sentences.

For weeks I had been bored and depressed, sitting listlessly in my room and fingering my guitar or playing my same records over and over again on the stereo. I had even lost interest in going with the gang to the local drive-in — the same old drive-in where the same old people ordered the same old Whacko-burgers with the same old, soggy french fries. *So I joined the army.*

Exercise 15-1   Self-study: Creating emphasis

Revise the following sentences to achieve better emphasis. Follow the instructions provided. Your answers may differ somewhat from the model sentences in the answer column.

Answer column

1. Professor Dull's course is awful, with its monotonous lectures, its confusing textbook, and its disorganized labs. (Revise to form a periodic sentence.)

1. With its monotonous lectures, its confusing textbook, and its disorganized labs, Professor Dull's course is awful.

2. Our trip to Montana — the homemade ice cream, the horseback rides, the rattlesnake striking my boot, the smell of barbecued steak, even the hikes along mountain trails — all this lives happily in my memory. (Arrange details in order of climax.)

2. Our trip to Montana — the homemade ice cream, the horseback rides, the smell of barbecued steak, the hikes along mountain trails, even the rattlesnake striking my boot — all this lives happily in my memory.

3. Scientists can operate only in a world where much is known and much unknown, according to Dr. Carl Sagan. (Relocate weak ending.)

3. Scientists, according to Dr. Carl Sagan, can operate only in a world where much is known and much unknown.

4. Susan walked out of the room. She was swinging the tassel on her belt. She was also smiling mysteriously. Also she was humming a tune. (Create a cumulative sentence ending with participial phrases.)

4. Susan walked out of the room, swinging the tassel on her belt, smiling mysteriously, and humming a tune.

5. The professor slammed his briefcase on the desk. His face was tight and drawn. His eyes glared at the students in the front row. (Create a cumulative sentence using absolute phrases.)

6. In the dark of the night, the fraternity's entire collection of *Playboy* magazines was stolen by a task force of sorority pledges. (Revise sentence using the active voice.)

7. Sam complained about everything. He didn't like the dorm food. His roommate's messiness bothered him. He thought his calculus teacher's lectures were boring. Even his mailbox was too low. (Revise this passage by using effective repetition of the word *complained*.)

8. Maxwell didn't want to help us put the cow in the dean's office. In truth, old Max was a coward, although he argued for two days that the prank was an old one, that students of our generation should be able to think of a more innovative practical joke, and that a cow might do permanent damage to the dean's office. (Revise for emphasis by putting the assertion that Max was a coward into a short sentence at the end.)

9. What is especially liked by me on hot summer afternoons is a banana milkshake. (Use active voice.)

10. The library's new fine schedule is a mistake because it discriminates against undergraduate students and because the notification system is too confusing. (Emphasize the main point by converting to a periodic sentence.)

11. The world has too many environmentalists who don't care a fig about the needs of business, says Senator Jones. (Revise for a stronger ending.)

12. Don't tell me about being a liberated male. I grew up in a house where my father cooked, ironed, knitted sweaters, and even mopped floors. (Arrange in order of climax.)

13. The butterfly landed on the rose. Its wings were folded back in perfect symmetry. The color was an exquisite deep purple. (Convert to a cumulative sentence using absolute phrases.)

14. Sharon slurped the milkshake. She made gurgling sounds with the straw. She also winked at Jefferson across the table. (Convert to a periodic sentence beginning with participial phrases.)

5. The professor slammed his briefcase on the desk, his face tight and drawn, his eyes glaring at the students in the front row.

6. In the dark of the night, a task force of sorority pledges stole the fraternity's entire collection of *Playboy* magazines.

7. Sam complained about everything. He complained about the dorm food. He complained about his roommate's messiness. He complained about his calculus teacher's lectures. He even complained about the height of his mailbox.

8. Maxwell didn't want to help us put the cow in the dean's office. He argued for two days that the prank was an old one, that students of our generation should be able to think of a more innovative practical joke, and that a cow might do permanent damage to parts of the dean's office. In truth, however, old Max was a coward.

9. What I especially like on hot summer afternoons is a banana milkshake.

10. Because it discriminates against undergraduate students and because the notification system is confusing, the library's new fine schedule is a mistake.

11. The world has too many environmentalists, says Senator Jones, who don't care a fig about the needs of business.

12. Don't tell me about being a liberated male. I grew up in a house where my father cooked, ironed, mopped floors, and even knitted sweaters.

13. The butterfly landed on the rose, its wings folded back in perfect symmetry, its color an exquisite deep purple.

14. Making gurgling sounds with the straw and winking at Jefferson across the table, Sharon slurped the milkshake.

OR

Slurping the milkshake and making gurgling sounds with the straw, Sharon winked at Jefferson across the table. [Note the different emphases in these two options.]

Exercise 15-2   Mastery exercise: Sentence emphasis

Revise the following sentences in any fashion that seems appropriate in order to improve the emphasis. In the column at the right, explain the principles you used, such as "periodic sentence," "stronger ending," "order of climax," "cumulative sentence using participles or absolutes," "active voice," "repetition of key words or phrases," or "putting main point into short sentence." There are no single "right answers."

Example:

Principles used

Three deaths were caused by the earthquake, according to the first reports from the police.

According to the first reports from the police, the earthquake caused three deaths.

periodic sentence with stronger ending; active voice

1. The Milky Way galaxy is one of billions just like it. These galaxies are strewn through space. The space is vast. Thus the Milky Way galaxy is unremarkable.

2. The clock struck 6:00 A.M. yesterday morning. At exactly that moment the lieutenant was slugged by Corporal Jones.

3. Jefferson Square was filled with a flock of pigeons. The pigeons were running around. They were flapping their wings. They hovered like vultures. They were waiting for people to throw them bread crumbs.

_____

_____

_____

_____

_____

4. The Indians moved slowly through the white settlement. Two dozen braves were on horseback. Chief Spotted Horse brought up the rear. Spotted Horse had a rifle slung across his back. His face was painted with the blood-red stripes of war.

_____

_____

_____

_____

_____

5. She was too tired to write her essay. She was also too fatigued to open her chemistry book. She had just enough energy to pour bubbles into a hot bath. She was even too tired to practice her flute.

_____

_____

_____

_____

6. Ideas are often invented by me through free-writing. A blank sheet of paper is pulled from my notebook. Then the pen is placed on the paper and writing goes on nonstop for ten straight minutes. Sometimes ideas about my childhood are thought of, such as the times we would walk in the park on Sundays where my hands would be held by my parents and I would be swung back and forth. At other times aspects of my present life in college will be thought of, such as last Sunday when homework was done while sitting on the bank by the river.

7. My girlfriend wanted me to sign up for tennis lessons. I was also asked to become social chairman for my dorm. After I told both my girlfriend and our dorm president "no," I was also asked by my choir director to sing a solo at the next concert and then my parents asked me to get a different jacket, but I told them "no" also.

8. His nose began to itch. He walked out of the bargain center. His arms were loaded with packages.

_____

_____

_____

_____

_____

9. "Knowing fundamental laws of physics gives students a basis for solving problems rationally," says the physicist Judith Franz. Scientists are often more interested in doing their own research than in teaching, nevertheless. Universities sell their students short, as a result.

_____

_____

_____

_____

_____

10. Juanita bandaged the wound swiftly. Her strong hands ripped the sheets into strips. Her fingers were deft and sure as she tied the bandage around LeRoy's arm.

_____

_____

_____

_____

_____

Variety

If you want your readers not only to understand your message but also to enjoy reading your prose because it is lively and interesting, then practice varying the length and structure of your sentences.

16A Learn to vary the patterns and lengths of your sentences for effect.

The most common sentence pattern begins with the subject and ends with the predicate. You can achieve variety, however, by departing from this pattern. One technique is to open sentences occasionally with modifiers of some type.

Eagerly, without looking back, she ran across the lawn into his waiting arms.

As he watched her approach, he felt the old longing ache within him.

Seeing the tears well in her eyes, he hugged her tightly to his chest.

Her lips quivering, her voice choked with emotion, she whispered softly, "I'm sorry."

To write romance novels, you have to learn the clichés.

You can also achieve variety by varying the length of your sentences and by inserting modifying elements within the sentence rather than at the beginning.

Monotonous:

Martin watched carefully for loose rocks. He picked his way along the edge of the cliff. Martin didn't hear the rattles at first, but then he suddenly froze with fear when he heard them for sure. A timber rattler was about 2 feet away, and it was coiled like a garden hose. The rattler's neck was arched and its fangs looked like twin needles of death. [Each sentence starts with the subject; the sentences are about the same length.]

Improved:

Watching carefully for loose rocks as he picked his way along the edge of the cliff, Martin suddenly froze with fear. At first he didn't hear the rattles. Then he heard them for sure. About 2 feet away, coiled like a garden hose, was a timber rattler, its neck arched, its fangs looking like twin needles of death. [Longest sentence is twenty-four words; shortest is six words. The short sentence places the emphasis on the dramatically important moments.]

16B   Achieve variety by occasionally asking a rhetorical question.

A rhetorical question, followed by the answer, can highlight an important point. When used sparingly, rhetorical questions can invite your readers to participate more actively in your prose.

> An expository essay is built around a thesis statement. But just what is a thesis statement? Strictly speaking, a thesis statement is a one-sentence summary of the whole argument of an essay. Written out in its long form, a thesis statement is the essay's main point along with a summary of the essay's supporting arguments. Although the thesis statement does not have to appear in the essay itself, it must have been clearly present in the writer's mind. [Try reading this passage again, eliminating the rhetorical question (sentence two). Can you see how the rhetorical question emphasizes the subsequent definition of *thesis statement* and, in effect, justifies the amount of time the writer spends on it?]

16C   On rare occasions, you can use an exclamation mark for special effect.

Overuse of exclamation marks can be an annoying habit that is sometimes common among inexperienced writers. However, a professional writer will occasionally use an exclamation mark. When used rarely, it can give special emphasis to a sentence.

> There she was again! Every morning when Hampton walked across the field, he saw the apparition. This time she was sitting on a branch above the stream.

16D   Occasionally invert the subject and the verb, or begin a sentence with a direct object.

Because an inverted pattern conveys a studied, artificial effect, it receives more than ordinary emphasis. The effect is lost, however, if overused.

> On a branch above the stream appeared the apparition. [Predicate comes before the subject.]

> A strange emblem she held in her hands. [Direct object comes first.]

Exercise 16-1   Writing varied sentences

One way to get a feel for variety in sentence structure is to practice saying the same thing in as many ways as possible. Rewrite each of the following sentences in as many different ways as you can think of. Which ones do you like the best?

Example:
A good massage can settle your nerves.

To settle your nerves, try a good massage.
There is nothing like a good massage to settle your nerves.
Settling your nerves is easy with a good massage.
After a good massage, your nerves will feel settled.
If you want to settle your nerves, a good massage is the answer.
Your nerves will be settled with a good massage.

1. Catsup is disgusting on macaroni and cheese.

2. In baseball a walk is as good as a hit.

3. A good hunting dog points at pheasants but doesn't chase them.

4. A word processor is a valuable aid for writers.

5. To make your prose lively and interesting, vary your sentence structure.

Exercise 16-2 Mastery exercise: Creating sentence variety in paragraphs

In the following paragraph, the unvarying length and pattern of the sentences make the prose monotonous. Revise the paragraph by varying sentence length and structure, combining sentences in any way you choose. Although there is no correct answer (obviously) for an exercise like this, we have used as our "answer" in the example the original version written by a professional writer.

Example passage:
You are out driving and hear a disturbing noise. It sounds like the squeak of a rusty gate and is really grating. Or you might say it sounds like a puppy and this puppy has just had its tail stepped on. This disturbing sound seems to be coming from your front tires. You should therefore stop your car and investigate this disturbing sound. Suppose you notice that the noise comes mainly when you make a turn. Then you can hope it is something inexpensive like low tire pressure. But suppose the car also drifts to the right or left; then maybe your wheels are out of alignment. First you should check your tire pressure to see if that is satisfactory. Next you should have your wheel alignment checked. Correct tire pressure and wheel alignment will help your tires wear evenly.

Professional version:
If you hear a noise like the grating screech of a rusty gate hinge or the high-pitched squeal of a puppy whose tail has just been stepped on, and it appears to be coming from the front tires, stop your car and investigate. If the noise comes as you make a turn, hope for something inexpensive such as low tire pressure. If the noise is accompanied by a drifting of the car to the right or left, it may mean that the wheels are out of alignment as well. So, first check the air pressure in your tires. Not low? Then have the alignment checked. If you neglect either of these problems, your tires will eventually wear unevenly. [Rose R. Olney, "10 Car Noises You Shouldn't Ignore," *Reader's Digest* (April 1983).]

Djenne is an African city in the middle of the River Niger's inland delta. Its pace of life is slow and is governed by the tropical sun which is relentless. Dustdevils and lizards are the only moving things in the heat of the middle of the day. The city stirs with life in the mornings, for donkey carts arrive. They are laden with fruit and fish, and the central market buzzes with activity. This central market is as big as a football field. The women sit on low stools and sell their wares. They are dressed in brilliantly colored robes and their wares are spread out before them. A few of these women wear gold earrings, and these earrings are enormous. The earrings denote status and wealth and link these women to a past that was more prosperous than the present. [Based on Ronald Trigs, "To Timbuktu and Beyond: A Journey to Africa's Past," *Travel/Holiday* (March 1983).]

17
Appropriate Diction

Another way to increase the enjoyment and clarity of your prose for readers is to create a style that is appropriate to your subject, neither too informal and breezy nor too formal and stuffy. You can vary your style through your choice of words and sentence structure. In anything you write, your choice of style will depend upon your audience and purpose. As you revise, make sure your words convey the exact meanings you intend.

Sometimes inexperienced writers create an ineffective style by asserting their own emotions or judgments in essays without providing the detail upon which their feelings are based. This editorializing can annoy readers, who generally want to form their own judgments. For example, if you are angry about an assignment your teacher gave, try downplaying your own emotions, providing instead the details about the assignment that particularly angered you.

Less effective:

Dr. Jackson's journal assignments are absurd. Anyone who thinks that dumb assignments like these should be given to freshmen students ought to be placed in an asylum. They are a total waste of time. [This writer's opinion is clear, but why the writer feels this way remains unclear.]

More effective:

Dr. Jackson asks students to write twenty minutes per day in a journal on topics that I find either uninteresting or offensive. For example, we had to write for a whole week on dancing (I hate dancing) and then for another week on restroom graffiti. He gives us no freedom of choice, nor does he read what we write. This kind of busy work is making me dislike English. [In this version the writer provides specific details which help readers form their own judgments.]

Try also to achieve a style that steers a middle course between breeziness and excessive formality.

Breezy tone:

So, friend, you think the computer is just for freaky hackers in basements. Well, let me tell you about a new development. Computers are now *with it* in ballet. Yup, I said *ballet!* Close your peepers and imagine this scene. Twenty-five dancers wearing shorts and leg warmers come leaping and twirling across the stage rehearsing *The Wild Boy* with Mikhail Baryshnikov as the lead honcho.

But this is no standard rehearsal. This little number, my friends, has been choreographed by computer.

Stuffy, excessively formal style:

Throughout the entire history of the noble art of ballet, professional dancers and directors have been hampered by the absence of a notational system that will enable them to make a permanent written record of the intricate movements of a ballet. But this serious shortcoming in the art form may at last be eliminated. Technological developments in computer graphics can now permit permanent machine storage of the dance patterns, which can be programmed into a computer and displayed on a suitable videoscreen with color enhancement capabilities.

Actual version written by a professional writer:

Twenty-five dancers, wearing rumpled shorts and leg warmers, move across the stage in an eerie stalk uncharacteristic of traditional ballet. It is a rehearsal for the premier staging of *The Wild Boy* with Mikhail Baryshnikov in the lead role. For the first time in history, the intricate movements of this new ballet may be preserved for future generations, for this dance has been choreographed with the aid of a computer. [Adapted from Joseph Menosky, "Videographics & Grand Jetés," *Science 82* (May 1982).]

Exercise 17-1   Creating effective style

Revise the following passages, which are marred by unsupported emotion or judgment. Use details that show the specific cause of the writer's feelings. Make up any details that you prefer. Use extra paper if needed.

> *Example:*
> My grandfather is the nicest man you can imagine. I just love to be with him on Saturday afternoons. He is so sweet and kind.

Revised: My grandfather is the nicest man you can imagine. On Saturday afternoons when I was a child my grandfather used to take me to the park. We would feed the squirrels together and throw bread crumbs at the ducks and swans. Often he would buy me an ice cream cone on the way home. Although he is too old now to walk to the park, when I visited him last Saturday he gave me a painting of a little girl on a bicycle in a park. He had painted it himself.

1. The Jones' children are the biggest brats I have ever babysat. I can't stand to be around them! The horrid little monsters! They drive me crazy!

2. Bubblebrook Park is so beautiful you wouldn't believe it. It is my favorite place to go in the whole world. When I go there I feel so serene and peaceful. I can spend hours just sitting there and never get bored.

3. The gymnastics team is unbelievably exciting to watch. I will just hold my breath and then gasp at the things they can do. The athletic ability of some of those gymnasts just leaves me in awe.

Exercise 17-2 Creating different styles

In this exercise, rewrite the provided passage in two ways. First make the passage overly informal and breezy. Then go to the opposite extreme by making it overly formal, stuffy, and pretentious. Use the two headings shown below in the example. Have fun with this exercise. Experiment with different voices. Use your own paper for this exercise.

Example:
I didn't know, at 21, that life could be good for a woman when she grew older. I thought that the best role in life was Pretty Young Thing. I thought that time could only bring me losses. [From the introduction to "In Praise of Older Women" by Judith Viorst in *Redbook*.]

Rewritten: Too breezy

Listen up, sisters, to old wrinkle-face, here. When I was younger, I thought that growing old would be the pits. I thought the best role in life was being a foxy chick. Like wow, I thought, the old spin of the clock would do me in.

Rewritten: Too stuffy

I did not realize when I was at the end of my adolescent years that my satisfaction with life could be maintained as I progressed in age. My only consideration at that point in time was that the most rewarding life role was a function of my youth and beauty, and as these became lost that I would experience a downward trend of meaningful experience.

Car radios are not the latest creations Detroit has added to its lineup of options. But they're getting to be one of the most sophisticated gadgets you'll find on a car's dashboard. The traveling music they produce is something this side of magic.

In fact, the 1980 radio models from Detroit are so streamlined some don't need knobs, dial faces or gears and pulleys to change stations. They've gone electronic and, if the trend persists, may become teeny on-board computers. They already have logic circuits, memories and other digital delights. [Leon Buckwaller, "Music Magic on the Road," *Mechanix Illustrated* (November 1979).]

17A Avoid the inappropriate use of slang.

Slang is the special vocabulary of particular groups of people. Slang words come into the language quickly and often quickly disappear. Because such words as *groovy, funky, laid back,* and *out of sight* have no universal definitions, they may not be understood by all readers, and they create an uncomfortably informal tone inappropriate for most writing in or out of college.

Inappropriate for most occasions:

The new major in Industrial Management is a real humdinger for students hoping to make kilobucks after graduation.

Better:

The new major in Industrial Management should be especially appealing to students looking for careers promising large incomes.

17B Use dialect with caution.

Dialect is a kind of prose in which the spelling of words is altered to reflect the speech sounds of particular groups of people. Although experienced writers can sometimes show the ethnic or regional origins of people by using dialect, they are always in danger of seeming inadvertently to be laughing at the people they are writing about. It is probably best to avoid dialect.

Dialect:

> "You're a rucky boy, Jelly," he said.

Revised:

> "You're a lucky boy, Jerry," he said in his strong Chinese accent.

17C Avoid jargon.

Jargon is the specialized language of certain jobs or occupations, and it is thus easily understandable only to limited groups of people. Sometimes jargon is necessary to convey exact meanings, but often it is used pretentiously where ordinary language would convey the same ideas more economically and gracefully.

Extensive jargon (in this case from medical sociology):

> Aging is characterized by time-dependent alterations in the ability of an organism to adapt to environmental change. Confusion about what constitutes aging has arisen from the failure of much prior research to differentiate those decremental changes that are a function of the passage of time from those that occur with increasing age but are secondary to disease.

Revised:

> As people get older, they are less able to adapt to changes in their environment. Research on aging, however, hasn't always distinguished between loss of function due to the passage of time and loss due to diseases common among older people.

17D Avoid obsolete, foreign, or technical words.

Like jargon, obsolete, foreign, or unnecessary technical words can make your prose appear pretentious and often cloud your meaning.

Pretentious:

> She vacillated *betwixt ennui* and *angst*—the result perhaps of her no longer possessing the *theopathy* she felt as an adolescent.

Better:

> She vacillated between boredom and anxiety—the result, perhaps, of her no longer possessing the religious ecstasy she felt as an adolescent.

Exercise 17-3   Avoiding slang and jargon

1. Can you convert the following passage to standard language using ordinary vocabulary? (These slang terms are from the early seventies.) After trying to translate the passage, explain briefly the problems you had.

My friend Jake has a hangup about funky furniture. Of course he's laid back — no problem there — but he's got these real far-out ideas about how a frat room should look.

Your translation:

What problems did you have?

2. Suppose you really like Bill Jackson's car. Would you say his car is the "cat's pajamas"? "the bee's knees"? "groovy"? "far out"? "awesome"? Would you say Bill is "a real cool cat"? Why or why not?

How would you describe his car in your own contemporary slang?

3. Now write a short passage about a topic of your choice that includes at least three currently popular slang words in your own social group. Then rewrite the passage eliminating the slang terms. Be prepared to discuss the problems of converting slang into standard English vocabulary. Can you translate the meanings exactly? Is slang less precise or more precise than a standard vocabulary?

Slang version:

Standard vocabulary version:

Observations about the two versions:

4. The following passage relies heavily on jargon and technical language common in many professional academic journals. Try to rewrite it in a more informal and readable style suitable for a general audience (use extra paper if needed). The passage is about a training program for increasing the thinking skills of preschool and grade school children.

Another of our goals is probably the one that marks the uniqueness of our method as compared with other programs oriented toward the development of cognitive processes. It represents an attempt to produce in the learner an intrinsic need for adequate cognitive functioning that will render his or her functioning independent of external conditions. Development of an intrinsic need system is a necessity stemming from the fact that many of those children whose cognitive modifiability is low continue to live in environments that will not provide them with the extrinsic need systems liable to elicit from them higher mental processes. This lack of extrinsic need to use proper cognitive processes may leave whatever is learned by the organism in a state of limited functional significance, and the individual who has learned to think may make very little use of his or her thought processes because of the limited need to do so. [From R. Feverstein and J. Mogens, "Instrumental Enrichment: Theoretical Basis, Goals, and Instruments," *Educational Forum* (1980).]

17E Use idioms according to standard practice.

An **idiom** is a customary arrangement or ordering of words peculiar to a language, often without logical justification. We cannot explain why English speakers say "She entered the building" rather than "She entered into the building" (the French would add the *into*) or "I am looking for my keys" rather than "I am looking my keys" (the French would omit the *for*). They just do. Often idioms involve the correct choice of a preposition.

Faulty	Correct
I was acquitted of blame.	I was acquitted from blame.
I was acquitted from the crime.	I was acquitted of the crime.
He acquitted from himself well.	He acquitted himself well.
I stayed at Boston.	I stayed in Boston.
I stayed in Georgia's house.	I stayed at Georgia's house.

In the last instance both *in Georgia's house* and *at Georgia's house* are correct, but they have slightly different meanings. "I stayed in Georgia's house" stresses being inside, perhaps while something else was happening: "I stayed in Georgia's house during the hailstorm." Similarly, the following sentences have slightly different meanings:

> We agreed with Ralph. [We entered into an agreement with Ralph.]

> We agreed on Ralph. [We couldn't decide who should chair the meeting — Ralph or Sally. Finally we agreed on Ralph.]

No single book can possibly list all the idioms in English. You have to trust your ear (very difficult, of course, if you are not a native English speaker) and rely on a good dictionary for help.

17F Choose words with connotations appropriate to your meaning and purpose.

Note the different feelings you have about the italicized words in these examples:

a *used* Porsche	a *preowned* Porsche
a *bland* taco sauce	a *mild* taco sauce
a *difficult* assignment	a *challenging* assignment

Words have both *denotation* and *connotation.* A word's *denotation* is its dictionary or primary meaning. The pairs of words above have approximately the same denotations. A word's *connotation* is the associations that the word evokes or the secondary meanings that it implies. For example, you might say that your friend wrote an essay "easily," "facilely," or "effortlessly." *Easily* is relatively neutral. It means "without much difficulty." *Effortlessly* implies that your friend has so much skill that the essay seemed to flow almost automatically from her typewriter. *Facilely,* however, implies that your friend had an easy time with the essay because she didn't think or try very hard; her work is shallow. Thus three words with approximately the same denotations have quite different connotations. A good dictionary will help you examine the various nuances of synonyms like these.

Be especially careful of connotations when you use figurative language (see Chapter 18). There is a considerable difference in feeling between "She hammered out the essay in an hour" versus "She bludgeoned out the essay in an hour" or between "Her eyes are as green as emeralds" versus "Her eyes are as green as leeks."

Exercise 17-4 Self-study: Using idioms correctly

A. The following exercise will help you appreciate problems associated with idiom. Choose the word in parentheses that completes the idiom. Because idioms are illogical, there are no rules that will help you master general principles. The following sentences, of course, are only illustrations of various kinds of problems with idiom; they are not an exhaustive list.

	Answer column
1. I like to do my work independent (of, from) other people.	1. of
2. A cafeteria in New York is very different (from, than) a cafe in Paris.	2. from
3. I was a frog during a (previous, prior) life.	3. previous
4. I stroke my backhand differently (from, than) the way she does.	4. from
5. (Before, previous to) the class, the professor spent eighteen hours developing the lecture.	5. before
6. Jim and Rebecca joined the firm (in, on) March 1983.	6. in
7. Jim and Rebecca joined the firm (in, on) March 8, 1983.	7. on
8. The university mistakenly charged me (with, for) tuition during summer quarter.	8. for
9. The university mistakenly charged me (with, for) plagiarism on a history term paper.	9. with
10. The university accepted me (with, for) the honors program.	10. for
11. The university was pleased (with, by) my application for the honors program.	11. with
12. Your answer does not correspond (to, with) reality.	12. to
13. Have you corresponded (to, with) the professor about your final grade?	13. with
14. We waited (on, for) the delivery of the new stereo.	14. for

B. In the remaining exercises, use a good dictionary for assistance.

15. Write a sentence of your own that uses the word *complied*.

16. Write a sentence that uses the words *waited on*.

17. Write sentences of your own using:
   a. *differ with*

   b. *differ from*

c. *differ about*

18. Write sentences of your own using:
a. *part from*

b. *part with*

19. Write a sentence of your own using the word *conform* followed by a preposition.

20. Write four sentences of your own using the word *make* followed by different particles to create verbs with different meanings (for example, *make up, make off, make out,* and *make way*).

Exercise 17-5   Denotation and connotation

A. Using a dictionary for assistance, explain the different connotations of the following words:

Example:
forgetful neutral term meaning the person is apt to forget things

senile   much more intense term suggesting a person forgets because of a deterioration of the brain. Senility is an age-related disease and usually affects an older person. When used in describing a young person, it is often a sarcastic term.

1. manly

   macho

   virile

   masculine

   boyish

2. stubborn

   persistent

   obstinate

3. depressed

sad

pensive

melancholy

inconsolable

4. feminine

feminist

ladylike

womanly

5. fault

error

mistake

sin

crime

B. The following excerpts from advertisements show obvious awareness of connotation. For each example, underline words that seem chosen especially for their connotations and explain how the connotations contribute to the effect of the advertisement.

6. The Porsche 928S is one of the fastest production automobiles in the world. It accelerates from 0 to 50 mph in 5.6 seconds and has reached speeds of 146 mph on the track. Its powerplant is a 4.7-liter V-8 engine with a light alloy block and cylinder heads.

7. Once upon a time there was a pioneer woman who captured the vitality of the Old West as well as its peace. Her name was Cinnamon Rose.

The herb tea that bears her name blends serenity with a taste for the adventurous. . . . For a delicious, soothing treat, sit back with a legend: Cinnamon Rose.

8. MERIT MAKING TASTE HISTORY. SIGNIFICANT MAJORITY RATES *MERIT* TASTE EQUAL TO OR BETTER THAN LEADING HIGH TARS. *Smoker research conclusive:* Nationwide tests with thousands of smokers continue to confirm the MERIT breakthrough in key areas of taste and overall preference.

9. *Le Menu.* You won't find too many frozen dinners that can hold a candle to Le Menu.

Le Menu is a whole line of premium dinners. Each gives you three perfectly orchestrated dishes. Like Pepper Steak: tender slices of sirloin beef garnished with green peppers alongside long grain rice and crisp Oriental vegetables.

18

Imagery and Figurative Language

Writers frequently improve their prose by using concrete language that invokes images in the reader's mind. Another technique is to use figurative language in which you compare thing A to thing B, using vivid, specific qualities of B to enhance the reader's understanding of A. Concrete language and figurative language, when used appropriately, can add a richness to your prose unattainable in any other way.

18A **You can also create richer, more vivid prose if you use concrete, specific language rather than vague, all-purpose language.**

Vague:

The child was bothered by the teacher's testing methods. [It is difficult for the reader to imagine vividly what the writer means by *bothered* or to understand what is meant by *teaching methods.*]

Richer:

Seeing the world complexly, Susan was infuriated by the teacher's multiple-choice exams, which didn't allow her to explain why more than one answer might be correct. [Concrete language allows us to understand Susan's predicament more clearly.]

Vague:

A lot of things about her speech interested me. [What things? What do you mean by *interested?*]

Richer:

Her anecdotes about people who hated group therapy, especially her story of Rita spitting on the therapist's shoes and running from the room, taught me to be skeptical about psychologist's claims. [Now we know what the speaker said and what interested the writer.]

265

18B To make your prose more vivid, you can often use metaphors and similes, but be sure that these figures of speech are appropriate to your subject, your tone, and your audience.

A **simile** makes a comparison by using the words *like* or *as*.

> He gobbled his food *like a hungry wolf.*
>
> Language without figures of speech is as boring *as a drone plane at an airshow.*

A **metaphor** makes its comparison directly, omitting the *like* or *as*. It asserts that thing A *is* thing B. A metaphor is more compressed than a simile and often has more power.

> He *wolfed* down his food.
>
> Her figures of speech *spun, dove, rolled, climbed:* She was *a stunt pilot with words.*

If writers aren't careful with their use of figurative language, they may unintentionally confuse or amuse their readers. If you compare thing A to thing B and midway through switch to a comparison with thing C, you will have created a *mixed metaphor.*

> Like a caterpillar on a cabbage leaf, he wolfed down his food. [Although caterpillars and wolves both eat a lot, the different comparisons in the same sentence create unintentional humor, causing us to imagine a ferocious, wolf-like caterpillar.]
>
> Her figures of speech spun, rolled, dived, climbed: She was a wizard with language. [We imagine stunt planes spinning, rolling, diving, and climbing, but not wizards.]

Sometimes, also, writers may inadvertently choose a figure of speech with associations inappropriate for their purpose, tone, or intended audience. For example, if you were describing the pleasant feeling of lying in bed listening to rain on a tin roof, it would probably be inappropriate to compare the sound to machine gun fire.

18C Avoid using worn-out expressions or clichés.

The effect of a good figure of speech is surprise — the creation of an apt comparison that brings your reader new insight or new appreciation. When you use trite expressions or clichés ("She was as blind as a bat." "He was as hungry as a horse." "After stubbing her toe, Sara hopped around like a chicken with its head cut off."), you borrow rather than create language. Because these expressions have lost their freshness, they fail to bring readers new insights, and they make the writer look careless and unimaginative.

Exercise 18-1   Appreciating figurative language

In the following passages, underline words or phrases that strike you vividly as figurative language. Then take one of the passages and try to rewrite it without using any figures of speech. What effect do the figures of speech have on the passage?

1. As the lead runner approaches the finish line, his eyes stare straight ahead in a state just preceding physical exhaustion. Sweat plasters his hair to his head, glues his shirt to his chest, and drips from his shorts. Although he still runs with the pumping stride of a trained athlete, it is clearly his will that propels him. He stumbles through the tape and lurches forward like a rubber mannequin, collapsing into the arms of the bystanders. [William Jordan, "The Bee Complex," *Science 84.*]
   Try to rewrite the passage without figures of speech. [NOTE: Many language experts argue that language is rooted in figures of speech (the previous word *rooted* is a figure of speech), so that it is impossible to eliminate them from any passage. But try to eliminate them if you can.]

What did you discover from trying to do this exercise?

2. Like their mountains, New Englanders are weather resistant; like their mountains, they are often obdurate, scratched, and striated. They are stubborn, frugal, and permanent. They are slow to change, isolated, and they will always be the dominant, if silent, presence in this place where they live. And they are seen by lesser folk in the balance of the nation as a necessary heritage, a cultural landmark, a monument to the nation's beginnings and a memorial to rugged truths. [John N. Cole, "The Crystal Hills," *Country Journal*.]

Rewrite the above passage, trying to eliminate figurative language—that is, try to make the writer's point about the New England people without comparing them to the New England mountains.

What is lost from the passage when figurative language is omitted? What function does figurative language serve?

Exercise 18-2   Creating figurative language

Learning to use figurative language can be fun if you think of yourself as playing with words. For experienced writers, figurative language tends to come naturally during the process of composing. Figures of speech seldom work if the writer consciously seeks them or tries to add them artificially to drafts for "effect," like adding catsup to a dull meatloaf. Beginning writers, however, can get the feel of figurative language by consciously trying to create it.

A. In the following exercises create some "Charlie Brown" metaphors ("Happiness is a warm puppy." "Happiness is finding your lost blanket."). Create three different metaphors for each exercise.

Example:
Happiness is . . .

getting a B on an exam you thought you had flunked.
hearing a friend's voice at a strange party.
finally finding your car keys.

1. Fear is . . .

2. Wonder is . . .

3. Surprise is . . .

B. Another way to appreciate figures of speech is to examine their implications. Often, for example, you will discover new insights about thing A as you explore its connection to thing B. In fact, exploring the implications of metaphors is an excellent way to expand your thinking on a topic.

The following exercise asks you to use metaphors to explore the topic "writing an essay." For each of the metaphors do five minutes of nonstop writing in which you explore the connections between the two ideas being compared. At the end of the exercise, explain any new insights you might have gotten, either about writing an essay or about figurative language. Use your own paper.

Example:
Writing an essay is like falling in love.

Let's see. When you fall in love, it just suddenly happens to you. You didn't expect it and then suddenly, whammo, you are swept off your feet. Sometimes writing an essay is like that. You don't have any idea what you are going to write about and then suddenly you get an idea and start writing. While you are writing, you are totally absorbed in what you are doing just as you are totally absorbed by love. Sometimes you fall out of love as quickly as you fell into it. You look at your former lover and wonder, "What did I see in that person?" This is how you look at your rough draft the next morning. While you were writing it, you were excited, but now you have fallen out of love with it.

4. Writing an essay is like building a house (or baking a cake).

5. Writing an essay is like building a sand castle.

6. Writing an essay is like having a baby.

7. Writing an essay is like spending a night in jail.

8. Writing an essay is like _____. (Make up your own comparison.)

9. What did you learn about writing an essay from the above exercise? What did you learn about making figures of speech?

Exercise 18-3   Creating fresh language, avoiding clichés

A. The sentences below are unimaginative and colorless. Rewrite them in two ways. First, rewrite them by using clichés and trite diction. Have fun making them as boring as possible. Then rewrite them again, this time using your own figurative language to illuminate, clarify, or explain. Your second versions should genuinely enliven the sentences, making them more surprising and vivid. Add details as needed.

Example:
Professor Smith's lecture was boring.

Rewritten with clichés

Professor Smith's voice was as boring as an old tennis shoe, and his lecture was as dull as dirt.

Rewritten with fresh figures of speech

Professor Smith's voice buzzed on and on, like the hum of a faulty light fixture; his lecture itself was like a TV test pattern at two o'clock in the morning.

1. My ten-year-old brother ate his breakfast cereal with bad manners.

   Cliché version

   Fresh version

2. When I opened the window, the fresh smell of spring entered my nostrils.

   Cliché version

   Fresh version

B. The following passages are technically correct but flat and lifeless. Rewrite them in any way that seems appropriate. Sometimes you may choose to use figurative language. At other times you may wish to replace all-purpose abstract words with specific, concrete words. Invent any details you need.

Example:

His first experiences on the summer job taught him an important lesson. [What job? What lesson? (Make up your own details.)]

After two days setting chokers in the Douglas fir forests of western Washington, he learned what he had wished he'd known six months earlier: you have to be in shape to be a lumberjack.

3. That time my mother's advice really helped me a lot.

4. If this situation isn't solved soon, we'll all be in big trouble.

5. As a child I loved to enter the old country store with all its old-fashioned things. Mrs. Holderman would stand behind the counter and take a piece of candy out of the jar and give it to me. It tasted wonderful. Then I would go outside and watch people sitting on the bench in front of the store. I can still remember what they looked like and hear the sounds coming from the street.

19

Including Needed Words

Writers can sometimes confuse readers by omitting needed words. Proofread your final drafts carefully—reading slowly aloud is a good strategy—to make sure your sentences are clear and complete.

19A Include all necessary parts of verbs.

Some dialects of English omit helping verbs in some of the tenses. In writing standard edited English, be sure to include the necessary helping verbs.

is
My mom working right now.
　　　∧

has
He seen plenty of deer on this mountain.
　∧

In order to avoid confusion, include all needed verb parts in compound constructions where the tense of one verb is different from the tense of the other.

written
In college I have and will continue to write many essays.
　　　　　　∧

19B Include the conjunction *that* when you need it for clarity.

that
The speaker suggested violence and pornography are more closely related than
　　　　　　　　　∧
we used to believe. [At first, the speaker seems to be suggesting violence and pornography. The *that* prevents momentary misreading.]

19C Include necessary articles, prepositions, and pronouns. Be especially careful to include needed words when making comparisons.

of
He seemed afraid to go in front or behind the horse.
　　　　　　　　　　　∧

in
Our foreparents believed and were willing to die for liberty.
　　　　　　　　　∧

When composing drafts, writers often forget to include needed words in comparisons. Watch for the following problems when you edit your drafts:

- When comparing items that contain possessives, make sure that you include a possessive (either a word with an apostrophe or the preposition *of*) in both sides of the comparison.

Shakespeare's plays are a lot harder to read than ~~Ibsen~~. [Ibsen's]

OR

Shakespeare's plays are a lot harder to read than Ibsen. [those of]

- Use the words *other* or *else* to distinguish a particular member of a group from all the other members to which it is being compared.

The new Plymouth Laser is more beautiful than any car on the market. [Without the *other* the sentence implies that the Laser is not a car.] [other]

Judy does more work than anyone in the family. [This sentence is correct both ways. Without the *else*, Judy is not a member of the family, and she does more work than anyone who is in the family. With the *else*, Judy is a member of the family and does more work than the others in the family.] [else]

Exercise 19-1   Self-study: Including needed words

In the following sentences add words needed to make the sentences clear and grammatically complete.

Answer column

1. My grandparents' automobile was made in France in the 1920s and surprisingly fast for its time.

1. My grandparents' automobile was made in France in the 1920s and *was* surprisingly fast for its time. [Repeat *was* since it is used two different ways: first as a helping verb in a passive construction; then as a linking verb.]

2. Shakespeare's *Hamlet* is better than any Renaissance play.

2. Shakespeare's *Hamlet* is better than any *other* Renaissance play. [*Hamlet* is a Renaissance play. The *other* separates *Hamlet* from other members of its class.]

3. My aunt has both knowledge and love for Egyptian mythology.

3. My aunt has both knowledge *of* and love for Egyptian mythology. [One has love *for* something but knowledge *of* something.]

4. Professor Jones struggling to get the movie projector down the stairs.

4. Professor Jones *is* struggling to get the movie projector down the stairs. [Standard edited English uses the helping verb *is*.]

5. He has and always will be certain of his love for me.

6. Sam Jones has more steals and assists than anyone in the league.

7. Your job is a lot more exciting than mother.

8. After the teacher bawled Sam out, he was meek as a mouse.

9. This computer is as good or better than the ones being sold in the bookstore.

10. I told the union people are not going to keep paying those high prices.

11. Texas is larger than any state in the union.

12. She noticed many animals in the zoo seemed unusually lazy.

13. I have both an interest and talent for computer programming.

14. You are more conceited than anyone in this room.

15. Watch your sentences carefully to make sure you don't any needed words.

---

5. He has ^been and always will be certain of his love for me. [Complete the first verb *has been* before switching to the second verb *will be.*]

6. Sam Jones has more steals and assists than anyone ^else in the league. [Corrected version means that Sam Jones is a member of the league.]

7. Your job is a lot more exciting than ~~mother.~~ mother's [Compare possessives with other possessives.]

8. After the teacher bawled Sam out, he was ^as meek as a mouse. [Use the word *as* twice in comparisons.]

9. This computer is as good ^as or better than the ones being sold in the bookstore [Complete the first comparison *as good as* before moving to the second *better than.*]

10. I told the union ^that people are not going to keep paying those high prices. [*That* prevents the momentary confusion that you were talking to union people.]

11. Texas is larger than any ^other state in the union. [Without the *other*, Texas does not seem to be in the union.]

12. She noticed ^that many animals in the zoo seemed unusually lazy.

13. I have both an interest ^in and talent for computer programming.

14. You are more conceited than anyone ^else in this room. [Without the *else*, you do not seem to be in the room.]

15. Watch your sentences carefully to make sure you don't ^omit any needed words.

20
Avoiding Wordiness

Readers like efficient prose that makes its point cleanly and concisely without using unnecessary words or padding. Avoiding wordiness does not mean eliminating details or cutting into the muscle of your essay. It means eliminating fat by cutting out inefficient words that take up space without adding meaning.

20A Edit carefully, eliminating unnecessary words.

Good writers typically write first drafts that are much longer than their final versions. In fact, excessive wordiness in a rough draft is often the sign of a healthy writing process. However, you should later edit your drafts carefully to achieve conciseness. Here is a passage from a typical first draft:

> One of the conclusions that the communications committee came up with is that it is difficult if not impossible to improve a student's communications ability without that student being assigned requirements where they have to use that ability and receive feedback on a regular basis throughout the four years of their curriculum. [fifty-two words]

Here is how the passage appeared on the next draft:

> The committee's major conclusion is that improvement of students' communications skills will be possible only if students are required to do written and oral work, and receive appropriate feedback, regularly throughout the four years of their curriculum. [thirty-seven words]

And here is the final version:

> The committee concluded that students' communication skills will improve only if faculty require written and oral work and provide appropriate feedback regularly throughout the undergraduate curriculum. [twenty-six words]

20B Eliminate deadwood phrases that take up space without adding meaning.

Wordy (deadwood phrases are italicized):

> *By virtue of the fact that in many cases* students don't revise their essays before turning them in, professors *are in a position* to help *in this area* by requiring students *on no uncertain terms* to exchange rough drafts with each other two weeks before the due dates assigned for the essays.

Better:

> Because students often don't revise their essays before turning them in, professors should require students to exchange rough drafts with each other two weeks before essays are due.

20C   Combine sentences to avoid wordiness.

Another cause of wordiness is the inefficient use of short, choppy sentences, which cause frequent repetition of words and phrases.

Wordy:

> Jim Maxwell took two years to build his solar building. This included nearly one year of planning. His solar building was intended mainly as a grain dryer. But it also provided a warm winter shop. Additionally he had the advantage of a machinery shed. This kept his machinery dry. His new solar building would pay dividends for years to come.

Revised:

> It took two years to build, including nearly one year of planning, but when Jim Maxwell finished his solar building, he had a grain dryer, a warm winter shop, and a dry machinery shed that would pay dividends for years to come. [Based on a passage by Alan Guebert, *Successful Farming.*]

20D   Avoid inflating your prose with jargon and other overblown language.

Inflated:

> Text production of a referential document involves simply reproducing or explaining world events. Text production of a persuasive document, on the other hand, can initiate or change such world events.

Better:

> Referential writing simply describes or explains events. Persuasive writing, on the other hand, can change events.

Exercise 20-1   Self-study: Eliminating wordiness

Improve the style and interest of the following sentences by cutting out deadwood, recasting the words, or combining elements to eliminate wordiness. The answers at the right are models only. Other ways of eliminating wordiness are also possible.

Answer column

1. She is an expert in the field of atomic engineering.
2. After the close of the war Harold Krebs returned back to his hometown.
3. He is an interesting person, but he is also a selfish one.

1. She is an expert in atomic engineering.
2. After the war, Harold Krebs returned home.
3. He is interesting but selfish.

4. He hopes that his essay will have the effect of causing those people who hear the essay to reconsider in their own minds what they believe are the fundamental and primary purposes of our higher educational schools and colleges.

4. He hopes his essay will cause people to reconsider the purpose of higher education.

5. The Continental Congress was sitting in New York City in 1787. Its purpose at that time was to be busy with arrangements for the Constitutional Convention. The Constitutional Convention met in Philadelphia that spring.

5. The Continental Congress, sitting in New York City in 1787, was busy with arrangements for the Constitutional Convention that met in Philadelphia that spring.

6. In recent times a new interest has been apparent among many people to make the language as it is used by specialists in the areas of government, law, and medicine more available to be understood and appreciated by readers who are not specialists in the above-mentioned areas.

6. Recently there has been new interest in making the language of government, law, and medicine more available to the nonspecialist reader.

7. As a result of the labor policies established by Bismarck, the working-class people in Germany were convinced that revolution was unnecessary for the attainment of their goals and purposes.

7. Bismarck's labor policies convinced the German working class that revolution was unnecessary.

8. If the present writer were placed in the dilemma of having to choose a month that he thought was his favorite month, the month he would probably choose would be the month of October or at least that month would surely rank near the top.

8. If I had to choose a favorite month, October would rank near the top.

9. It has been deemed an impossibility to take a superannuated member of the canine species and teach that organism new behavioral responses to stimuli in that organism's physical environment.

9. You can't teach an old dog new tricks.

10. At the present time it can be considered a truism that families with incomes neither too far above nor too far below the median income for families in this country can send their children to expensive colleges with no more out-of-pocket charges and expenses than it would cost to send those same children to colleges whose tuition and related expenses are much lower.

10. The truth is that for average-income families an expensive college costs no more than a cheap one.

Exercise 20-2   Playing with wordiness

A. One way to appreciate wordiness is to create it purposely. Have fun turning the following sayings into the most pompous, jargon-laden, wordy monstrosities that you can.

Example:
To know him is to love him.

To become acquainted with his behavioral traits as those traits reveal characteristics of his inner psyche, disposition, and character is to possess for this person a reverential attitude.

1. Better late than never.

2. Whatever can go wrong will.

3. Cleanliness is next to godliness.

4. Eat your spinach because children are starving in India.

5. Don't kill the goose that lays the golden egg.

Exercise 20-3   Mastery exercise: Eliminating wordiness

A. Improve the style and interest of the following sentences by cutting out deadwood, recasting the words, or combining elements to eliminate wordiness.

Example:
At this moment in time she seems to appear to be acting in a manner that makes one think that she is a nervous kind of person.

Right now she is acting nervously.

1. It appears to me that he seems to be an unusually quiet person but also that he is the kind of person who really cares a lot about other people.

2. If a person is the kind of person who hurries rapidly when that person tries to do things, then that person is apt to find that he or she has wasted a lot of valuable time and material by trying to do the events too rapidly.

3. Molly was interested in finding out the answer to a question that she had recently been puzzling about. The question was this: What is the important and essential difference between a disease that most people would call "mental illness" and a disease that is simply a disease of the brain?

4. It is unfortunate that the mayor acted in this manner. The mayor settled the issue. But before he settled the issue he made a mistake. He fostered a public debate that was very bitter. The debate pitted some of his subordinates against each other (and these were key subordinates too). It also caused many other people to feel inflamed passions and fears as a result of the way the mayor handled the whole affair.

5. She spoke in a very low and hard-to-hear voice that at the present time all the people who run for political office can't be trusted on account of the fact that they have to misrepresent the way various issues are complex to get the votes of people who belong to groups that have special interests.

B. Revise the following passage by combining short, choppy sentences into longer, more graceful ones, thereby reducing wordiness.

Western physicians often work in the Third World. In doing so they find themselves competing with unfamiliar health systems. Many of these unfamiliar practices seem useless. Often they also seem dangerous. Take, for example, a ritual in Ethiopia. In this ritual the tooth buds of infants are removed. This often leads to infection. Yet sometimes there is wisdom in these practices. Where antibiotics are scarce, popular folk medicine may be better than Westerners realize. In Uganda tetanus, or lockjaw, is extremely common. At puberty healers perform a special ritual. They remove two lower teeth from the person entering puberty. If this person later gets lockjaw, this ritual at puberty may save the person's life. The spaces where the teeth were removed make it possible to feed the person. They feed the person through a straw. This allows food to enter the person if his or her jaw is locked. Even more bizarre practices may have scientific merit. One treatment for malaria is particularly bizarre. The sick person drinks cow's urine. One doctor suggests that perhaps this treatment helps. The urine contains ammonia. Perhaps the ammonia prevents brain swelling. This in turn prevents convulsions. [Based on a passage by Elisabeth Rosenthal, *Science Digest.*]

21
Avoiding Sexist Language

Many contemporary writers appreciate how the language we have inherited subtly reflects a male-dominated society. Although people cannot change a language overnight, they can become aware of sexual biases in our language and try, whenever possible, to phrase sentences so as to avoid them.

21A Avoid language that implies sexist labels or stereotypes.

Referring to women as "the weaker sex," "the ladies," "the girls," or "the distaff side" implies offensive role stereotyping even if the writer doesn't intend it. Equally offensive is to refer to women as if they were somehow the appendages of men — by identifying them primarily as wives or mothers of males — or to refer to their physical attractiveness or style of dress in a context where that would be irrelevant. As a rule of thumb, never describe a woman differently from the way you would describe a man.

Sexist:

Janet Peterson, looking stunning in her new blue-sequined evening gown, gave the keynote address at the annual mayors' conference. [Would you say, "Robert Peterson, looking stunning in his new tuxedo with ruffled collar and sleeves, gave the keynote address at the annual mayors' conference"?]

Revised:

Janet Peterson, newly elected mayor of the state's third largest city, gave the keynote address at the annual mayors' conference. [You could, of course, go on to describe her appearance *if* you are sure you would have done likewise had she been male.]

21B Whenever possible, revise sentences to avoid using the masculine pronouns *he, him, his,* and *himself* to refer indefinitely to people of both sexes.

English speakers have traditionally used masculine pronouns to refer indefinitely to people of both sexes. However, this usage is coming increasingly to seem biased against women. The most satisfactory way to solve this problem is to use plural forms since the pronouns *they, them, their,* and *themselves* do not indicate gender.

Sexist:

> If a person wants to bring his text to the exam, he may.

Revised:

> If persons want to bring their texts to the exam, they may.

In quite informal writing, you can also use *you* and *your* to avoid sexist usage; similarly, in formal prose you can use *one* and *one's.*

> If you want to bring your texts to the exam, you may.
> If one wants to bring one's text to the exam, one may.

Another strategy is to alternate between masculine and feminine forms. Thus, if in one paragraph you had a sentence like this:

> At the revising stage, the writer should go over his draft carefully, making sure that the central idea of each paragraph is clear.

in the next paragraph you could switch to feminine pronouns:

> At the editing stage a writer's focus shifts. Now she should check for sentence-level problems, paying particular attention to spelling, punctuation, and problems of usage.

NOTE: This practice, although now common in some academic journals, is not yet widely accepted.

21C   In general, avoid cumbersome constructions such as *his or her, him/her,* or *s/he.*

These strategies for avoiding masculine pronouns are awkward and distracting. While *him or her* can be satisfactory when used occasionally, if it is repeated frequently the construction becomes unbearable.

At present, then, there seems to be no completely satisfactory way of avoiding the masculine pronoun. As a result, some professional writers still use *he* or *him* to refer to both sexes. In doing so, however, these writers identify themselves as linguistically conservative and imply that they are politically conservative also, at least on feminist issues. If you are willing to accept that risk, then you are free to make your own decision about pronoun usage.

21D   Try to avoid the use of *man* as a suffix in such words as *repairman* or *mailman,* but also try to avoid coinages that are cumbersome to read and to write.

Sometimes the suffix *person* is an acceptable substitute for *man,* as in *chairperson* and *salesperson,* which are becoming increasingly acceptable in formal usage. However, *policeperson, fireperson,* or *weatherperson* still sounds odd, as does "Joan is a new freshperson at state college." Often alternative expressions can be found—*journalist* for *newsman, firefighter* for *fireman,* or *supervisor* for *foreman*—but sometimes these coinages can be clumsy too (*refuse disposal specialist* as opposed to *garbage man).*

Exercise 21-1 Revising to avoid sexist language

You are executive secretary to I. M. Macho, President of Mush Machine Corporation. Lately he has been trying to overcome some of his sexist language habits, but he is still having a bit of trouble. He has just asked you to look over this rough draft of a letter. On the letter, mark the changes he should make to overcome sexist use of language.

An Open Letter to the Employees of Mush Machines:

As everyone has heard by now, Bill Thompson has resigned from his position as chairman of the planning committee. Several of our lady employees have expressed interest in being elected to chair that committee and indeed, as president of Mush Machine Corporation, I think it is time we gave the gals a chance.

So I am asking every employee to submit to me his recommendations for nominations. The only thing I insist upon is that we select the best man we can for the position, regardless of sex.

Remember that the planning committee includes men from every level of the company: stock boys, furnace men, salesmen, shop foremen, cleaning ladies, secretaries (except for the women who work directly in the president's office), and, of course, the professional men at the executive level. This means that the chairman should be able to communicate well with everyone he encounters in this delicate and crucial position.

May I also remind you how crucial the planning committee is now that manpower needs are so hard to project. In a company such as ours, which produces the best machines that mankind can make, planning can make the difference between success and failure. If you remember the speech made last week by Elaine Martin, mother of two and wife of Jake Martin over in sales, you will appreciate how much a misestimation of just one phase of our company's operation can jeopardize every man's future. So please take great care with your nominations. And if it comes to pass that one of the weaker sex gets the job, then maybe we will all be the stronger for it.

Sincerely,

I. M. Macho,
President

22
Using Dictionaries and the Thesaurus

A good dictionary is an essential tool for a writer. Use it regularly to check meanings, spelling, usage, pronunciation, or syllabication of a word.

22A Choose an appropriate dictionary.

There are many different types of dictionaries, but the most appropriate for college students are the hardbound, abridged dictionaries containing between 140,000 and 170,000 words. Not all dictionaries are alike, so you should choose one that fits your needs and your attitude toward language.

22B Learn how to read the entries in a standard desk dictionary.

To use your dictionary effectively, study the information guide in the front. This information will explain abbreviations, usage labels, order of definitions, and so forth.

1 Spelling, syllabication, and pronunciation

Learn to use your dictionary's system for indicating pronunciation and also its method for indicating preferred pronunciations when two or more pronunciations are common. Use the information on syllabication when you need to hyphenate words at the end of typed lines.

2 Parts of speech and changes in a word's form as it shifts from one part of speech to another

Symbols like *n.* (noun) or *v.tr.* (transitive verb) indicate the parts of speech a word can play. Definitions are usually grouped by parts of speech. Thus all definitions for *table* as a noun (the kitchen table, a water table) will be given, followed by definitions of *table* as a verb (as in, "We tabled the motion."). The various forms a word can take as it shifts from one part of speech to another are also indicated. (For example, *impassive,* adj., can become *impassively,* adv., and *impassivity,* n.)

3 Definitions

The several meanings a word can have are grouped by parts of speech. Dictionaries differ in the way they order definitions: Some go from earliest definitions to most recent; some from most frequent to least frequent; others from least frequent to most frequent. Be sure you know how your dictionary arranges definitions.

4 Word origins

Most dictionaries also tell you the *etymology* of a word, that is, the origins of a word or how it entered the English language. A study of origins often gives you revealing insights into why words mean what they mean.

5 Usage

Some dictionaries (particularly the *American Heritage Dictionary of the English Language*) give you detailed information about how current professional writers handle particular usage problems. Other dictionaries label certain words as *nonstandard, archaic, obsolete, slang,* and so forth. If a word has no usage label, it is generally an acceptable word for formal essays. Check how your dictionary determines usage labels. Be aware that different dictionaries use different criteria for labeling words. *Webster's Ninth New Collegiate Dictionary,* for example, accepts *like* as a conjunction, while *American Heritage* calls that usage *nonstandard.*

6 Synonyms and antonyms

Some dictionaries list synonyms (words with similar meanings) for many words and indicate the slight shades of difference in their connotations. Often dictionaries provide antonyms also (words with opposite meanings).

7 Geographical and biographical entries

Most hardbound desk dictionaries include a geographical section to help you identify, spell, and pronounce the names of important places *(Kyushu)* and a biographical section to help you identify, spell, and pronounce the names of important people *(Kosygin, Aleksei Nikolayevich).* Learn where your dictionary gives such listings.

22C Use a thesaurus with caution.

Thesauruses, such as *Roget's International Thesaurus,* give extensive listings of synonyms for words. These are useful for finding a word that exactly expresses an intended meaning. Many inexperienced writers, however, go through a "thesaurus" stage in their language growth, where they substitute exotic-looking words for everyday words, imagining that the high-sounding language seems more mature and intellectual. Generally, however, you should prefer a plain style to a fancy style.

Thesauruses, then, are an excellent way to expand your vocabulary and to have fun exploring the richness of our word-stock. But use them with caution. Never use a word from a thesaurus without also looking it up in your dictionary (thesauruses do not provide definitions). Be sure that your chosen word both denotes and connotes (see page 257) what you intend.

Exercise 22-1   Using your dictionary

Use your own college-level desk dictionary to answer the questions in the following exercises.

Name of your dictionary _____

Publisher _____

Date of publication _____

Learning your dictionary's abbreviations and symbols

A. Read your dictionary's explanations of its abbreviations and symbols. Then indicate below the symbol, abbreviation, or other method used by your dictionary to indicate the following:

Example:

An intransitive verb   _____v.i._____

1. A word borrowed from the Tagalog language   1. _____

2. A word whose origin is uncertain   2. _____

3. A variant spelling that is just as acceptable as the first listed spelling (HINT: look up *ax*; then reread explanations in the front of your dictionary.)   3. _____

4. A variant spelling that is sometimes used but is not as acceptable as the first listed spelling (HINT: look up *woolly.*)   4. _____

5. A word or definition that is no longer used at all   5. _____

6. A word that used to be common but is now used only rarely and seems old-fashioned   6. _____

7. An adverb   7. _____

8. The pronunciation of the *si* sound in *vision*   8. _____

9. The pronunciation of the *ear* sound in *heard*   9. _____

Spelling, syllabication, and pronunciation

B. In the provided blanks, copy *exactly* the way your dictionary enters the indicated words (including syllable divisions) and shows pronunciation.

Example (from Webster's Ninth):
mathematics   *math·e·mat·ics \ ˌmath-ə-'mat-iks*

10. government

11. grimace

12. inchoate

13. Gloucestershire (a county in England)

14. the plural of *index*

C. Does your dictionary tell you to spell the following as one word, as a hyphenated word, or as two words?

15. waterbuffalo _____

16. waterbuck _____

17. watercolor _____

18. waterrepellent _____

Using definitions

D. Use your dictionary to answer the following questions.

19. In what order does your dictionary list definitions?

20. How many meanings does your dictionary list for the noun *jump?*

21. How many meanings does your dictionary list for the verb *jump?*

E. In the following sentences, copy the single definition in your dictionary that best explains the meaning of the underlined word. Also indicate the part of speech under which your definition is listed.

Example (from **American Heritage**):
I refuse to *accede* to your demands.

intr. v. to give one's assent; to consent; agree (first of three definitions)

22. Ms. Jones began *canvassing* her district in early March.

23. She *induced* me to take calculus.

24. From my stammering, stuttering, and blushing, she *induced* that I didn't want to take Sex Education.

25. Sir Thomas left his beloved lady safely in the *keep* and proceeded on horseback to the dragon's lair.

26. Beethoven was deaf when he *composed* his most famous symphonies.

27. She sat there in the front row perfectly *composed.*

Word origins

F. Show the origin of each of the following words by citing the original meaning of the word in its original language. Do not use abbreviations.

Example (*from* **American Heritage**):

decimate

from Latin decimāre, from decimus meaning tenth

28. zest

29. crescent

30. pseudonym

31. complex (adj.)

32. lieutenant

Understanding usage labels

G. What usage label does your dictionary give to the italicized words below when used in the context indicated by the sentence? If possible, check your answers with those of students using different dictionaries.

Example (from Webster's Ninth)
One critic rather liked the new movie, but the other *knocked* it horribly.

This dictionary apparently accepts the usage. It gives a definition "to find fault with" and doesn't indicate any problem with that usage.

33. A successful businessperson enters the office in the morning, makes a quick list of all the tasks to be accomplished that day, and then *prioritizes* the entries.

34. Then a fight began to brew *betwixt* Sir Robert and Sir Thomas.

35. *Fetch* me the *cannikin*, please.

36. If she asks me to revise this essay one more time, I am going to *croak*.

37. "I love this little *critter*," said Judy, hugging her puppy.

Working with synonyms

H. Many dictionaries list synonyms for words and explain slight differences in their connotations. Using your dictionary, explain the slight differences in meaning in each of the following phrases.

Example (based on Webster's Seventh, which has fuller information on synonyms than the Ninth):
a proficient writer/an adept writer

Proficient and adept both mean "highly skilled." However, "proficient" suggests that the skill comes from training, while "adept" suggests it comes more from an innate ability.

38. to be prejudiced against something/to be biased against something

39. to ignore something/to disregard something/to neglect something/to overlook something

40. It was his imagination at work./It was his fancy at work.

Geographical and biographical entries

I. Answer the following questions using your dictionary.

41. When was St. Thomas Aquinas born?

42. Where and what is Huila?

43. What is the approximate population of Cochabamba, and where is it?

23

End Marks

Use periods, question marks, and exclamation points to mark the ends of sentences and to indicate other special operations in writing.

23A **Use periods to end sentences that make statements, give mild commands, ask courtesy questions, or ask questions indirectly.**

Statement:

The parade is at four o'clock this afternoon.

Mild command:

Please return the form by 5:00 P.M., Friday.

Courtesy question:

Would you please return the form in the enclosed envelope. [Without a question mark in this "courtesy question," the writer implies that the addressee is not really being offered a choice. The question structure is a form of politeness only.]

Indirect question:

He asked if we intended to go also.

23B **Use a question mark at the end of a direct question but not an indirect one.**

Direct questions:

Where are you going?

He asked, "Where are you going?"

Indirect question:

He asked me where I was going.

NOTE: When a quoted question is inserted within another sentence, do not follow the question mark with a comma or period.

Faulty:

> "Can we go with you?," she asked. She asked, "Can we go with you?".

Correct:

> "Can we go with you?" she asked. She asked, "Can we go with you?"

When quotation marks and a question mark appear together, the question mark goes inside the quotation marks if only the quotation is a question and outside if the whole sentence is a question.

> The professor asked, "Can you solve the fox and chicken puzzle?"
> Did you hear the professor talk about a "fox and chicken puzzle"?

You can also use a question mark to change a statement into a question.

> You said that? John lost the moneybox?

You can also use question marks, usually inside parentheses, to indicate conjectures about unknowns as distinct from known facts, usually with dates.

> *Beowulf* (A.D. 700?) is an epic poem in Old English.

NOTE: Do not use question marks to indicate sarcasm or to express uncertainty about information that can be located.

23C Use exclamation marks sparingly to express strong emotion, shock, or surprise.

> No! I can't believe he would have done it!

NOTE: Use exclamation marks sparingly, since overuse weakens the power of an occasional exclamation. Use periods after mildly exclamatory sentences and commas after mildly exclamatory interjections.

Exercise 23-1 Self-study: End marks

A. In the following sentences, add end marks (periods, question marks, exclamation points) as needed. Also add commas as needed for sentences with quotations.

	Answer column
1. I'll be happy to meet you at the restaurant for dinner	1. I'll be happy to meet you at the restaurant for dinner.
2. Will you please meet me at the restaurant for dinner	2. Will you please meet me at the restaurant for dinner?
3. Will you kindly fill out the questionnaire and return it to me by eight o'clock tomorrow morning	3. Will you kindly fill out the questionnaire and return it to me by eight o'clock tomorrow morning. [Period indicates a courtesy question, not a real question.]
4. Be at the restaurant by dinnertime	4. Be at the restaurant by dinnertime.
5. He asked me if I would be at the restaurant by dinnertime	5. He asked me if I would be at the restaurant by dinnertime.

6. "Will you be at the restaurant by dinnertime " he asked

7. He asked "Will you be at the restaurant by dinner-time "

8. "Will you " he asked "be at the restaurant by din-nertime "

9. "No " I shouted "Not that restaurant " The old horror returned to my mind — the burned ham-burger, the soggy french fries, the tattooed cook

10. "Can we go to the restaurant with you " Polly askcd

11. "Did Polly ask if she could go to the restaurant with us " George asked

12. Polly asked if she could go to the restaurant with us

13. George asked "Were Polly's words 'Can I go to the restaurant with you' "

14. Did Polly say the "restaurant" or the "department store"

15. George asked quizzically, "Did Polly say the 'res-taurant' or the 'department store' "

6. "Will you be at the restaurant by dinnertime?" he asked.

7. He asked, "Will you be at the restaurant by dinner-time?"

8. "Will you," he asked, "be at the restaurant by din-nertime?"

9. "No!" I shouted. "Not that restaurant!" The old horror returned to my mind — the burned ham-burger, the soggy french fries, and tattooed cook.

10. "Can we go to the restaurant with you?" Polly asked.

11. "Did Polly ask if she could go to the restaurant with us?" George asked.

12. Polly asked if she could go to the restaurant with us.

13. George asked, "Were Polly's words 'Can I go to the restaurant with you?' "

14. Did Polly say the "restaurant" or the "department store"?

15. George asked quizzically, "Did Polly say the 'res-taurant' or the 'department store'?"

Exercise 23-2 Mastery exercise: End marks

A. Punctuate the following sentences correctly by using the appropriate end marks (periods, question marks, exclamation points). In sentences with quotations, also use commas appropriately.

Example:

Did Pete say "Boise Street" or "Boise Avenue "?

1. The committee will meet in Room 107 tomorrow morning at eight o'clock sharp

2. Ask Mr. Thompson if he will be there

3. Will you be there, Mr. Thompson

4. Did William ask Mr. Thompson if he would be there

5. "Will you be there, Mr. Thompson " William asked

6. William asked "Will you be there, Mr. Thompson "

7. Will you kindly return the requested information on the form provided

8. Mr. Thompson plans to address the committee on the question "Should Martin's Marshmallow Company get into the hot chocolate business "

9. Did you say "Room 107" or "Room 108 " I have to know right now what information to put on my memo to Mr. Thompson

10. "What information should I put in my memo to Mr. Thompson " William asked "Room 107 or Room 108 "

Commas

24

The comma is the most frequently used mark of *internal* punctuation. A comma mistakenly used as an end mark creates a comma splice (see Chapter 4).

Because commas generally mark places where the voice naturally pauses or changes tone, writers can eliminate many of their comma problems by reading their sentences aloud in a natural voice. Sometimes commas are used to separate elements such as items in series or main clauses joined by coordinating conjunctions. (When you *separate* items, you place a single comma between the items being separated.) Most of the time, however, you use commas *to set off* items. In these cases you always use commas in pairs (one comma before the item, one comma after the item) unless the item comes at the very beginning or end of the sentence where the sentence boundary takes the place of one of the commas. You should learn to identify the core of your sentences—the core is the subject, verb, and accompanying complements (direct object, indirect object, subject complement, objective complement)—and then remember that inside this core you generally use commas in pairs. For example, a single comma is never used to separate a subject from a verb or a verb from a complement.

The pattern for setting off items is therefore as follows:

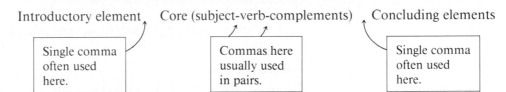

Introductory element | Core (subject-verb-complements) | Concluding elements

| Single comma often used here. | Commas here usually used in pairs. | Single comma often used here. |

24A Use commas to separate independent clauses joined by coordinating conjunctions (*and, but, or, nor, for, yet,* and *so*).

I released the dog's leash, *and* the dog trotted off across the field.

I have made plenty of cookies, *but* I don't want you to eat any until after dinner.

I couldn't wait to look through the telescope, *for* I had always wanted to see the rings of Saturn.

If the main clauses are very short, some writers omit the comma before the coordinating conjunction, but you are never wrong to include it. If the clauses are very long and include numerous internal commas, you can raise the comma preceding the coordinating conjunction to a semicolon.

Correct:

He left, *and* I was sorry. He left *and* I was sorry. [either version]

Correct:

Having lost her job as a secretary, my mother went back to school and finished her degree, completing three years in two and simultaneously caring for three children; *but* she was never fully happy until she found a new job. [semicolon used because the clauses are long and contain internal commas]

24B Use a comma to set off most introductory adverb clauses and long modifying phrases.

The pattern for this rule is as follows:

introductory element, core

- Set off most introductory adverb clauses. If the introductory clause is short and if no confusion results, some writers omit the comma, but the use of a comma is generally preferred.

When I get home from work, I always fix myself a big sardine sandwich.

Because Jo Anne can't stand messes, she keeps her office desk incredibly neat.

NOTE: When the adverb clause comes at the end of a sentence, it is normally not set off unless it expresses a contrary element (usually introduced by *although*) or unless the voice clearly pauses when the sentence is read aloud.

I always fix myself a sardine sandwich *when* I get home from work.

Jo Anne keeps her office desk incredibly neat *because* she can't stand messes.

I always fix myself a sardine sandwich for a snack, *although* I prefer anchovies and pickled herring. [Here *although* introduces a contrary element.]

- Set off introductory verbal phrases and other long phrases used as modifiers.

Participial phrase:

Having lost my balance, I began waving my arms frantically.

Infinitive phrase:

To understand Einstein's theories, you should ride in a barely moving train next to a stationary train and try to decide which one is moving.

Long prepositional phrases:

Behind the glass doors at the entrance to the elaborately decorated parlor, the burglar crouched quietly.

NOTE: Initial gerund phrases or infinitive phrases used as sentence subjects must not be set off because they are part of the sentence core.

To know him is to love him. [COMPARE: To know him, you must first know his dog.]

Playing her guitar every evening is Sally's way of relaxing. [COMPARE: Playing her guitar every evening, Sally expects eventually to join a rock band.]

• Set off introductory transitional elements. Writers generally set off transitional words and phrases such as *on the other hand, in summary, however, moreover,* and *in short* (see Chapter 4 for a list of these expressions).

On the other hand, bicycle racing involved an astonishing amount of strategy.

Moreover, the Atomic Energy Commission has already challenged the court order.

24C Use commas to set off absolute phrases.

An absolute phrase consists of a noun followed by a participle (sometimes the participle *being* is understood but absent from the phrase). These phrases are "absolute" because they are complete in themselves, modifying the whole sentence to which they are attached rather than an individual word within the sentence (see page 98). Wherever absolute phrases occur, they are always set off with commas.

His hand wrapped in a blanket, Harvey hobbled toward the ambulance.

The bear reared on its hind legs, *its teeth looking razor sharp in the glaring sun.*

The students, *their term papers written and typed,* headed happily toward the game room.

24D Use commas to set off participial phrases at the end of a sentence if they modify the subject.

The doctor rushed quickly toward the accident victim, *fumbling to get his black bag open, yelling at spectators to call an ambulance.* [The participles *fumbling* and *yelling* modify the subject of the sentence *doctor;* hence they are set off by commas.]

NOTE: Do not set off a participial phrase at the end of the sentence if it modifies the immediately preceding noun.

The doctor rushed quickly toward the accident victim *lying face forward on the soft shoulder of the road.* [Here the participial phrase modifies the preceding noun *victim* instead of the sentence subject. Hence it is not set off with commas.]

24E Use commas wherever needed to separate sentence elements if failure to separate them would create confusion.

Possibly confusing:

Every time John ate his dog wanted to be fed too.

Clear:

Every time John ate, his dog wanted to be fed too.

Exercise 24-1   Self-study: Punctuating main clauses, adverb clauses, participial phrases, and absolute phrases

In the following sentences, use commas wherever appropriate. Be able to explain your decisions on the basis of the rules and principles discussed in this chapter.

A. In this first set of exercises, use commas to separate main clauses joined with a coordinating conjunction.

Answer column

1. Sally left for the dance and I followed after her on my motorcycle.

    1. Sally left for the dance, and I followed after her on my motorcycle.

2. I was desperate to find her for she had taken with her my little black book of phone numbers.

    2. I was desperate to find her, for she had taken with her my little black book of phone numbers.

3. I couldn't find her so I called Juanita.

    3. I couldn't find her, so I called Juanita.

4. Day in and day out the garbage collectors make their rounds in all kinds of foul weather but still their job doesn't gain from the general public the recognition it deserves.

    4. Day in and day out the garbage collectors make their rounds in all kinds of foul weather, but still their job doesn't gain from the general public the recognition it deserves.

5. The old man whom I met at the baseball game still hasn't received the free tickets he won for catching the foul ball so he has begun to call the main ticket office on a regular schedule twice a day.

    5. The old man whom I met at the baseball game still hasn't received the free tickets he won for catching the foul ball, so he has begun to call the main ticket office on a regular schedule twice a day.

B. In the next set of sentences, use a comma to set off an introductory adverb clause or other long modifying phrase at the beginning of a sentence.

6. After Juanita received my phone call she immediately set out in her car to find Sally.

    6. After Juanita received my phone call, she immediately set out in her car to find Sally. [introductory adverb clause]

7. Juanita set out in her car to find Sally immediately after she received my phone call.

    7. [no commas; adverb clause at end]

8. Because Sally had decided not to go to the dance after all none of us could find her.

    8. Because Sally had decided not to go to the dance after all, none of us could find her. [introductory adverb clause]

9. None of us could find Sally because she decided not to go to the dance after all.

    9. [no commas; adverb clause at end]

10. Having spent more than an hour wandering among the couples on the crowded ballroom floor Juanita and I decided to go have a root beer float.

    10. Having spent more than an hour wandering among the couples on the crowded ballroom floor, Juanita and I decided to go have a root beer float. [introductory participial phrase]

C. In the following sentences use commas to set off absolute phrases or participial phrases at the end of a sentence if they modify the subject.

11. His head shaking back and forth in disgust the cook left the customer and reentered the kitchen.

    11. His head shaking back and forth in disgust, the cook left the customer and reentered the kitchen. [sets off absolute phrase]

12. His eyes squinting in the morning sun the farmer stood in the bed of the truck wiping his glasses with a handkerchief.

    12. His eyes squinting in the morning sun, the farmer stood in the bed of the truck, wiping his glasses with a handkerchief. [First comma sets off absolute phrase; second comma sets off participial phrase at end modifying subject.]

13. The eagle lifted off from the top of the pine tree its wings beating gracefully and soared higher and higher into the evening sky.

13. The eagle lifted off from the top of the pine tree, its wings beating gracefully, and soared higher and higher into the evening sky. [Pair of commas sets off absolute phrase interrupting core of sentence.]

14. The little girl walked into the department store her hand clutching a new purse her eyes gleaming.

14. The little girl walked into the department store, her hand clutching a new purse, her eyes gleaming. [Commas set off two absolute phrases at end of sentence.]

15. The police found Sam singing in the shower.

15. [No comma since final participial phrase modifies Sam; if comma were placed after *Sam,* then sentence would mean the police were singing in the shower.]

D. In the following sentences, determine when commas are needed to join main clauses and when they are not needed. These sentences will help you identify some of the places where beginning writers frequently make errors in using commas.

16. Ralph walked unsuspectingly into the supermarket and saw a robbery in process.

16. [No commas needed; the *and* joins two verbs *walked* and *saw* but not two clauses.]

17. Kneeling behind a counter Ralph watched the robbers carefully but he was unable to creep close enough to the thugs to get a good look at their faces.

17. Kneeling behind a counter, Ralph watched the robbers carefully, but he was unable to creep close enough to the thugs to get a good look at their faces. [First comma sets off an introductory participial phrase; the second comma separates two main clauses joined by the coordinating conjunction *but.*]

18. Suddenly he froze in fear when he saw the snub-nosed pistols protruding from beneath the crooks' overcoats.

18. [No commas needed; *when* is a subordinating conjunction; the participle *protruding* modifies *pistols,* not the subject of the sentence.]

19. Suddenly he froze in fear for he had seen snub-nosed pistols in the crooks' hands.

19. Suddenly he froze in fear, for he had seen snub-nosed pistols in the crooks' hands. [Comma separates main clauses joined by the coordinating conjunction *for.*]

20. Suddenly he froze in fear because he had seen snub-nosed pistols in the crooks' hands.

20. [No commas needed; *because* is a subordinating conjunction.]

24F Use commas to set off nonrestrictive clauses and phrases and nonrestrictive appositives.

Adjective Clauses and Phrases

Adjective modifiers following a noun are either restrictive or nonrestrictive depending on whether they are needed to identify the noun they modify. If their presence in the sentence is not needed for identification of the noun, they are nonrestrictive and must be set off with commas.

Restrictive clause:

My father dislikes people who ride noisy motorcycles. [The father doesn't dislike all people — just those people who ride noisy motorcycles. The adjective clause *restricts* the meaning of *people* — therefore no commas are used.]

Nonrestrictive clause:

My father dislikes Billy Stevens, who rides a noisy motorcycle. [Here we know whom father dislikes—Billy Stevens. The adjective clause does not further restrict the meaning of Billy Stevens but simply adds additional information about him. Therefore add a comma.]

Restrictive phrase:

The cat watching the swinging cord looks like a calico. [The phrase *watching the swinging cord* identifies which cat looks like a calico. The implication is that there are two or more cats. ("The cat watching the swinging cord looks like a calico; the cat sleeping on the sofa is a Siamese.") The phrase restricts *cat,* identifying the particular one meant. Therefore no commas.]

Nonrestrictive phrase:

Our cat Koshka, watching the swinging cord, begins stalking toward it. [Here the phrase merely adds information about an already identified cat.]

Appositives

An appositive is a noun immediately following another noun and referring to the same person, place, or thing. An appositive is restrictive if it is needed to identify the preceding noun and nonrestrictive if it simply adds information. As with nonrestrictive adjective clauses and phrases, set off nonrestrictive appositives.

Restrictive:

His brother Pete just sent him an autographed baseball. [The appositive *Pete* identifies which of several brothers is meant. The sentence implies that he has more than one brother.]

His brother, Pete, sent him an autographed baseball. [Here the appositive implies the writer has only one brother. The name of the brother is extra information.]

His brother Pete, a big league pitcher, just sent him an autographed baseball. [We know that Pete is the brother who sent him the baseball; *big league pitcher* adds extra information.]

Exercise 24-2   Self-study: Special help with restrictive and nonrestrictive clauses and phrases

Students can sometimes understand restrictive and nonrestrictive clauses and phrases more easily if they start out envisioning a simple diagram. Consider the following sentence:

Students who do nonstop writing before constructing a first draft often write well-developed essays.

We could draw a large circle to represent all students:

and then a smaller circle inside the larger one to represent that small group of students who do nonstop writing before constructing rough drafts:

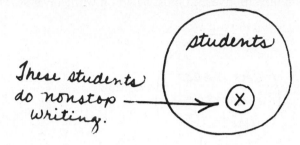

Now this sentence clearly means that the people who write well-developed essays are not the large group of all students but the subgroup of students who begin by doing nonstop writing.

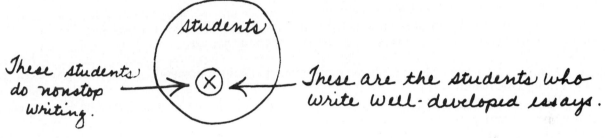

Thus the relative clause *who do nonstop writing before constructing a first draft* restricts the meaning of students to a narrow subgroup of students — those who begin by doing nonstop writing. This clause is therefore called *restrictive,* and it is not set off by commas. You have to have the information "who do nonstop writing before constructing a first draft" to know what is meant by *students.*

On the other hand, consider this sentence:

Marilyn Washington, who does nonstop writing before she constructs a first draft, generally writes well-developed essays.

If we diagrammed this sentence, we would not have a small circle inside a larger circle but two circles side by side. The first circle represents Marilyn Washington:

and the second circle represents additional information about her:

We know who writes well-developed essays — Marilyn Washington — so we don't need the extra information "who does nonstop writing before constructing a first draft" in order to identify which person writes the well-developed essays. Therefore this clause is nonrestrictive and must be set off with commas.

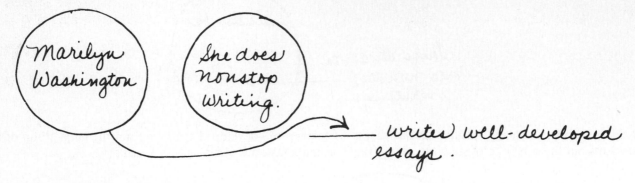

Often a sentence can be correctly punctuated either by setting off the relative clause (nonrestrictive) or by not setting it off (restrictive), but the two versions will have different meanings.

1. My history professors who have had special training in writing-across-the-curriculum give us interesting writing assignments.
2. My history professors, who have had special training in writing-across-the-curriculum, give us interesting writing assignments.

Sentence 1 means that some of my history professors have had special training in writing-across-the-curriculum and some haven't; only those who have had the training give interesting writing assignments.

Sentence 2 means that all my history teachers have had the special training and all of them give interesting writing assignments.

In the following sentences locate all restrictive and nonrestrictive clauses and phrases. Place commas around the nonrestrictive clauses and phrases. If the use of circle diagrams helps you visualize the difference between restrictive and nonrestrictive elements, try using them. Circle diagrams are shown for the first two answers.

Answer column

1. Did you see the person who just walked around the corner of the building?

1. [restrictive — no commas needed]

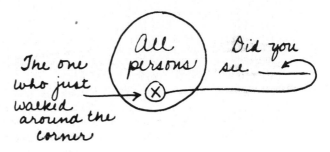

2. Did you see Mrs. Jones who just walked around the corner of the building?

2. Did you see Mrs. Jones, who. . . . [nonrestrictive — comma needed after *Mrs. Jones*]

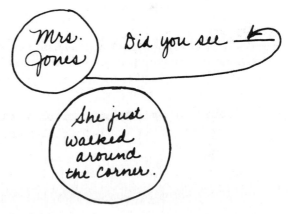

3. Tennis which requires an extended arm swing differs from racquetball which requires mainly a wrist swing.

3. Tennis, which . . . swing, differs from racquetball, which . . . wrist swing. [nonrestrictive]

4. Most colleges which have a wide variety of night classes attract older students.

4. Correct either way. [If you set off *which. . . classes,* you mean that most colleges have night classes and all these attract older students. If you don't set the *which* clause off, you mean that only those colleges that have the night classes attract older students.]

5. The magazine lying on the coffee table has a fascinating article about exploring in Africa.

5. [*Lying on the coffee table* is a necessary modifier identifying which magazine is meant. No commas.]

6. The new *National Geographic* lying on the coffee table has a fascinating article about exploring in Africa.

6. The new National Geographic, lying on the coffee table, has. . . . [Set off *lying on the coffee table* because the magazine is already identified.]

7. America which in 1850 was in the throes of a huge shifting of social and economic forces would soon be ripped apart by civil war.

7. America, which . . . forces, would. . . . [Clause isn't needed to identify America. Nonrestrictive—needs commas.]

8. In the decade before Lincoln's election, the production of Northern industry which almost doubled greatly outstripped economic growth in the
South.

8. In the decade before Lincoln's election, the production of Northern industry, which almost doubled, greatly outstripped economic growth. . . .
[*Which almost doubled* is a nonrestrictive clause. It
isn't needed to identify the production of Northern
industry. Therefore set off with commas.]

9. I think joggers who run in the street should have to
get licenses like cars and motorcycles.

9. Correct either way, depending on the meaning intended. [If the writer means all joggers run in the
street and they all should get licenses, commas
should be inserted around *who run in the street.* If
the writer means that only some joggers run in the
street and only those should get licenses, then no
commas are needed.]

10. Those old, single-speed, balloon-tired bicycles of
the 1950s which could hop curbs, rumble across
vacant lots, and take all the abuse we kids could
give them were in many ways a lot more practical
than today's ten-speed racing bikes.

10. Those old, single-speed, balloon-tired bicycles of
the 1950s, which could hop curbs, rumble across
vacant lots, and take all the abuse we kids could
give them, were. . . . [*Which could . . . give
them* is probably nonrestrictive and needs
commas. The writer probably means that all those
old bikes could hop curbs and so forth.]

11. The bikes that I like best are those classic, old, balloon-tired bikes of the 1950s.

11. [Restrictive—no commas. *That I like best* identifies which bikes are meant.]

12. My grandfather gets annoyed at sports figures who advertise beer on TV.

12. [Restrictive; my grandfather doesn't get annoyed at all sports figures, just those who advertise beer on TV.]

13. My grandfather gets annoyed at Billy Martin who advertises beer on TV.

13. My grandfather gets annoyed at Billy Martin, who advertises beer on TV. [Nonrestrictive; we know whom grandfather gets annoyed at — Billy Martin. The relative clause just gives us extra information about him.]

14. People who live in glass houses shouldn't throw stones.

14. People who live in glass houses shouldn't throw stones. [Restrictive; some people can throw stones; those who can't are just those who live in glass houses.]

15. Peter and Polly Patterson who just built themselves a glass house shouldn't throw stones at those of us who still live in wooden structures.

15. Peter and Polly Patterson, who just built themselves a glass house, shouldn't throw stones at those of us who still live in wooden structures. [The first relative clause is nonrestrictive because Peter and Polly Patterson are already identified; the second clause is restrictive since we need the relative clause to know what people are meant by *us*.]

24G   Use commas to separate items in series.

A series is a set of three or more nouns, pronouns, adjectives, adverbs, phrases, or clauses. Place commas after each item in the series.

He especially likes golf, jogging, *and* swimming. [Some writers omit the comma in front of the conjunction if no confusion would result, but most authorities prefer the comma.]

We went to the movies, had dinner downtown, *and* then went bowling.

24H   Use commas to separate coordinate adjectives preceding a noun.

Coordinate adjectives in series are separated by commas. Adjectives are coordinate if they can be separated by *and* and placed in a different order.

Coordinate adjectives:

A nearsighted, tall, thin, grumpy-looking man walked slowly down the street. [We could say a "thin and grumpy-looking and nearsighted and tall man.]

Noncoordinate adjectives:

Three aluminum-plated frying pans sat on the shelf. [We would not say "frying and aluminum-plated and three pans.]

NOTE: Do not place a comma after the last coordinated adjective in a series.

Faulty:

A lightweight, sleekly designed, ten-speed, bicycle was my summer's dream.

Correct:

A lightweight, sleekly designed, ten-speed bicycle was my summer's dream.

Exercise 24-3   Self-study: Items in series; coordinate adjectives

In this exercise use commas to separate items in series or to separate coordinate adjectives. Be sure to place a comma before the final *and* in a series (see 24P) but not to place a comma between the last coordinated adjective and the noun being modified.

1. José dislikes dogs cats hamsters and oysters.

   Answer: 1. José dislikes dogs, cats, hamsters, and oysters.

2. José dislikes dogs that bark cats that howl in the middle of the night hamsters that get out of their cages and oysters that fail to make pearls.

   Answer: 2. José dislikes dogs that bark, cats that howl in the middle of the night, hamsters that get out of their cages, and oysters that fail to make pearls.

3. The old gaunt tired and apparently depressed cowboy walked into the bunkhouse took off his boots and lay on the bed.

   Answer: 3. The old, gaunt, tired, and apparently depressed cowboy walked into the bunkhouse, took off his boots, and lay on the bed.

4. I believe that this university doesn't care about its students because it doesn't have an effective student evaluation system because the Student Union building is poorly maintained and because they raise tuition every year without warning.

   Answer: 4. I believe that this university doesn't care about its students because it doesn't have an effective student evaluation system, because the Student Union building is poorly maintained, and because they raise tuition every year without warning.

5. The tall stately dome of the capitol building stood against the twilight sky, in contrast to the fierce blood-red sweep of the gathering clouds.

   Answer: 5. The tall, stately dome of the capitol building stood against the twilight sky, in contrast to the fierce, blood-red sweep of the gathering clouds.

6. You don't really think I would eat those disgusting putrid moldy hamburgers, do you?

   Answer: 6. You don't really think I would eat those disgusting, putrid, moldy hamburgers, do you?

7. Let me tell you that those hamburgers are the most disgusting putrid and moldy specimens of meat that I have ever seen.

   Answer: 7. Let me tell you that those hamburgers are the most disgusting, putrid, and moldy specimens of meat that I have ever seen.

8. The chef laid out his prize hamburgers—succulent aromatic bathed in special sauces topped with delicately melting cheddar cheese—a dramatic contrast from the disgusting putrid moldy garp I had been eating the previous night.

   Answer: 8. The chef laid out his prize hamburgers—succulent, aromatic, bathed in special sauces, topped with delicately melting cheddar cheese—a dramatic contrast from the disgusting, putrid, moldy garp I had been eating the previous night.

9. Do you think that these wonderfully luscious Boy Scout peanut butter cookies deserve to stay on the plate?

   Answer: 9. Do you think that these wonderfully luscious Boy Scout peanut butter cookies deserve to stay on the plate?
   [These adjectives are noncoordinate and thus are not separated by commas; you would not say "these peanut butter and wonderfully luscious and Boy Scout cookies."]

10. What most bothers my mother is my little brother's messy room my sister's tangle of hair-care apparatus in the bathroom and our dog's tendency to spread his dinner all over the bedroom rug.

    Answer: 10. What most bothers my mother is my little brother's messy room, my sister's tangle of hair-care apparatus in the bathroom, and our dog's tendency to spread his dinner all over the bedroom rug.

24I   Use commas to set off parenthetical words, phrases, or clauses and other similar elements that interrupt the flow of the sentence.

By reading your sentences aloud in a natural voice, you can generally hear and thus identify parenthetical material that interrupts the flow of a sentence. Such material should be set off by commas. The following are common examples of interrupting material:

- Set off contrasting elements introduced by *but, not, although,* or other words that suggest a change of direction in thought:

The woman at the front desk, *not the mechanic,* was the one who quoted me the price.

Rosa, *although unwilling,* completed the assigned schedules.

He finished repairing the lawnmover, *but not without effort.* [Some writers do not set off contrasting elements introduced by *but* unless the voice pauses noticeably when the sentence is read aloud.]

- Set off words of direct address, *yes* or *no,* and mild interjections:

I tell you, *Jim,* your plan won't work. [Jim is addressed directly.]

Yes, I will be happy to do so. [*Yes* or *no* as answers to questions are set off.]

Well, I have decided to go, but, *jiminy crickets,* I don't want to. [Set off mild interjections.]

- Set off transitions, sources of indirect quotation or of authority, and other interrupting material:

She will, *however,* demand more money. [Transition expressions are generally set off except for occasional single-word transitions when the voice makes almost no pause.]

This new car, *according to latest government reports,* gets below-average mileage. [Phrases citing sources of authority are usually set off.]

My old pickup, *because of its broken front windshield,* isn't very safe on the highway. [Here one needs to trust one's ear that the phrase interrupts the flow of the sentence.]

24J   Set off attributive material accompanying direct quotations.

"To be a successful student," *my adviser told me,* "you have to enjoy learning."

24K   Use a comma to set off the name of a person being addressed.

Thank you, *Sam,* for your help in this matter.

24L   Use commas to substitute for words intentionally omitted from a sentence.

Occasionally a writer will omit several words from a sentence if the context is clear. Use a comma to substitute for the missing words.

Full sentence:

I said he was a good teacher, but I did not say he was a good lecturer.

Intentionally omitted words:

> I said he was a good teacher, not a good lecturer.

Frequently writers omit *and* before the last item of a series.

Full sentence:

> Dr. Smith was foolishly dressed, boring, and arrogant.

Intentionally omitted word:

> Dr. Smith was foolishly dressed, boring, arrogant.

24M   Occasionally you can set off an item for emphasis even if it would not normally be set off.

Normal:

> All the way home I endured the noise from a crying baby and from four yapping puppies.

Emphatic:

> All the way home I endured the noise from a crying baby, and from four yapping puppies.

24N, O   Use commas for separating or setting off elements in places and addresses and also for setting off the year when it is included with the month and date.

> He drove to Grand Forks, North Dakota, on July 5, 1971, in an old blue Ford. [The name of the state and the year are set off.]

24P   Put a comma before the coordinating conjunction in a series.

> Although British writers and some American writers omit the comma before the coordinating conjunction in a series, sentences are generally clearer if the comma is included.

Confusing:

> I like three kinds of pizza: pepperoni, Canadian bacon and pineapple and Italian sausage.

Clear:

> I like three kinds of pizza: pepperoni, Canadian bacon and pineapple, and Italian sausage.

24Q   Avoid needless commas.

> Because beginning writers tend to use too many commas rather than too few, try to avoid commas unless a specific rule calls for one. Especially avoid commas in the following cases—all of which are sources of frequent error in student papers.

- Do not use a comma to separate a subject from its verb or a verb from its complements. Remember that once inside the core of a sentence, you use commas *in pairs* to set off nonrestrictive or interrupting elements.

Faulty:

The man in the apartment next to mine, swallowed a goldfish. [Comma separates subject from verb.]

Faulty:

My brother, who recently won a pole-sitting contest swallowed a goldfish. [Here a comma occurs on one side of a nonrestrictive clause but not on the other side.]

Correct:

The man in the apartment next to mine swallowed a goldfish.

My brother, who recently won a pole-sitting contest, swallowed a goldfish.

- Do not set off items in the core of a sentence unless they are truly parenthetical or nonrestrictive or noticeably interrupting.

Faulty:

The rest of the goldfish, in the bowl, seemed delighted that my brother got sick.

Correct:

The rest of the goldfish in the bowl seemed delighted that my brother got sick.

- Do not use a comma before an *and* if it joins only two words or phrases.

Faulty:

I like golf, and basketball.

Correct:

I like golf and basketball. [Only two items are being joined.]

Faulty:

She pedaled uphill for twenty minutes straight, and won the race by several lengths.

Correct:

She pedaled uphill for twenty minutes straight and won the race by several lengths. [Compound predicate has only two verbs being connected.]

Exercise 24-4 Self-study: Using commas to set off parenthetical or interrupting elements, dates, and addresses.

A. In the following sentences use commas as needed to set off parenthetical or contrasting material that interrupts the flow of a sentence.

1. This particular sausage according to Pablo Bilboa is made from a special recipe from the Basque country of Spain.

2. It is hard work not hard play that most accounts for an athlete's success.

3. Transcendental meditation still among the most popular relaxation techniques on the West Coast is not really a form of religion.

4. Listen to him Sarah; you are not you know exactly guiltless yourself.

5. "I will not however go with you on the trip to New York" said Katrina not without a touch of anger in her voice.

1. This particular sausage, according to Pablo Bilboa, is made from a special recipe from the Basque country of Spain. [See 24I.]

2. It is hard work, not hard play, that most accounts for an athlete's success.

3. Transcendental meditation, still among the most popular relaxation techniques on the West Coast, is not really a form of religion.

4. Listen to him, Sarah; you are not, you know, exactly guiltless yourself.

5. "I will not, however, go with you on the trip to New York," said Katrina, not without a touch of anger in her voice.

B. In the following sentences use commas wherever needed to avoid misreading or to follow standard conventions for use of commas in dates and addresses.

6. After you walk the dog wants to walk too.

7. She said she arrived from Denver Colorado on January 8 1979 by Greyhound bus.

8. I am glad you asked but no I really don't want to do that.

9. I bought two records on the 15th; on the 17th, three; on the 19th six; and on the 24th a whopping twelve.

10. Hey Pete when you finish eating the garbage needs to be taken out.

6. After you walk, the dog wants to walk too.

7. She said she arrived from Denver, Colorado, on January 8, 1979, by Greyhound bus.

8. I am glad you asked, but, no, I really don't want to do that.

9. I bought two records on the 15th; on the 17th, three; on the 19th, six; and on the 24th, a whopping twelve.
[See 24L.]

10. Hey, Pete, when you finish eating, the garbage needs to be taken out.

Exercise 24-5 Self-study: Common problems of comma usage

In the following exercises insert commas where needed. These exercises are designed to illustrate places where beginning writers often make errors. Since beginning writers commonly err on the side of too many commas rather than too few, follow this piece of advice: "When in doubt, leave them out." Put in commas wherever you know a rule calls for them. Otherwise leave them out.

1. The snow was falling lightly so we bundled up the kids and went for a walk in the park.

1. The snow was falling lightly, so we bundled up the kids and went for a walk in the park. [Main clauses are joined with coordinating conjunction; no comma in front of *and* because it joins two verbs only.]

2. Doing sit-ups in the corner of the gym the wrestlers their faces covered with sweat continued training for next week's championship matches.

2. Doing sit-ups in the corner of the gym, the wrestlers, their faces covered with sweat, continued training for next week's championship matches. [First comma sets off introductory participial

3. Having lived in Phoenix Arizona since 1963 as an engineering consultant for Sun Belt Industries my fishing partner knew something about living with heat.

3. Having lived in Phoenix, Arizona, since 1963, as an engineering consultant for Sun Belt Industries, my fishing partner knew something about living with heat. [Commas on both sides of *Arizona* set off state; comma after *Industries* sets off the whole introductory participial phrase.]

4. I cannot give you a beginner the same privileges I give Tom Smithson an experienced craftsperson.

4. I cannot give you, a beginner, the same privileges I give Tom Smithson, an experienced craftsperson. [Commas set off nonrestrictive appositive. Be sure to put commas on both sides of *a beginner* because that appositive comes in the middle of the sentence.]

5. That dog over on the other side of the pond on the other hand is an expensive purebred but it is not as smart as old Rover here a genuine mutt.

5. That dog over on the other side of the pond, on the other hand, is an expensive purebred, but it is not as smart as old Rover here, a genuine mutt. [Commas on both sides of *on the other hand* set off an interrupting transition in the middle of the sentence; comma before *but* separates main clauses joined with a coordinating conjunction; comma before *a genuine mutt* sets off a nonrestrictive appositive.]

6. The chief of the engineering section personally approved all requests for office supplies and warned all of us against unnecessary spending.

6. The chief of the engineering section personally approved all requests for office supplies and warned all of us against unnecessary spending. [No commas; the *and* joins two verbs — *approved* and *warned* — not two main clauses.]

7. Experienced writers usually want trusted colleagues to read their developing essays in draft form for they know that they need readers' reactions in order to understand how to revise.

7. Experienced writers usually want trusted colleagues to read their developing essays in draft form, for they know that they need readers' reactions in order to understand how to revise. [Comma separates main clauses joined by coordinating conjunction; no other punctuation is needed.]

8. I can no longer eat candy because the doctors have forbidden me to eat sweets in any form.

8. I can no longer eat candy because the doctors have forbidden me to eat sweets in any form. [No punctuation needed because the adverb clause comes at the end of the sentence.]

9. I was more or less anesthetized by the cold and braced myself not to collapse until we reached the cowshed.

9. I was more or less anesthetized by the cold and braced myself not to collapse until we reached the cowshed. [No punctuation needed; *and* joins two verbs, not two main clauses; the adverb clause *until we reached the cowshed* comes at the end of the sentence.]

10. Unless we become serious critics of the educational system and the society behind it there is not much hope my art professor believes for the future of the humanities in America. Moreover this same professor thinks that most of us will never care to

10. Unless we become serious critics of the educational system and the society behind it, there is not much hope, my art professor believes, for the future of the humanities in America. Moreover, this same professor thinks that most of us will never care to

criticize our culture because we enjoy too much the mindless pleasures of watching TV and buying imitation wood-grain furniture.

11. "Animals" my professor continues "eat drink have sex and even work all their adult lives but only humans create music and listen to it with pleasure."

12. Sam let's see how much this guy really likes music. Let's come to class tomorrow with both of us plugged into your Sony Walkman.

13. He was however an unusually tall lad bold proud courageous and athletic and he took to running on the beaches for hours at a time when he was a teenager.

14. Forever setting his sights on distant horizons this tall lad from Scotland got the wanderlust bought passage on a freighter and headed for America.

---

criticize our culture because we enjoy too much the mindless pleasures of watching TV and buying imitation wood-grain furniture. [First comma sets off introductory adverb clause; next, commas go on both sides of the parenthetical clause *my art professor believes;* in the next sentence *moreover* is an introductory transition word and is therefore set off; no more commas are needed.]

11. "Animals," my professor continues, "eat, drink, have sex, and even work all their adult lives, but only humans create music and listen to it with pleasure." [First two commas set off the attributive phrase *my professor continues;* commas after *eat, drink,* and *sex* separate items in series; comma after *lives* separates main clauses joined by a coordinating conjunction.]

12. Sam, let's see how much this guy really likes music. Let's come to class tomorrow with both of us plugged into your Sony Walkman. [Comma sets off a noun of address.]

13. He was, however, an unusually tall lad, bold, proud, courageous, and athletic, and he took to running on the beaches for hours at a time when he was a teenager. [Commas around *however* set off an interrupting transition in the middle of the sentence; commas after *lad* and *athletic* set off adjectives coming after the noun and therefore interrupting the flow of the sentence (comma after *athletic* does double duty because it also separates main clauses joined by a coordinating conjunction); commas after *bold, proud,* and *courageous* separate coordinate adjectives.]

14. Forever setting his sights on distant horizons, this tall lad from Scotland got the wanderlust, bought passage on a freighter, and headed for America. [Comma after *horizons* sets off introductory participial phrase; commas after *wanderlust* and *freighter* separate verbs in series.]

Exercise 24-6   Self-study: Identifying comma rules

The following passage was written by a professional science writer. Explain each comma in terms of the rules given in this chapter.

Human beings go into suspended animation only within the pages of science fiction, yet hibernating animals manage

this near deathlike state for four to six months each year. When a ground squirrel, for instance, curls up for the

winter, its body temperature drops from the normal mammalian level of about 98 degrees Fahrenheit to as low as 34

or 35 degrees, and its heart, over a period of three to four hours, slows from 350 beats a minute to two to four beats a minute. How do animals survive this drop in body temperature and metabolic level? And how do animals hibernate in the first place?

⁸
"We don't really know," says Roland Aloai. . . . Hibernation conserves energy. It is a way animals can avoid the lean, cold winter. As Aloia points out, "An animal that can reduce its metabolic activity by 98 percent when there isn't much food around is way ahead."

Although people associate hibernation with bears, only small mammals like ground squirrels, hamsters, hedgehogs, woodchucks, and bats can enter the torpor that defines true hibernation. Some animals, including various species of snakes, land snails, and lizards, enter a state of dormancy, or estivation, in the summer when water is scarce. In bears, the ratio of surface area to body mass is not great enough to dissipate the heat required to lower the animal's temperature to hibernation levels. A wintering bear's temperature rarely falls below 86 degrees Fahrenheit, so they are rather easily awakened; it takes a true hibernator several hours to arouse from a near-freezing body temperature.

[From Carrol B. Fleming, "How Do Animals Hibernate?" *Science 84* (Jan/Feb 1984), p. 28.

Answers

1. Separates main clauses joined by a coordinating conjunction. (24A)

2 and 3. Set off an interrupting transition expression. (24I)

4. Sets off an introductory adverb clause. (24B)

5. Separates main clauses joined by a coordinating conjunction. (24A)

6 and 7. Set off phrases that interrupt the flow of the sentence. (24I)

8. Sets off an attributive phrase used with quotations. (24J)

9. Separates coordinate adjectives. (24H)

10. Sets off an attributive phrase used with quotations. (24J)

11. Sets off an introductory adverb clause (24B)

12, 13, 14, and 15. Separate items in series. (24G)

16 and 19. Set off the interrupting phrase beginning with *including.* (24I)

17 and 18. Separate items in series. (24G)

20 and 21. Set off a nonrestrictive appositive. (24F)

22. Sets off an introductory phrase. (24B)
(This phrase is so short that many writers would choose to omit the comma.)

23. Separates main clauses joined by a coordinating conjunction. (24A)

Exercise 24-7   Using commas in extended passages

In the following passage, which is a continuation of the article on hibernation in animals used in Exercise 24-6, all commas have been omitted. Insert the commas where you think the original author placed them, and state the rule governing your choice. Number each of your commas and then cite the rule in the space below the passage. The first one has been done for you as an example.

For years scientists thought that the cooler weather of autumn triggered the onset of hibernation, but golden-mantled ground squirrels kept in a constant temperature of 95 degrees Fahrenheit show signs of hibernation every 300 to 360 days or so. The squirrel cannot lower its body temperature in such heat but it will lose weight as if in hibernation.

This seems to indicate the presence of an internal body rhythm according to Eric Pengelley at the University of California at Riverside who has found that many other ground squirrel species also have self-contained clocks. The internal clock which may or may not exist in other hibernators apparently directs the metabolic changes that occur in ground squirrels every year.

Researchers have spent a great deal of time in the last 15 years trying to find what triggers hibernation. At the Stritch School of Medicine of Loyola University in Maywood Illinois Albert Dawe and Wilma Spurrier isolated a substance from the blood serum of hibernating woodchucks and one ground squirrel species. When Dawe and Spurrier's "trigger substance" is injected into ground squirrels it results in hibernation.

Trigger substance may work in combination with another secretion called antitrigger. Dawe and Spurrier hypothesise the antitrigger in the bloodstream keeps an animal active throughout spring and summer. The production of trigger substance continues however and by fall it overrides antitrigger and the animal hibernates. The animal becomes active again when enough antitrigger is produced in the spring. As Dawe and Spurrier see it these substances hold the key to understanding the complex mechanisms of hibernation.

Rules for each comma:

1. Separates main clauses joined by a coordinating conjunction. (2A)

Exercise 24-8   Mastery exercise: Comma usage

Insert commas where needed in the following sentences.

1. Whenever I go home to Bismarck North Dakota for Christmas vacation the dinner conversation turns to cross-country skiing.

2. On my last visit during dessert my dad who is an expert skier asked me if I wanted to try dogsled racing.

3. "I've wanted to try dogsledding for years " Dad said "but we've never had the equipment or the dogs. Now however my friend Jake Jackson the new agent for Smith Insurance has just bought a team and wants his friends to give it a try."

4. Rock shrimp unlike some other species have hard shells that make them difficult to peel.

5. Hiking or biking through southern Germany you will discover a rich mosaic of towns regional foods colors sounds and smells of the rural countryside and historic Black Forest region.

6. Instead of riding on busy boulevards you can pedal on a network of narrow paved roads built for farm vehicles or on graveled paths through lush green forests.

7. According to historian Daniel T. Rodgers a central question that divided workers and employers in the nineteenth and early twentieth centuries was how many hours a day the average worker should work.

8. Believing strongly in tradition the early factory owners thought their workers should follow the old sunrise to sunset work schedule of agricultural laborers.

9. This schedule which meant fourteen-hour workdays during the summer could also be maintained during the winter thanks to the invention of artificial light which owners rapidly installed in their factories.

10. Spurred on by their desire to create a shorter working day laborers began to organize into forerunners of today's labor unions and used their collective powers to strive for change.

11. Their faces painted in strange haunting colors from the juice of berries the warriors began drinking at dawn and by midmorning the tribal dances began with chanting rhythmic stomping and drumming.

12. Early every morning in hopes of gaining better information about the tribe the anthropologist would call on an elder medicine man in his hut.

13. According to an advertisement from the Lockheed Corporation a new space telescope which will soon be launched into a 320-mile-high orbit by the space shuttle will be the finest galactic telescope system ever built a masterpiece of advanced technology in optics instrumentation communications and pointing control.

14. On the desk over in the corner of the abandoned room the missing beaker sat its mysterious liquid jelled into a moldy sponge-like substance its power lost its purpose forgotten.

15. It was my chemistry professor not my physics professor who told me the story of the lost beaker and insisted that if I could find it I would never again fail another exam.

25

Semicolons

25A Use a semicolon to join main clauses that are not joined by a comma and a coordinating conjunction.

A semicolon is stronger than a comma and can be used to join two independent sentences into a single sentence with two main clauses. The semicolon indicates a close relationship between the meanings in the two main clauses and creates a sentence with two balanced, equal parts. Of course, you have the option also of joining the clauses with a comma and a coordinating conjunction *(and, or, but, nor, for, so,* and *yet).* (Joining two main clauses with only a comma creates a *comma splice*—see Chapter 4. Remember that a main clause has a complete subject and predicate and can stand alone as an independent sentence.)

I asked the professor for an extension on my essay; she told me I was out of luck. [These clauses could also be treated as independent sentences and separated with a period and capital letter. The semicolon, however, indicates a closer relationship between their meanings than does a period and a capital letter.]

Graduate schools typically employ their graduate students as teaching assistants; at some universities these assistants teach most of the introductory classes. [Again, the semicolon indicates a close connection of ideas between the clauses.]

25B Use a semicolon to join main clauses linked by a conjunctive adverb.

Conjunctive adverbs (see Chapters 4 and 9) are words like *however, therefore, nevertheless,* and *thus.* They are not grammatically equivalent to coordinating conjunctions and cannot join main clauses either by themselves or with a comma. When linking main clauses, they must be used with a semicolon.

Comma splices:

He spent all morning baking the pie, nevertheless, nobody seemed to appreciate his efforts.

I loved astronomy as a child, therefore, I signed up for physics in college.

Corrected:

He spent all morning baking the pie; nevertheless, nobody seemed to appreciate his efforts.

I loved astronomy as a child; therefore, I signed up for physics in college.

25C Use a semicolon to separate elements in a series when some of those elements contain commas.

> On vacation we went to Laramie, Wyoming; Denver, Colorado; Salt Lake City, Utah; and Boise, Idaho. [Since commas are used here to separate the cities from the states, semicolons are needed to separate the items in series. Without the semicolons such a sentence would be confusing because a reader might think that Laramie and Wyoming were two separate places instead of one, and so forth.]

25D Use a semicolon to separate elements in elliptical constructions, where words left out are clearly understood and where a semicolon would otherwise be appropriate.

> I left my heart in San Francisco; my wallet in Reno. [In this sentence the understood meaning is this: "I left my heart in San Francisco; I left my wallet in Reno." The semicolon is used as if the missing words were present in the sentence.]

25E Use semicolons to separate elements in reference notes when those notes contain other punctuation marks.

> Please read *Hamlet* III.ii.25 – 90; IV.iv.1 – 10; and all of Acts I and V.

Exercise 25-1   Self-study: Semicolons and commas

In the following sentences insert semicolons and commas as needed.

Answer column

1. We ate two hot fudge sundaes and then we had the nerve to weigh ourselves at the drugstore.

1. We ate two hot fudge sundaes, and then we had the nerve to weigh ourselves at the drugstore. [Main clauses are joined by comma and coordinating conjunction.]

2. We ate two hot fudge sundaes moreover we had the nerve to weigh ourselves at the drugstore.

2. We ate two hot fudge sundaes; moreover, we had the nerve to weigh ourselves at the drugstore. [Main clauses are joined by a semicolon — presence of conjunctive adverb *moreover* doesn't change the way the sentence is punctuated.]

3. We ate two hot fudge sundaes we had the nerve moreover to weigh ourselves at the drugstore.

3. We ate two hot fudge sundaes; we had the nerve, moreover, to weigh ourselves at the drugstore. [Note how the conjunctive adverb *moreover* can move in its clause; compare with sentence 2.]

4. We ate two hot fudge sundaes yet we had the nerve to weigh ourselves at the drugstore.

4. We ate two hot fudge sundaes, yet we had the nerve to weigh ourselves at the drugstore. [*Yet* is a coordinating conjunction.]

5. Although we ate two hot fudge sundaes we still had the nerve to weigh ourselves at the drugstore.

5. Although we ate two hot fudge sundaes, we still had the nerve to weigh ourselves at the drugstore. [*Although* is a subordinating conjunction, making the opening clause a subordinate rather than main clause.]

6. Having eaten two hot fudge sundaes we still had the nerve to weigh ourselves at the drugstore.

6. Having eaten two hot fudge sundaes, we still had the nerve to weigh ourselves at the drugstore. [Here the comma sets off an opening participial phrase.]

7. We invited Sarah president of the student body Mark the vice-president Garcia the student body treasurer and Professor Tungsu the faculty adviser.

7. We invited Sarah, president of the student body; Mark, the vice-president; Garcia, the student body treasurer; and Professor Tungsu, the faculty adviser. [Since commas are needed to separate the names from the offices, semicolons are needed to separate the items in series.]

8. We told them to bring bats balls and gloves plenty of crackers cheese and drinks and enough books towels and blankets for a whole day of fun.

8. We told them to bring bats, balls, and gloves; plenty of crackers, cheese, and drinks; and enough books, towels, and blankets for a whole day of fun.

9. The second factor that suggests it could be a close election is the number of unemployed these voters are going to go heavily for Bilboa and Ferlazzo.

9. The second factor that suggests it could be a close election is the number of unemployed; these voters are going to go heavily for Bilboa and Ferlazzo. [If you didn't want the reader to see these two main clauses as one closely linked unit, you could use a period instead of the semicolon and capitalize the *t* in *these.*

10. One startling revelation is that even children less than a year old are not as selfish as people once believed instead these infants show an early capacity for empathy.

10. One startling revelation is that even children less than a year old are not as selfish as people once believed; instead, these infants show an early capacity for empathy.

11. Eight of the persons tested received plain aspirin the other eight aspirin plus caffeine.

11. Eight of the persons tested received plain aspirin; the other eight, aspirin plus caffeine. [Punctuate as if no words were omitted from the second clause.]

12. Rubbing elbows with the natives is what Munich's famed Oktoberfest is all about fun-loving Bavarians celebrate night after night for sixteen days.

12. Rubbing elbows with the natives is what Munich's famed Oktoberfest is all about; fun-loving Bavarians celebrate night after night for sixteen days.

13. Although you can trace the chemical name and find out the hard facts there also are alternative sources of information.

13. Although you can trace the chemical name and find out the hard facts, there also are alternative sources of information. [*Although* is a subordinating conjunction.]

14. Since most lawns contain one or two different soil types you should take two samples from your property.

14. Since most lawns contain one or two different soil types, you should take two samples from your property. [*Since* is a subordinating conjunction.]

15. I have spent hours thumbing through these magazines however I haven't found a single good idea for my essay.

15. I have spent hours thumbing through these magazines; however, I haven't found a single good idea for my essay.

Exercise 25-2   Self-study: Sentence-combining using different connectives

Combine the following sentences into a single sentence with two main clauses. Use either a coordinating conjunction or a conjunctive adverb, along with appropriate punctuation, as indicated. Choose a coordinating conjunction or conjunctive adverb whose meaning links the clauses logically. The point of this exercise is to help you appreciate the logical meaning of different connectives as well as to increase your skill at punctuating sentences that use different kinds of connectives.

Example:
It is raining. I must take my umbrella. (conjunctive adverb)

It is raining; therefore I must take my umbrella.

1. That 1972 Nash Rambler at the OK Used Car Corral was an ugly piece of junk. It was at least $200 overpriced. (conjunctive adverb)

2. I want to go to the dance badly. I don't have enough money for a new suit. (coordinating conjunction)

3. Tuition will probably be raised again next year. The administration just announced a shocking increase in the cost of heating and other utilities. (coordinating conjunction)

4. Bill Jackson's family claim they are too poor to contribute more than a few dollars to the United Way. They just bought a new Mercedes Benz. (conjunctive adverb)

5. Professor Jones disagreed with almost everything I said all term. I was surprised when I got an A for the course. (conjunctive adverb)

6. Professor Jones disagreed with almost everything I said all term. I was surprised when I got an A for the course. (coordinating conjunction)

7. Professor Jones disagreed with almost everything I said all term. I still got an A for the course. (conjunctive adverb)

8. Professor Jones disagreed with almost everything I said all term. I still got an A for the course. (coordinating conjunction)

9. I love pizza. It is not on my diet. (conjunctive adverb)

10. Pizza is not on my diet. I shouldn't have any. (coordinating conjunction)

1. That 1972 Nash Rambler at the OK Used Car Corral was an ugly piece of junk; moreover, it was at least $200 overpriced. [Note that connectives such as *however* and *therefore* would be illogical. However, in place of *moreover,* you might have *furthermore, also,* or *in addition.*]

2. I want to go to the dance badly, but I don't have enough money for a new suit.

3. Tuition will probably be raised again next year, for the administration just announced a shocking increase in the cost of heating and other utilities.

4. Bill Jackson's family claim they are too poor to contribute more than a few dollars to the United Way; however, they just bought a new Mercedes Benz.

5. Professor Jones disagreed with almost everything I said all term; therefore, I was surprised when I got an A for the course.

6. Professor Jones disagreed with almost everything I said all term, so I was surprised when I got an A for the course.

7. Professor Jones disagreed with almost everything I said all term; however, I still got an A for the course.

8. Professor Jones disagreed with almost everything I said all term, yet (but) I still got an A for the course.

9. I love pizza; however, it is not on my diet.

10. Pizza is not on my diet, so I shouldn't have any.

Exercise 25-3   Mastery exercise: Semicolons and commas

In the following sentences insert semicolons and commas as needed. Some sentences may need no additional punctuation. Make sure that your marks of punctuation can be easily read.

Example:

She walked slowly into the lawyer's office$\overset{;}{\wedge}$however$\overset{,}{\wedge}$the receptionist apparently did not recognize her.

1. The two men defended themselves before the justice of the peace in Bilford across the river a similar case was being tried with attorneys and a full jury.

2. She claimed that most teenage shoplifters are never caught moreover those that are caught are seldom punished.

3. I admit that I went to the party I did not however enjoy it.

4. I admit that I went to the party but I did not enjoy it.

5. Although I went to the party I did not enjoy it.

6. When the party ended our apartment was in chaos from one end of the living room to the other end of the bedroom a fine layer of confetti blanketed everything like snow.

7. Within twenty minutes of leaving the trail we saw an antelope two elk one of which had begun to shed the velvet on its antlers an assortment of squirrels gophers and chipmunks and most startling of all a large black bear with two cubs.

8. An effective education does not consist of passive rote learning rather it consists of active problem-solving.

9. Failure to introduce and to use calculators and computers in school creates needless barriers for teachers and learners furthermore computer literacy is rapidly becoming a basic skill for the new millennium.

10. We watched the interminable slides of their vacation for what seemed like an eternity — Toledo Ohio Columbus Missouri Topeka Kansas Omaha Nebraska and on and on across the continent.

26
Apostrophes

The apostrophe is used mainly for showing possession, but it is also used to form special plurals and to indicate missing letters in contractions and in words showing regional dialects.

26A Use the apostrophe to show possession of nouns and indefinite pronouns.

Possessive constructions show both a possessor and a thing possessed. The thing possessed occurs last in the construction. The person or thing doing the possessing (the possessor) comes first, and it is this word that contains an apostrophe. Possession can also be shown through the use of a prepositional or participial phrase.

Possessor	Thing possessed	Alternative construction
Sally's	car	car belonging to Sally
men's	coats	coats for men
cats'	fur	fur of cats
three minutes'	work	work lasting three minutes

1 Do not confuse plural and possessive forms.

Because both plurals and possessives are formed in speech with an *s* sound, they seem identical to the ear. However, to the eye they are easily distinguished because the possessive form has an apostrophe. (Although an apostrophe is occasionally used to form a plural, this usage is so rare that you should associate apostrophes in your mind with possessive forms. See Rule 26C for the only times you use apostrophes for making plurals.)

		Identical sound	
Singular	**Plural**	**Singular possessive**	**Plural possessive**
cat	cats	cat's	cats'
horse	horses	horse's	horses'

Be sure that you signal your meaning to your reader by using the correct spelling.

333

Faulty:

We have two horse's and ten cat's on our farm.

Correct:

We have two horses and ten cats on our farm. [Plural forms only; no possession is intended.]

2 To form the possessive, add an apostrophe and an *s* (*'s*) to nouns and pronouns not already ending in *s* whether they are singular or plural.

Possessor	Possessive form
George (singular)	George's book
cattle (plural)	cattle's health
children (plural)	children's shot records
child (singular)	child's toy

3 Add only an apostrophe (') to words already ending in *s* whether these words are singular or plural.

Possessor	Possessive form
Louis (singular)	Louis' dog
plumbers (plural)	plumbers' tools
bosses (plural)	bosses' worries
boss (singular)	the boss' letter

NOTE: Some writers add an apostrophe and an *s* (*'s*) to short, singular nouns already ending in *s*. Either method is acceptable.

boss's letter	Louis's dog

Exercise 26-1 Self-study: Apostrophes

Form the possessive case of the noun in parentheses by adding an apostrophe or an apostrophe and an *s* as needed. Then in your own words explain what the phrase means, indicating the number (singular or plural) of both the possessor and the thing possessed.

Example:
the (frogs) warts   *the frogs' warts (There are at least two warts, and at least two frogs possess them.)*

Answer column

1. the (dog) bone

1. the dog's bone [There is only one bone, and only one dog possesses it.]

2. the (dog) bones

2. the dog's bones [There is now more than one bone, but only one dog possesses them.]

3. the (dogs) bones

3. the dogs' bones [Now more than one dog possesses the bones. Note that the apostrophe comes after the *s* in *dogs*, indicating that *dogs* is plural.]

4. the (baby) rattle	4. the baby's rattle [one baby, one rattle]
5. the (babies) rattles	5. the babies' rattles [more than one baby, more than one rattle]
6. the (babies) rattle	6. the babies' rattle [Now two or more babies are going to have to share a single rattle.]
7. the (baby) rattles	7. the baby's rattles [Now one baby has plenty of rattles.]
8. my (boss) temper	8. my boss' (or boss's) temper [You have only one boss. Because *boss* ends in *s*, you do not need to add an *s* after the apostrophe, but you can choose to do so. Either method is correct.]
9. my (bosses) tempers	9. my bosses' tempers [Now you are in trouble. You have more than one boss, and they all have tempers.]
10. (Louis) temper	10. Louis' (or Louis's) temper [Because *Louis* ends in *s*, you can add just an apostrophe or you can add an apostrophe and an *s*.]

4 To form the possessive of hyphenated words and compound words and word groups, add an apostrophe and an s ('s) to the last word only.

her mother-in-law's silverware

the ladies-in-waiting's formal gowns.

5 To express joint ownership by two or more people, use the possessive for the last name only; to express individual ownership, use the possessive for each name.

Paul's and his sister's sailboats [Each owns a separate sailboat.]

Paul and his sister's sailboat [Together they own one sailboat.]

26B Use an apostrophe (') to indicate omitted letters in contractions and in words showing regional dialect.

you're [you are]   it's [it is]   isn't [is not]   spring of '34 [spring of 1934]   "nothin' doin' 'round here" ["nothing doing around here"]

NOTE: Be sure the apostrophe is inserted in exactly the place where the missing letters would be.

Faulty:

is'nt

Correct:

isn't [is *no*t]

26C Use an apostrophe and an s ('s) to form the plural of letters, numbers, and words referred to as words.

On your test I can't distinguish between your *t*'s and your *E*'s. [The final apostrophe and *s* are not italicized (underlined in typing or handwriting).]

NOTE: Some writers omit the apostrophes in these plurals if no confusion would result.

On your test I can't distinguish between your *t*s and your *E*s.

26D Do not use apostrophes with the possessive forms of personal and relative pronouns (*yours, his, hers, ours, theirs, its, whose*).

His bike looks as if *it's* [it is] losing *its* front tire.

NOTE: When an apostrophe is used with these pronouns, it indicates a contraction.

Possessive	Contraction
The dog chases *its* tail.	*It's* a funny dog. [it is]
Your tie is crooked.	*You're* a sloppy dresser. [you are]
Whose dog is that?	*Who's* at the door? [who is]

Exercise 26-2   Self-study: Apostrophes

A. Form the possessive case of the following nouns and pronouns by adding an apostrophe or apostrophe and an *s* as needed. For each word make up your own "thing possessed" to form a possessive phrase.

Example:
Judy

Judy's car

Answer column

1. pickle _____ pickle's taste

2. James _____ James' book

3. Jim _____ Jim's book

4. everyone _____ everyone's happiness

5. four hours _____ four hours' wait

6. pickles _____ pickles' taste

7. sister-in-law _____ sister-in-law's coat

8. Sam and Janet (joint ownership) _____ Sam and Janet's lunch

9. Sam and Janet (individual ownership) _____ Sam's and Janet's lunches

10. horse _____ horse's tail

11. horses _____ horses' tails

12. mice _____ mice's cages

13. mouse _____ mouse's cage

14. St. Thomas _____ St. Thomas' influence

15. movies _____ movies' directors

B. Add apostrophes as needed in the following passage.

16. Pete and Lois asked us whose car that was with its windows rolled down during the rainstorm. We thought at first it was Rachael and Bobs car, but then someone said it was Georges brother-in-laws old 62 Cadillac. Whoever owned the car, its seats were soaked. "Its a mess," said Lois. "Lets move the car into the Jones garage and put some heat lamps over the seats. Its too bad that Georges brother-in-law isnt here right now so that we could ask him what to do." Finally we decided to leave him a note. "How many *l*s does *Cadillac* have?" Pete asked. "Thats hard to spell," I agreed. "Anyway," said Pete as he finished the note, "this mornings rainstorm wasnt nearly as bad as last Thursdays. Although it rained for only thirty minutes, we got three hours worth of water at this mornings rates. The seats on Lois and Bobs cars were sopping wet, yet both cars windows were rolled up. Theyre still trying to get them dry."

Answers

Pete and Lois asked us whose car that was with its windows rolled down during the rainstorm. We thought at first it was Rachael and Bob's car, but then someone said it was George's brother-in-law's old '62 Cadillac. Whoever owned the car, its seats were soaked. "It's a mess," said Lois. "Let's move the car into the Jones' garage and put some heat lamps over the seats. It's too bad that George's brother-in-law isn't here right now so that we could ask him what to do." Finally we decided to leave him a note. "How many *l*'s does *Cadillac* have?" Pete asked. "That's hard to spell," I agreed. "Anyway," said Pete as he finished the note, "this morning's rainstorm wasn't nearly as bad as last Thursday's. Although it rained for only thirty minutes, we got three hours' worth of water at this morning's rates. The seats on Lois' and Bob's cars were sopping wet, yet both cars' windows were rolled up. They're still trying to get them dry."

27
Quotation Marks

Use quotation marks to set off words, phrases, and sentences that you wish to indicate are someone else's actual spoken words or that you have copied from another source such as a book or magazine article. Also use quotation marks to set off titles of short works and to indicate words used in a special sense. Quotation marks always occur in pairs, one marking the beginning and the other marking the ending of the quoted material.

27A   Use quotation marks to enclose a passage copied from another source.

Original passage:

> A society cannot be free and stay free if it tries to enforce equality of wealth. [Fritz Machlup]

Ways of Quoting:

> Fritz Machlup once said, "A society cannot be free and stay free if it tries to enforce equality of wealth." [quotes the whole passage]

> According to Fritz Machlup, trying "to enforce equality of wealth" will destroy a society's freedom. [quotes only a part of the original passage]

Paraphrase:

> Fritz Machlup once claimed that a society's freedom will be destroyed if its government tries to equalize everyone's wealth. [The paraphrase puts the original version into the writer's own words, thereby avoiding direct quotation. Note, however, that the writer still indicates that Fritz Machlup is the source of the idea.]

Also use quotation marks to indicate words spoken by someone.

Direct quotation:

> "Can I go to the show?" Sally asked her mother. [shows Sally's direct words]

Indirect quotation:

> Sally asked her mother if she could go to the show. [Indirect quotation is like a paraphrase: It shows Sally's meaning but doesn't use her direct words; hence no quotation marks.]

If a quotation takes more than five lines, you should use *block indentation* rather than quotation marks to set off the quotation. Single-space the quotation, indenting every line five spaces from the left margin. Do *not* put quotation marks around the blocked passage.

Example of a Passage Using a Block Quotation
The economist Fritz Machlup has frequently pointed up inconsistencies in liberal values, particularly those bearing on equality and freedom. According to Machlup, "A society cannot be free and stay free if it tries to enforce equality of wealth." Machlup then continues:

> Young people should evaluate the concept that each person should get the same amount of everything. If wealth were equalized, it would have to be done again in ten years unless incomes were regulated also. If incomes were equalized, our economy would break down completely.

When quoting long passages from literature, including poetry, use block indentation. For short quotations, use quotation marks within the text. (Indicate line divisions in poetry with slash marks.)

I love Blake's lines, "Tyger! Tyger! burning bright/In the forests of the night."

In American practice, use a single quotation mark (made with an apostrophe on the typewriter) to set off a quotation within a quotation.

Molly told her discussion group angrily, "Every time I ask my husband to help me with the ironing, he says 'Men don't iron clothes!' and stalks out of the room in a huff."

27B Place other marks of punctuation inside or outside of quotation marks according to the following current conventions:

- Place commas and periods inside quotation marks.

He said "Buzz off," and then went about his business.

He said "Buzz off." Then he went about his business.

- Place colons and semicolons outside the final quotation mark.

He said "Buzz off"; then he went about his business.

My husband wants his "privileges": *Monday Night Football* and no housework chores.

- Place question marks or exclamation marks inside quotation marks if they belong to the quotation; place them outside quotation marks if they belong to a whole sentence of which the quotation is only a part.

"Buzz off!" my husband told me.

Did your husband really tell you to "buzz off"?

"Should I buzz off?" my husband asked.

27C **Use quotation marks for titles of essays, short stories, short poems, songs, chapters of books, and other sections that occur within books or periodicals.**

> I loved the Rolling Stones' "Satisfaction."

> Chapter One, "Planning, Developing, and Revising Papers," really helped me understand the writing process.

> I liked Spenser's sonnet "Most Glorious Lord of Lyfe" better than *The Faerie Queene.* [Both the sonnet and *The Faerie Queene* are poems, but the latter is italicized (underlined) because it is long. (See Chapter 32.)]

27D **Use quotation marks to show that someone else has used a word or phrase in a special way, one that you or the general public may not use or agree with completely.**

> My husband refuses to do what he considers "woman's work." [The quotation marks indicate that you would not use the phrase *woman's work* and that you and your husband have different ideas about what it means.]

> A story isn't "tragic," in Aristotle's sense of the word, just because it has an unhappy ending. [The quotation marks call attention to a specialized use of *tragic*—Aristotle's use of the term.]

27E **Avoid setting off slang or clichés in quotation marks as an attempt to apologize for them.**

> Inexperienced writers sometimes think it is all right to use trite language if they "apologize" for it by using quotation marks. Instead, rephrase your sentence to eliminate the triteness.

> *Weak:*

> She was "happy as a lark" to get the job.

> *Better:*

> She was elated to get the job.

Exercise 27-1   Self-study: Quotation marks

Insert double or single quotation marks as needed in the following sentences. Some sentences may not require any.

Answer column

1. Can I borrow some sugar? she asked me.

2. She asked me, Can I borrow some sugar?

3. She asked me if she could borrow some sugar.

4. When Hamlet says To be or not to be, my professor told us yesterday, he is not really contemplating suicide.

5. I hate you! screamed Sophia.

6. Did Sophia really say I hate you?

1. "Can I borrow some sugar?" she asked me.

2. She asked me, "Can I borrow some sugar?"

3. She asked me if she could borrow some sugar. [indirect quotation]

4. "When Hamlet says 'To be or not to be,'" my professor told us yesterday, "he is not really contemplating suicide."

5. "I hate you!" screamed Sophia.

6. Did Sophia really say "I hate you"? [Question is the whole sentence, not the quotation. Hence question mark goes outside the quotation mark.]

7. In Emily Dickinson's A Bird Came Down the Walk, the bird is said to Row him softer home/ Than oars divide the ocean.

8. She called him, in her own words, an exquisite poet; however, she really thinks his poetry is boring.

9. The Bard of Avon is what some people call Shakespeare.

10. The sergeant gritted his teeth and barked Forward march!

11. Do you mean to tell me, said Colonel Baker, that after the lieutenant told him to dismiss the troops, the sergeant turned around and said Forward march?

12. What he calls childlike I call childish.

13. Captain Jones reported to Colonel Baker that the sergeant's command to move the troops forward was an act of insubordination.

14. Although the end of Emily Dickinson's poem uses impressionistic images such as banks of noon or leap plashless as they swim, the beginning of the poem seems realistic:

    A bird came down the walk
    He did not know I saw;
    He bit an angleworm in halves
    And ate the fellow, raw.

15. Did Dickinson say, asked Sarah, that the bird ate the fellow, raw?

---

7. In Emily Dickinson's "A Bird Came Down the Walk," the bird is said to "Row him softer home/ Than oars divide the ocean."

8. She called him, in her own words, an "exquisite poet"; however, she really thinks his poetry is boring. [Semicolons go outside of quotation marks.]

9. The "Bard of Avon" is what some people call Shakespeare.

10. The sergeant gritted his teeth and barked "Forward march!" [Exclamation point is inside quotation mark because it is part of the quotation.]

11. "Do you mean to tell me," said Colonel Baker, "that after the lieutenant told him to dismiss the troops, the sergeant turned around and said 'Forward march'?" [The question is the whole sentence asked by Colonel Baker; hence the question mark goes inside the double quotation. However, the question is not part of the sergeant's words "Forward march"; hence the question mark goes outside the single quotation.]

12. What he calls "childlike" I call "childish."

13. Captain Jones reported to Colonel Baker that the sergeant's command to move the troops forward was an act of insubordination.

14. Although the end of Emily Dickinson's poem uses impressionistic images such as "banks of noon" or "leap plashless as they swim," the beginning of the poem seems realistic:

    A bird came down the walk
    He did not know I saw;
    He bit an angleworm in halves
    And ate the fellow, raw.

[Do not put quotation marks around the block quotation since the block indentation itself indicates quoted matter.]

15. "Did Dickinson say," asked Sarah, "that the bird 'ate the fellow, raw'?"

Exercise 27-2   Mastery exercise: Apostrophes and quotation marks

A. In the following sentences add apostrophes as needed. Place a caret (∧) in the space where an apostrophe is to be inserted, and then write out the whole word, with the apostrophe, in the space at the right. The number of blank lines do not necessarily indicate the number of words needing apostrophes.

Example:
Jim∧s cats were fighting for thirty minutes.   _____*Jim's*_____

1. Its a good thing that the notebook is hers.   1. _____
                                                                            _____

2. Their fathers-in-laws coats were left in the hallway by mistake next to the womens   2. _____
   powder room.   _____
                                                                            _____

3. The songs mood, created through its beautiful melody and words, is one of Rogers   3. _____
   and Hammersteins greatest achievements.   _____
                                                                            _____

4. She told us to mind our *p*s and *q*s unless we wanted to have our ears boxed.   4. _____
                                                                            _____
                                                                            _____

5. Thomas stereo speakers aren't as good as the Jones, whose speakers are one of our   5. _____
   neighborhoods greatest attractions.   _____
                                                                            _____

B. In the next sentences add single or double quotation marks as needed. Place a caret (∧) in the exact place where a quotation mark should be inserted and then indicate the mark in the space above the word. Be sure that a grader can tell whether a mark goes inside or outside other punctuation marks. If no changes are needed, place *OK* next to the sentence in the right margin.

Example:
Did Molly say∧"Please pass the catsup∧"?

6. My mother told me that she didn't want me to buy a car until I had a permanent part-time job.

7. Jake has his little quirks, as Molly calls them, but he is still lovable.

8. My adviser recently remarked: The nervous student who encounters a professor who states, Twenty percent of this class usually fails, must learn to say, Not me, instead of giving up.

9. How many of you have read John Donne's poem The Ecstasy? asked Professor Jones.

10. The meaning of the terms role conflict and role strain are among the most important concepts you learn in Introduction to Sociology.

11. Did your teacher really say Attendance is necessary in this class?

C. In the following passage, insert apostrophes and single or double quotation marks as needed. Indicate clearly where the punctuation marks go by placing a caret (∧) in the appropriate place and then writing the correct punctuation marks above the caret.

Example:

∧"Jim∧'s cat,∧" said Sally,∧" is driving me nuts.∧"

12. We are guilty of gross misuse of language, continued the speaker, whenever we use disinterested to mean uninterested.

13. Aunt Sally called the top drawer of her desk the Shame to Throw It Away Drawer: a chaos of string, rubber bands, paper clips, old photographs, and notes from friends dated ten years earlier.

14. How many *p*s are there in the tongue twister Peter Piper picked a peck of pickled peppers? asked Martha.

15. I spent two hours worth of good homework time, complained Thomas friend Karen, trying to invent a tongue twister that would make people stand up and shout Thats a masterpiece!

28
Other Marks of Punctuation

Use the dash, the colon, parentheses, brackets, the slash, and ellipses according to current conventions.

28A   **Use the dash to set off words, phrases, and sometimes whole sentences so that they receive special emphasis.**

Think of the dash as a very strong comma, used to indicate pauses that give special emphasis to the material being set off. On a typewriter, make a dash with two unspaced hyphens connected without spaces to the preceding and following words.

Sir Walter Raleigh brought the potato—as well as tobacco—to Queen Elizabeth I on his return from Virginia. [In the above example a pair of commas could replace the pair of dashes: The dashes, however, emphasize the material inside them.]

Sometimes the dash is used to set off nouns placed for special emphasis at the beginning of a sentence. The nouns are then summarized by a pronoun following the dash.

Joy, happiness, prosperity—all this is promised to investors in the new Whackoburger fast-food chain.

For many uses of the dash, commas will also suffice and are often the better choice. To make dashes effective, use them sparingly.

28B   **Use the colon for linking independent clauses when the second clause completes a meaning predicted in the first clause, for introducing block quotations or lists, and for setting off some words and phrases at the end of a sentence.**

If you wish to join two independent clauses and indicate that the second clause is a direct explanation of the first, use a colon.

The professor agreed to excuse Jack's late paper for two reasons: First, Jack had a case of strep throat early in the week, and second his cat had kittens on his typed copy. [The first clause sets up our anticipation for an immediate explanation; the clause following the colon provides the explanation.]

NOTE ON CAPITALIZATION: If what follows the colon is a complete sentence, you have the option of beginning the sentence with a capital letter. Usage varies. However, if what follows the colon is not a complete sentence, use a small letter.

A colon is also used to introduce a block quotation or any other quotation for emphasis.

His father replied slowly, carefully, thoughtfully: "Buying the tractor now, when we are already too deeply in debt, is not a good idea." [Although a comma could also be used to introduce this quotation, the colon is more formal and emphatic.]

Always use a colon if the quotation is printed in the block indentation format (see Chapter 27).

Use a colon to introduce lists when the list follows a grammatically complete independent clause.

We can win in two ways: changing our defense or adding Jones to the offensive lineup.

Do not use a colon in the middle of a clause:

Faulty:

We can win either by: changing our defense or adding Jones to the offensive lineup.

Correct:

We can win either by changing our defense or by adding Jones to the offensive lineup.

Faulty:

The guide gave us plenty of advice such as: taking along insect repellent, buying a good poncho, and rubbing petroleum jelly on tender spots on our feet.

Correct:

The guide gave us plenty of advice, such as taking along insect repellent, buying a good poncho, and rubbing petroleum jelly on tender spots on our feet.

OR

The guide gave us plenty of advice: taking along insect repellent, buying a good poncho, and rubbing petroleum jelly on tender spots on our feet. [Use a colon only when the material that precedes it could stand as a complete sentence. Note that the words *such as* mean approximately the same thing as a colon; use one or the other but not both.]

Use a colon to separate chapter from verse in biblical citations and to separate hours from minutes in time of day.

He quoted John 3:16. It is now 11:24 P.M.

28C Use parentheses to set off nonessential information that breaks the flow of thought within a sentence or a paragraph.

David Jones (my stepfather) and Daniel Jones (my real father) had unusually similar names. [Commas could also be used here, but they would give the enclosed information more emphasis, perhaps obscuring the point of the sentence.]

PUNCTUATION NOTE: When you place a complete sentence within parentheses, the concluding end mark goes inside the parentheses. When you end a sentence with parenthetical elements, the end mark goes outside the parentheses.

When visiting England, we watched a lot of cricket (a British game somewhat similar to American baseball).

When visiting England, we watched a lot of cricket. (Cricket is a British game something like American baseball.)

When inserting a parenthetical sentence within another sentence, do not begin the parenthetical sentence with a capital letter or end it with a period. However, you can end the parenthetical sentence with a question mark or exclamation point.

Easterners sometimes think (this misconception greatly annoys us Westerners) that Minnesota is next door to Oregon.

Easterners sometimes think (what could annoy us Westerners more?) that Minnesota is next door to Oregon.

Parentheses are sometimes used to enclose numbers or letters identifying each part of a list.

To graduate, a student must fill out three forms: (1) the transcript summary, (2) the request form, and (3) the adviser's sign-off sheet. [Use numbers within parentheses in this way mainly for bureaucratic and technical writing, not for most college essays.]

28D Use brackets to set off material within quoted matter that is not part of the quotation.

According to Joseph Menosky, "Courses offered to teach these skills [computer literacy] have popped up everywhere." [The source of the above quotation did not contain the words *computer literacy* following *these skills* since the context of the sentence explained what *these skills* meant. The writer must therefore insert *computer literacy* in brackets to make up for the missing context. The brackets mean that the enclosed material did not occur in the original version.]

Brackets are also used when you must change the grammar of a quotation slightly to make it fit the grammar of your own sentence.

Original source from an author named David McCracken:

I see computer literacy as the New Math of the 1980's.

> David McCracken says that "computer literacy [is] the New Math of the
> 1980's." [The writer had to change the original *as* to *is* to make it fit the
> grammar of the new sentence. This change is placed in brackets.]

If you quote a source containing an obvious mistake, you can insert *sic* in
brackets to indicate that the mistake is in the original source and is not your own.

> According to Joe Schmoe, not your greatest sportswriter, the home-run cham-
> pion is still "Baby *[sic]* Ruth."

28E Except in very informal language, use the slash only to divide lines of poetry written as a quotation within a sentence.

> When Keats said " 'Beauty is truth, truth beauty'—that is all/Ye know on
> earth, and all ye need to know," do you think he had ever taken a chemistry test?

Slashes are sometimes used to separate years or to indicate options, but these uses are
too informal for most essays.

> I was working at Safeway during 1982/83.
>
> He told me to take algebra and/or trigonometry.
>
> The catalog tells a student that he/she can take up to fifteen electives of his/her
> choice. [The above sentences might be acceptable in an informal memo in-
> tended for one or two readers who are also colleagues, but not in a formal essay.]

28F Use three spaced periods (called ellipsis points) to show words omitted from quotations.

> An ellipsis is formed with three spaced periods (. . .) and is used either to indicate
> that material has been omitted from a quotation or to indicate that in dialogue a
> speaker's words are halting, broken, or trailing off. When an ellipsis occurs at the end
> of a sentence, a fourth period is used as the end mark for the sentence (. . . .).

Original:

> The good Shakespeare critic must point out the patterns of the dance. He must
> find terms in which the opposition and conflicts and problems within a play can
> be stated while recognizing the reductiveness of those terms. He must fight the
> temptation to proclaim what it boils down to. [Norman Rabkin]

Ellipsis used to show omitted words:

> According to Norman Rabkin, the "good Shakespeare critic . . . must find
> terms in which the opposition and conflicts and problems within a play can be
> stated. . . . He must fight the temptation to proclaim what it boils down to."
> [The first set of ellipsis points indicates that words have been omitted within
> sentences. The second set indicates that the omission stops at the end of a

sentence — a period has been added to the set of three to serve as the end mark for the sentence.]

Ellipses used to show halting speech in dialogue:

"Help . . . ," he gasped. "I . . . can't . . . get my . . . breath."

Exercise 28-1   Self-study: Dash, colon, parentheses, brackets, ellipses

A. In the following exercises, insert dashes, colons, parentheses, or brackets as needed. Some sentences may be correct.

1. Anxiety, dread, fear of choosing all these are hallmarks of existentialism.

2. There are only two kinds of people those who make sweeping generalizations and those who don't.

3. "It don't *sic* make any difference to me," said the professor.

4. Of the seven students interviewed, only two both of them English majors complained about the quality of the student newspaper.

5. The distance between Piedmont and Pickleville 72 miles is too far for me by bicycle.

6. Her favorite courses in college were Modern Poetry, Ancient Greek History, and Contemporary Philosophy.

7. She liked a number of courses in college such as Modern Poetry, Ancient Greek History, and Contemporary Philosophy.

8. Her favorite courses in college were the following Modern Poetry, Ancient Greek History, and Contemporary Philosophy.

9. Her favorite courses in college Modern Poetry, Ancient Greek History, and Contemporary Philosophy all required extensive term papers.

---

1. Anxiety, dread, fear of choosing — all these are hallmarks of existentialism.

2. There are only two kinds of people: those who make sweeping generalizations and those who don't. [A dash would also be appropriate; the colon is slightly more emphatic.]

3. "It don't *[sic]* make any difference to me," said the professor. [The brackets indicate that the bad usage was the professor's and that you are indeed quoting accurately.]

4. Of the seven students interviewed, only two — both of them English majors — complained about the quality of the student newspaper. [Parentheses could also be used. The dashes place emphasis on the fact that the complainers are English majors; parentheses would suggest that this information is simply incidental.]

5. The distance between Piedmont and Pickleville (72 miles) is too far for me by bicycle. [Dashes are also possible: They would place greater emphasis on the 72 miles.]

6. Correct as it is. [No extra punctuation needed; a colon after *were* would be wrong because the preceding material would not form a complete, independent sentence.]

7. Correct as it stands. [Again, no extra punctuation is needed.]

8. Her favorite courses in college were the following: Modern Poetry, Ancient Greek History, and Contemporary Philosophy. [Here a colon is needed because the list now follows a complete independent sentence.]

9. Her favorite courses in college — Modern Poetry, Ancient Greek History, and Contemporary Philosophy — all required extensive term papers. [Parentheses would also be possible. What is the difference in meaning between using dashes and parentheses?]

10. I like this college except for one thing it costs too much.

10. I like this college except for one thing: It costs too much. [You could also use a dash. The colon places more formal emphasis on the last clause.]

B. Consider the next two passages as original sources for a quotation that you must write for a research essay. Quote the material in boldface print, using brackets, if necessary, to insert explanations or to make slight changes in grammar.

11. Critical thinking does not need to be redefined. What is needed is clarification and elaboration of a fairly loose concept. **Previous definitions are accurate but overly restrictive,** and, while the broader definitions of critical thinking provide a larger context for definition, they are so general that they provide little psychological or pedagogical guidance. [Robert Yinger]

Quote the boldface material from the above passage in a single sentence beginning "Yinger claims that. . . ."

Yinger claims that

Answer
Yinger claims that "[p]revious definitions [of critical thinking] are accurate but overly restrictive."

12. For nearly a century, **Brown County has been home to a prospering artists' colony amid the hills of southern Indiana.** [From an article in *Better Homes and Gardens.*]

Quote the boldface material in a sentence beginning: "In an article on family vacations, *Better Homes and Gardens* claims that. . . ." Change *has been* to *is.*

In an article on family vacations, *Better Homes and Gardens* claims that

Answer
In an article on family vacations, *Better Homes and Gardens* claims that "Brown County [is] home to a prospering artists' colony amid the hills of southern Indiana."

C. Quote the following passage using ellipsis points in place of the underlined portions. Begin your quotation, "As the physicists Wheeler and Kirkpatrick explain:"

13. Physics is the study of the material world. It is a search for an explanation of the behavior of objects in the universe. The search covers the entire range of material objects, from the smallest known particles—so small that it is meaningless to discuss what they look like, to the astronomical objects—millions of times bigger than our sun or so dense that a thimbleful of material would weigh a billion tons. The search also covers the entire span of time from the primordial firefall to the ultimate fate of the universe. Within this vast realm of space and time, the searchers have one goal: to comprehend the course of events in the whole world—to create a world view.

[Gerald F. Wheeler and Larry D. Kirkpatrick, *Physics: Building a World View,* Prentice-Hall, 1983.]

Answer
As the physicists Wheeler and Kirkpatrick explain:

Physics . . . is a search for an explanation of the behavior of objects in the universe. The search covers the entire range of material objects, from the smallest known particles . . . to the astronomical objects. . . . The search also covers the entire span of time from the primordial firefall to the ultimate fate of the universe. Within this vast realm of space and time, the searchers have one goal: . . . to create a world view.

NAME _____ DATE _____

Exercise 28-2 Mastery exercise: All uses of punctuation

A. The following passages by professional writers have been reproduced exactly as written except that all internal marks of punctuation have been omitted. Insert a caret (∧) wherever punctuation is missing and write the correct punctuation above the caret.

1. My mother almost never drank says Nancy Wexler president of the Hereditary Diseases Foundation yet one day as she was crossing the street a policeman said Arent you ashamed to be drunk so early in the morning! Those words terrified her mother for her father and her three older brothers had died of a frightening hereditary ailment called Huntingtons disease which made them lose their balance twitch uncontrollably and eventually lose their minds. Mrs Wexler thought she had been spared she was 58, past the age when symptoms of the disease usually begin. [Maya Pines, *Science 84.*]

2. Few Presidents in history have known how to set and hold the stage as well as Ronald Reagan does and thus he entered the political year via his State of the Union Message and his opening of the re-election campaign with a great splash. Reagans sense of theatre is unmatched in politics his use of language unique and his capacity for arrogating unto himself the symbols and values Americans hold dear flag family God patriotism national strength awesome. He is the master weaver of the national myths. *[Newsweek.]*

B. Quote the following passage, omitting the italicized words. Use ellipses appropriately to signify missing words. Begin your quotation with the words "According to Desmond Morris:"

3. Animals fight amongst themselves for one of two *very good* reasons: either to establish their dominance in a social hierarchy, or to establish their territorial rights *over a particular piece of ground.* Some species are purely hierarchical, with no fixed territories. Some are purely territorial, with no hierarchy problems. *Some have hierarchies on their territories and have to contend with both forms of aggression. We belong to the last group:* we have it both ways.
[From Desmond Morris, *The Naked Ape* (New York: McGraw-Hill, 1967).]

Spelling
29

Although many good writers are poor spellers, such writers would never submit a finished piece of work to readers without ensuring that all words are spelled correctly. You should consider correct spelling an essential quality of finished essays and get in the habit of editing for spelling as an important last step in the writing process.

29A   You can avoid some spelling errors by reading and pronouncing words carefully.

Often writers are led into misspelling a word because they don't pronounce it carefully.

Correct spelling	Correct pronunciation		Wrong pronunciation
athletics	ath**let**ics	*not*	ath**el**etics
government	govern**ment**	*not*	gover**ment**

A similar problem occurs when a writer confuses two different words that have the same sound.

There, their, they're

There (adverb) are two main reasons why they're (contraction for "they are") not doing their (possessive of "they") homework.

Exercise 29-1 Correcting misspellings due to mispronunciation or confusion of words that sound the same

A. Fill in the missing letters in the words below; clues to the meanings of the words to be spelled correctly are given in parentheses. Find the word in your dictionary and indicate its pronunciation by copying the word in the blank at the right exactly as its pronunciation appears in your dictionary. Indicate syllable divisions and location of primary accents.

Pronounciation column

Example:

Your sandals are sim __ila__ r to mine. (having a general likeness) *sĭm ĭ· lẽr*

1. As a nature lover, I believe in protecting the envir _____ t. (natural surroundings) 1. _____

2. I am a soph _____ e in college. (second-year student) 2. _____

3. She is a can _____ e for class president. (someone running for office) 3. _____

4. He is suppo _____ to be here by now. (ought to) 4. _____

5. My little sister has a misch _____ s personality. (impish) 5. _____

6. George is an eternal opt _____ t. (someone who looks on the bright side of things) 6. _____

7. Mount Shasta is wond _____ y beautiful. (adverb meaning "full of wonder") 7. _____

8. I think he's a p _____ rt. (someone who is morally corrupt) 8. _____

9. The doctor gave me a p _____ tion. (written order for medicine) 9. _____

10. That evidence is totally irr _____ t. (not pertinent) 10. _____

B. In the following sentences choose the correct word in parentheses. Write your answers in the blanks provided. Use your dictionary to check your answers.

Answer column

11. I wanted her to (accept/except) my apologies, (accept/except) I couldn't find her. 11. _____

_____

12. Of course my apology can't (alter/altar) what I did. 12. _____

13. She needs to see my point of view from a broader (prospective/perspective). 13. _____

14. (Two/too) boys are going (too/to) the movies (to/too). 14. _____

_____

_____

15. I think (its/it's) fun to watch a dog chase (its/it's) tail. 15. _____

_____

16. She is taller (then/than) I.

16. _____

17. If the cat gets (loose/lose) again, she said she would (loose/lose) her mind.

17. _____

_____

18. I don't know what (affect/effect) the playwright intended, but the play really (affected/effected) my mood.

18. _____

_____

29B Learn as many principles of spelling as you can, but when in doubt always consult a dictionary.

1 When trying to decide between *ie* and *ei* check both the sound and the previous letter.

Normally place *"i* before *e* except after *c*, unless the word is pronounced *ay* as in *neighbor* and *weigh."*

>   believe   grief   pierce   wield [*i* before *e*]
>
>   BUT
>
>   receive   conceit   ceiling [except after *c*]
>   feign   neighbor   eight [unless the word is pronounced *ay*]

Unfortunately there are some exceptions which you just have to memorize.

>   seize   caffeine   weird   height

2–4 Drop a final silent *e* from a root word when adding suffixes beginning with a vowel, but not from suffixes beginning with a consonant.

>   rave/raving   manage/managing   pile/piling   move/moving
>   force/forcible   advise/advisable   argue/arguable
>   debate/debatable   fame/famous   bride/bridal
>
>   BUT
>
>   love/lovely   hope/hopeful [Suffixes begin with consonant.]

There are only a few exceptions to this rule. When the silent *e* of the root word follows a soft *c* (a *c* that has an *s* sound) or a soft *g* (a *g* that has a *j* sound), do not drop the *e* when adding suffixes beginning with *a* or *o*. In such cases, the final *e* is needed to indicate the correct sound of the *c* or *g*.

>   peace/peaceable [The *c* is pronounced *s*.]
>   manage/manageable [The *g* is pronounced *j*.]

Also, do not drop a final *e* if the resulting word would be confusing.

>   dye/dyeing [to avoid confusion with *dying*]
>   singe/singeing [to avoid confusion with *singing,* but also to keep the soft *g*]

Other exceptions: true/truly   due/duly   awe/awful   judge/judgment

5 Keeping or dropping a final *y* depends on a few simple principles:

>   • Keep a final *y* when adding *ing*
>
>   fly/flying   study/studying   worry/worrying
>
>   • When the final *y* follows a consonant in the root word, change the *y* to *i* before adding any suffix other than *ing.*
>
>   beauty/beautiful   worry/worrier   happy/happiness

- When the final *y* follows a vowel in the root word, ordinarily keep the final *y* when adding a suffix.

    enjoy/enjoys/enjoyed   play/plays/played

There are a few exceptions to this rule when adding an *ed* ending.

    pay/pays/ BUT paid   say/says/ BUT said

6 Double a final consonant when you add a suffix beginning with a vowel (*ing, er, est, ed, ence, ance, ible, able, and ened*) if the final consonant is preceded by a single vowel and if it is in an accented syllable.

hop/hopping [Compare with hope/hoping; the double *p* in *hopping* keeps the sound of the *o* short.]

boat/boating [Final *t* is not doubled because it is preceded by two vowels, not a single vowel.]

confound/confounded [Final *d* is not doubled because it is preceded by another consonant, not a single vowel.]

occur/occurrence [Final consonant is in an accented syllable: oc**cur**rence.]

refer/referred [Final consonant is in an accented syllable: re**fer**red.]

refer/reference [Final consonant is in an unaccented syllable: **ref**erence.]

benefit/benefited [Final consonant is in an unaccented syllable: **ben**efited.]

7 When adding prefixes to the beginning of words, don't change the spelling of either the prefix or the root word.

unusual [un + usual]   unnatural [un + natural]
disappear [dis + appear]   dissatisfied [dis + satisfied]

Exercise 29-2   The *ie* or *ei* combination

Spell the following words correctly by deciding whether to use *ie* or *ei*. Remember the jingle *"i* before *e* except after *c* unless the word is pronounced *ay* as in *neighbor* and *weigh."* But remember also that there are some exceptions. Use your dictionary freely. After each word indicate whether it follows the rule or is an exception.

Example:

rec_____ve   *receive (follows rule)*

w_____rd   *weird (exception)*

1. bel_____ve

2. spec_____s

3. dec_____ve

4. l_____sure

5. consc_____nce

6. h_____ght

7. w_____ght

8. perc_____ve

9. sl_____gh

10. conc_____ted

11. caff_____ne

12. f_____gn

13. c_____ling

14. s_____ze

15. p_____rce

16. st_____n

17. ch_____f

18. y_____ld

19. gr_____f

20. n_____ther

Exercise 29-3   Adding suffixes and prefixes

Add suffixes or prefixes to the following words, making decisions about whether to drop a final *e*, double a final consonant, change a final *y* to *i*, or make other changes as needed. Use your dictionary to check your answer, but first try to determine the correct spelling by using the rules.

Example:

mop + ed   *mopped*

mope + ing   *moping*

1. come + ing   _____

2. run + ing   _____

3. write + ing   _____

4. compel + ed   _____

5. advantage + ous   _____

6. prefer + ed   _____

7. unforget + able   _____

8. forgot + en   _____

9. slope + ing   _____

10. slop + ing   _____

11. happy + ness   _____

12. party + ing   _____

13. un + involved   _____

14. non + negotiable   _____

15. transmit + ed   _____

16. pay + ing   _____

17. pay + ed   _____

18. hungry + ly   _____

19. value + able   _____

20. argue + ment   _____

21. cry + ed   _____

22. dismay + ed   _____

23. mercy + ful   _____

24. grace + ous   _____

25. beauty + ous   _____

29C The rules for forming plurals are usually straightforward and easy to learn.

1. With most nouns, form the plural by adding *s*, including the plural of acronyms and the plural of years.

    ball/balls   apple/apples   1980/the 1980s
    one IOU/two IOUs

2. When a noun ends in *s, x, ch,* or *sh,* add *es* to form the plural. (Note that the *es* plural adds an extra syllable to the word, so that you are really just spelling it the way you pronounce it.)

    hiss/hisses   box/boxes   lunch/lunches   bush/bushes

3. If the noun ends in a *y* preceded by a consonant, change the *y* to *i* and add *es*. If the final *y* is preceded by a vowel, just add the *s*.

    duty/duties   fly/flies   boy/boys   day/days

4. If a noun ends in *o*, you must memorize whether to add an *s* or an *es*. Generally, however, if the final *o* is preceded by a consonant, the plural takes an *es*.

    hero/heroes   potato/potatoes
    scenario/scenarios   BUT   solo/solos

5. For words ending in *f* or *f* plus silent *e*, generally form the plural by changing the *f* to *v* and adding *es*.

    life/lives   scarf/scarves   wolf/wolves
    But there are many exceptions:
    chief/chiefs   bluff/bluffs

6. For hyphenated words, generally form the plural by changing the first word, not the last one.

    mother-in-law/mothers-in-law [not mother-in-laws]

7. Memorize the plural forms of occasional irregular nouns.

    woman/women   ox/oxen   deer/deer   child/children

8. Some words borrowed directly from Greek or Latin still take their plural forms from the original language.

    datum/data   phenomenon/phenomena   alumnus/alumni

Exercise 29-4   Forming the plural

In the blank at the right, enter the plural form of each word. Check yourself by consulting your dictionary.

Example:

box   *boxes* _____

1. sheep   _____

2. dog   _____

3. puppy   _____

4. fox   _____

5. brother-in-law _____

6. TV   _____

7. cupful   _____

8. criterion   _____

9. series   _____

10. company   _____

11. chef   _____

12. shelf   _____

13. man   _____

14. buoy   _____

15. belief   _____

16. knife   _____

17. cargo   _____

18. piano   _____

19. library   _____

29D Use spelling lists to help improve your spelling.

The following list of words includes some of the most frequently misspelled words in English. Look it over carefully, searching for words that you know are particularly troublesome for you. Then keep this list handy whenever you are writing an essay.

absence	embarrass	maintenance	reminisce
abundance	environment	marriage	repetition
accommodate	equipment	mathematics	resemblance
acknowledge	exaggerate	misspelled	roommate
acquaintance	existence	mysterious	schedule
aggravate	familiar	necessary	secretary
all right	fascinate	noticeable	separate
already	foreign	occasionally	similar
analysis	forty	occurrence	sophomore
appearance	fourth	omission	succeed
argument	government	parallel	supersede
attendance	grammar	perform	temperament
believe	harass	precede	tendency
benefited	height	prejudice	tragedy
calendar	hindrance	privilege	truly
category	imaginary	procedure	undoubtedly
certain	immediately	proceed	usually
changeable	independent	pronunciation	vacuum
condemn	infinite	receive	valuable
conscience	irresistible	recommend	villain
definite	leisure	reference	weird
dependent	license	referring	writing

Exercise 29-5   Creating mnemonics

A **mnemonic** is a made-up saying to help you remember an important point. For example, here is a mnemonic to help you remember how to spell *separate:*

"There is *a rat* in *separate.*"

This mnemonic should help you remember that the middle letters of *separate* are *arat* rather than *erat*. Here is another mnemonic:

"*Accommodate* is greedy because it has to have two *c*'s and two *m*'s."

    For the following exercise look over the list of commonly misspelled words just given and choose eight words that you know you have trouble spelling. Then make up your own mnemonic to help you remember those words.

Word correctly spelled _____   **Your mnemonic** _____

1.

2.

3.

4.

5.

6.

7.

8.

29E Use hyphens to form certain compound words and to avoid confusion.

1, 2 Hyphens are often used to join two or more nouns into a new noun naming a single concept or to join adjectives to a noun for the same purpose.

> jack-in-the-box   great-grandfather [A *great grandfather* would be a grandfather that you thought was great.]   goof-off   clerk-typist   hair-raiser

Many words that you might suspect should be hyphenated are now considered either as one word or as two unhyphenated words. When in doubt, check your dictionary.

> hairsplitter   laboratory technician

3 Use a hyphen to join modifiers when the absence of a hyphen might cause confusion.

Confusing:
> I spent the summer babysitting for four year old children.

Clarified:
> I spent the summer babysitting for four year-old children. [four children, each one-year old]

> I spent the summer babysitting for four-year-old children. [an unspecified number of children who were four years old]

Confusion can also occur if a prefix added to a word creates a spelling identical to that of another word. In such cases use a hyphen.

> I never recovered from the trauma of trying to re-cover the davenport.

Also use hyphens to join elements of a compound adjective that you newly coin for your own purposes.

> Sam gave me his patented oh-teacher-you-didn't-tell-us-you-meant-*all*-students smile.

Compound adjectives are normally hyphenated when they occur in front of the noun they modify, but not when they come after it.

> This was a well-organized essay.
> This essay was well organized.

Do not use hyphens between an adverb and an adjective if the adverb ends in *ly*.

> This was a brilliantly organized essay.

4 Use hyphens to attach certain prefixes to words.

Most prefixes require no hyphens *(unnatural, disappear)*. However, use a hyphen if the prefix is connected to a capitalized word *(un-American, anti-Arab)*. Additionally, the prefixes *ex* and *self* are normally hyphenated *(ex-wife, self-interest)*. Also hyphenated are compound numbers from twenty-one to ninety-nine and fractions *(one hundred twenty-nine, three-fourths)*.

Exercise 29-6   Using hyphens

A. Combine each of the following sentences into a single sentence that uses a hyphen.

Example:
Sam operated out of interest. This interest was in himself.

Sam operated out of self-interest.

1. There is Pete. Pete used to be my husband.

2. The mouse uttered a squeak. This squeak seemed to say "Let me out of this cage."

3. Rover is a mean dog. He also has a short temper.

4. Ramsay was a man. He drank hard. He loved fun. He loved women.

5. He is a strong man. He has muscles like bricks.

B. Write out the following numbers, using hyphens when appropriate.

Example:

105 *one hundred five*

72 *seventy-two*

6. 13

7. 94

8. 1,994

9. $24\frac{2}{3}$

10. 24,000

C. Determine whether the words in parentheses should be hyphenated, left as they are, or combined into a single word. Use your dictionary freely. Write your answers in the space below each sentence.

Example:
The (first sergeant) radioed the base unit to commence firing the (anti aircraft) guns.

first sergeant   anti-aircraft

11. We felt that her strong (pro British) stance was (self serving).

12. There are so many (house flies) in the kitchen that I am starting to get my (so this is summer blues).

13. Although she studied (pre Renaissance) poetry and had a fondness for (thirteenth century) philosophy, her attitude toward religion was definitely (twentieth century); nevertheless, her dissertation, which her adviser said was the most (lucidly written) piece of (graduate work) he had ever read, showed unusual sensitivity to (religious feelings) throughout (Franco German) history.

14. She does a lot of (hot dog) skiing.

15. Although I was a (non partisan) in this affair, I still thought that they caught him (red handed).

30
Capitalization

Most writers agree on the conventions for using capital letters, but the conventions occasionally change. When in doubt about whether to capitalize a particular word, consult a good dictionary.

30A **Capitalize the first letter of the first word in every sentence and also in sentence fragments used for effect. In fragmentary questions placed in series, initial capital letters are optional.**

That man is a liar. A lousy scoundrel, in fact. What do you want me to do? Like him? Invite him to dinner? Offer him my money?

OR

What do you want me to do? like him? invite him to dinner? offer him my money?

30B **Use capitals for proper names of people, places, and things and for abbreviations of and words derived from proper names.**

• Specific people:

Pete Rose   George Washington   Emily Dickinson

BUT

a baseball player   a hero   a poet

• Titles of people when the titles precede names or when they follow names without an article but generally not when they follow names and include an article:

Doctor Sarah Smith   Professor John Jones   John Jones, Professor of Mathematics

BUT

Sarah Smith, a medical doctor   John Jones, a professor of mathematics

• Family relationships when used with a name. When used in place of a name, capitalization is optional:

Please Aunt Eloise, tell Grandfather [or grandfather] that dinner is ready.

BUT

my uncle   Tony's grandfather

375

- Specific geographical locations, areas, and regions, but not compass directions used as directions:

Mount Everest   the Pacific Northwest   Idaho   Main Street
the South

BUT

the northwest part of the United States   a main street in Boston
a mountain south of here

- Historical events, names, movements, and writings:

the Korean War   the Oregon Territory   the Articles of Confederation

BUT

a war in Korea   territory in Oregon   articles currently being considered
by congress

- Specific things identified by proper names (ships, buildings, brand names):

U.S.S. Missouri   the Empire State Building   Sanka

BUT

an important navy ship   a tall building   coffee

- Specific academic courses but not academic subject areas except English and foreign languages:

Chemistry 101   Ancient Roman History   Advanced Calculus

BUT

chemistry   history   mathematics   languages   Russian

- Specific times, days, months, and holidays, but not names of seasons:

Monday   the Fourth of July   Halloween

BUT

an important day   last year   autumn   winter

- Abbreviations derived from proper names:

N.F.L.   U.S.A.   RCA   U. of W.

- Words derived from proper names:

Shakespearean   Trumanesque   Octoberfest

30C   **In titles of books, articles, plays, musical pieces, and so forth, capitalize the first and last words, all other words except articles and prepositions or conjunctions with fewer than five letters, and any word after a colon or a semicolon.**

"Ain't No Such Thing as a Montana Cowboy"   "The World Beyond the Horizon"   "Star Symbols: A Study of Astrological Myth-Making"

30D Capitalize the first words of spoken dialogue but not the first word in the second half of a broken quotation coming after attributive words. Do not capitalize indirect quotations.

> She said, "Because it is raining, we won't go."
>
> "Because it is raining," she said, "we won't go."
>
> BUT
>
> She said that we wouldn't go because it is raining.

30E Use capitals consistently and avoid unnecessary capitals.

> Contemporary writers generally use capitals sparingly. When you have a choice, therefore, prefer small-case letters. Once you make a decision, stick with it consistently throughout your essay.

> *Inconsistent:*

> The new president of Bickerstaff College addressed the faculty, staff, and students. The President asked for cooperation, high standards, and good community relations. [Either capitalize *president* in both instances or use small letters in both instances.]

Exercise 30-1   Self-study: Capitalization

In the following sentences, add capital letters wherever needed.

Answer column

1. "she told me not to do it," my cousin barbara explained.

   1. "She told me not to do it," my cousin Barbara explained.

2. "she told me not to do it," cousin barbara explained.

   2. "She told me not to do it," Cousin Barbara explained. [The word *cousin* is capitalized here and not in sentence 1 above because here there is no *my* in front of it. Without the *my, cousin* becomes part of the name. However, some writers would not capitalize *cousin* in either case.]

3. my cousin explained that her mother told her not to do it.

   3. My cousin explained that her mother told her not to do it.

4. "she told me not to read *the sound and the fury,*" grandfather watson explained, "because I would find it too depressing, having been born and raised in the south."

   4. "She told me not to read *The Sound and the Fury,*" Grandfather Watson explained, "because I would find it too depressing, having been born and raised in the South." [*Because* is not capitalized because it is the second part of a broken quotation and is actually the middle of an ongoing sentence. *South* is capitalized because it is used here as the name of a region, rather than as a direction.]

5. "read some of the poet greg keeler's ballads about montana," grandfather told me. "they will keep you in stitches if you grew up anywhere south of canada and west of the mississippi river."

   5. "Read some of the poet Greg Keeler's ballads about Montana," Grandfather told me. "They will keep you in stitches if you grew up anywhere south of Canada and west of the Mississippi River." [*They* is capitalized because it begins a new sentence (compare with *because* in sentence 4 above; *south* and *west* are used as directions only.]

6. every memorial day my brother Sam, a professor of chemistry at liberty college, and dr. susanna bilboa, professor of biology at the same college (she is my brother's current "comrade") visit my grandfather's and grandmother's graves at hillside cemetery south of tamarack falls.

7. the president of the library association advised me to take lots of english courses and also history courses if I wanted to have a truly liberal education; however, I decided to major in chemical engineering. My first year I took nothing but science and math courses except for history of western civilization taught by professor joseph stubbs, who got his ph.d. from a university in western europe.

8. The title of his ph.d. dissertation was *from aristotle to thomas aquinas: a study of syllogistic thinking as a means of ascertaining truth.*

9. My roommate, who is majoring in creative writing, wrote a satirical poem mocking dr. stubb's dissertation; he calls it "stubbs's folly."

10. an islamic group on our campus founded a new club to enhance social opportunities for foreign students. next spring this group plans to rent a cabin on icepond lake and sponsor weekend retreats to discuss various social issues. they will invite people from all ethnic groups including blacks, chicanos, asians, caucasians, and native americans. several feminist leaders have also been invited to conduct discussions on women's issues, particularly the future of an e.r.a. amendment and the status of new day-care legislation at the state capitol. they hope that the governor and several important legislators can be persuaded to spend an evening with the group.

6. Every Memorial Day my brother Sam, a professor of chemistry at Liberty College, and Dr. Susanna Bilboa, Professor of Biology at the same college (she is my brother's current "comrade") visit my grandfather's and grandmother's graves at Hillside Cemetery south of Tamarack Falls. [*Professor of Biology* is capitalized because it is not preceded by an article; compare with *a professor of chemistry*, which is not capitalized.]

7. The president of the library association advised me to take lots of English courses and also history courses if I wanted to have a truly liberal education; however, I decided to major in chemical engineering. My first year I took nothing but science and math courses except for History of Western Civilization taught by Professor Joseph Stubbs, who got his Ph.D. from a university in western Europe. [*History of Western Civilization* names a specific course rather than a subject area and hence is capitalized.]

8. The title of his Ph.D. dissertation was *From Aristotle to Thomas Aquinas: A Study of Syllogistic Thinking as a Means of Ascertaining Truth.*

9. My roommate, who is majoring in creative writing, wrote a satirical poem mocking Dr. Stubb's dissertation; he calls it "Stubbs's Folly."

10. An Islamic group on our campus founded a new club to enhance social opportunities for foreign students. Next spring this group plans to rent a cabin on Icepond Lake and sponsor weekend retreats to discuss various social issues. They will invite people from all ethnic groups including Blacks, Chicanos, Asians, Caucasians, and Native Americans. Several feminist leaders have also been invited to conduct discussions on women's issues, particularly the future of an E.R.A. amendment and the status of new day-care legislation at the state capitol. They hope that the governor and several important legislators can be persuaded to spend an evening with the group.

31
Numbers and Abbreviations

Wherever it is necessary to save space—such as in tables, indexes, and footnotes—writers often use abbreviations and figures. In most kinds of informal and formal writing, however, writers rarely use abbreviations and use figures only for numbers that take more than two words to write out.

31A **Use words for numbers that take one or two words and also for numbers that begin a sentence (except for dates). For most other numbers use figures rather than words.**

ten dogs   ninety-nine cats   one thousand mice   112 goldfish

BUT

One hundred twelve goldfish were in the tank.

1981 was a bad year for grasshoppers.

31B **Use figures for numbers in prose containing much quantitative information. Generally use figures for dates, times of day, and addresses.**

Figures would commonly be used in the following instances:

- To express dates, especially when the year is included:

September 7, 1981

BUT

We came on September seventh. [September 7th is acceptable by some writers but not September 7th, 1981.]

- To express time of day followed by A.M. or P.M. but not by o'clock:

1:00 P.M. [or p.m.]

BUT

one o'clock in the afternoon

- To express addresses and zip codes:

1399 Fifth Avenue South, Pickleville, CA 76431 [When house number and street name come together, spell out the street name.]

- To express percentages, decimals, measurements, and statistical information:

12 feet   25 percent   3.17 earned run average

- To express numbers in series where easy comparison is important:

There were 700 persons at the professor's first public lecture, 270 at the second, and 42 at the third.

- To refer to the parts of a book:

Chapter 13   page 8

31C   In formal writing, spell out most words rather than abbreviate them.

Use abbreviations rarely and then only in those instances listed in rules 31D to G below. Be especially careful to spell out the word *and* (use the ampersand [&] only if it is part of an official name like *A & W Root Beer*); the names of countries, states, and cities; the names of months and the days of the week; people's names unless you are using only an initial *(Thomas R. White* but not *Thom. R. White)*; the words for pages, chapters, volumes, and editions; and such words as *company, brothers,* and *incorporated* unless they are part of an official title (The Smith brothers established an incorporated company called "Smith Bros. Inc.")

NOTE: Avoid using *etc.* (an abbreviation for the Latin *et cetera,* meaning "and so forth"). Prefer instead the English *and so forth, including,* or *such as;* better yet, rewrite your list to make it more inclusive. Never write *and etc.* since *et* means "and" in Latin.

Weak:

During one year I saw two ballets, one opera, four Shakespeare plays, etc.

Better:

During one year I saw many cultural events including two ballets, one opera, and four Shakespeare plays.

31D   Use abbreviations for academic degrees and the following common titles when used with a person's name.

Mr.   Ms.   Dr.   Jr.   Sr.   St. (Saint)

Other titles such as governor, colonel, professor, and reverend are spelled out:

The doctor asked Colonel Jones, Ms. Hemmings, and Professor Pruitt to present the portrait of St. Thomas to Judge Hogkins on the occasion of her getting a Ph.D. in religious studies.

31E   Use abbreviations for agencies, groups, people, places, and objects commonly known by capitalized initials.

FBI   I.O.O.F.   JFK   Washington D.C.   DNA molecules

NOTE: If your essay repeats frequently a word or group of words known by an abbreviation to a limited audience, identify the abbreviation for the general reader by spelling out the complete word or phrase the first time and placing the abbreviation in parentheses.

> We were notified by an official from the Fund for the Improvement of Postsecondary Education (FIPSE) that our university had received the grant. By telephone the FIPSE official explained. . . .

31F Use abbreviations for certain words and concepts conventionally occurring as abbreviations or symbols, especially in times, dates, and amounts.

> *A.D.* 1200   500 *B.C.* [*A.D.* always precedes the date; *B.C.* follows it.]   2:45 *P.M.* $15.05   *no.* 12 in a series

31G Use abbreviations for common Latin terms — to be used mainly for footnotes, bibliographies, or parenthetical comments. In formal writing, spell out the English equivalents.

> e.g. [for example]   i.e. [that is]   cf. [compare]

Exercise 31-1   Self-study: Numbers and abbreviations

In the following sentences write out any numbers or abbreviations that would not be acceptable in a formal essay.

Answer column

1. Prof. Jones, who is a dr. in biochemistry, is reputed to have stayed in her lab for 32 consecutive hrs. last Feb.

    1. Professor Jones, who is a doctor in biochemistry, is reputed to have stayed in her lab for thirty-two consecutive hours last February. [*Lab* isn't an abbreviation here but an informal shortened word that is generally accepted in informal essays. A formal essay would require *laboratory.*]

2. Both the English dept. & the history dept. have profs with M.A. degrees and Ph.D. degrees.

    2. Both the English department and the history department have professors with M.A. degrees and Ph.D. degrees. [Unlike *lab,* which is a shortened form of *laboratory* acceptable in informal essays, *prof* isn't considered a suitable substitute for *professor* even in informal essays.]

3. Sen. Crudwell and Rev. Jones both believe that the U.S.A. should promote better relations between the U.S.S.R. and China.

    3. Senator Crudwell and Reverend Jones both believe that the U.S.A. should promote better relations between the U.S.S.R. and China.

4. When we moved to Wichita, Ks, my little brother was 4 ft. 11 in. tall, my sister was 5 ft. 2 in. tall, and I was 5 ft. 8 in. tall. Now all of us have grown 2 in. except for my sister, who is still 5′ 2″.

    4. When we moved to Wichita, Kansas, my little brother was 4 feet 11 inches tall, my sister was 5 feet 2 inches tall, and I was 5 feet 8 inches tall. Now all of us have grown two inches except for my sister, who is still 5 feet 2 inches. [Figures are used in measurements.]

5. 3, 192 people crowded into the stands to watch the Jefferson Bros. Circus.

    5. Three thousand one hundred ninety-two people crowded into the stands to watch the Jefferson Bros. Circus. [To avoid spelling out such a large

number, rewrite the sentence so that it doesn't open with the number. "A total of 3192 people crowded. . . ."]

6. They live at 15 19th St.

7. They live at 15 Grant Street.

8. They live at 15th Ave. and Grant.

9. She came on 9 May, 1977.

10. She came on May 9, 1977.

11. She came on May 9th, 1977.

12. She came on May 9th.

13. She came on May ninth.

14. She came on May 9.

15. In A.D. 1600, major changes were clearly taking place in the psyches of Elizabethan theatergoers.

16. 6% of all people polled agreed completely with the proposal, while 72% strongly disagreed.

17. We counted 42 deer.

18. We counted 42 deer, 12 goats, 14 elk, and 211 prairie dogs.

19. The instructor told us specifically to read Ch. 5, especially pp. 200–204.

20. I don't want to make such promises, e.g., the promise to buy him the book.

6. They live at 15 Nineteenth Street.

7. OK

8. They live at 15th Avenue and Grant.

9. OK

10. OK

11. She came on May 9, 1977.

12. OK [*9th* can substitute for *ninth* if no year is present.]

13. OK

14. OK

15. OK

16. Six percent of all people polled agreed completely with the proposal, while 72 percent strongly disagreed.

17. We counted forty-two deer.

18. OK [Figures are needed for easy comparison.]

19. The instructor told us specifically to read Chapter 5, especially pages 200–204.

20. I don't want to make such promises, for example, the promise to buy him the book.

32

Italics

Use italic script (indicated by underlining in handwritten or typed papers) in the following instances:

32A Use italics for titles of books, magazines, journals, newspapers, plays, films, works of art, long poems, pamphlets, and musical works, but not for titles at the top center of initial pages of essays or on title pages.

> *Moby Dick*   *Newsweek*   *Star Wars*

EXCEPTIONS: Books of the Bible, the Bible itself, and court cases or government documents are not italicized.

NOTE: Italics and quotation marks can both be used for titles. Most writers, however, use quotation marks for short works or parts of longer ones (see Chapter 27) and italics for long works complete in themselves. Capitalize and italicize *a, an,* and *the* only if they are part of the title (the *Encyclopaedia Britannica,* but *The Sound and the Fury*).

32B Use italics for foreign words and phrases not part of the English language.

> He tasted the wine and pronounced it *un peu sec.*

32C Use italics for letters, numbers, words, and phrases referred to as words.

> To spell *separate* correctly, remember there is *a rat* in *separate.*

32D Use italics for names of ships, trains, and air or space vehicles.

> the *Portland Rose* [train]   a *Boeing 707* [plane]

32E Use italics for occasional emphasis.

> What am I doing? *What* am I doing? What *am* I doing? What am *I* doing? What am I *doing?*

NOTE: Although the use of italics in the above examples creates a slightly different meaning for each sentence, overuse of this technique is distracting. Use italics for emphasis sparingly; instead, rewrite your sentence to achieve emphasis through sentence structure and word choice. (See Chapter 15.)

Exercise 32-1 Self-study: Italics

In the sentences below, underline any words that should be placed in italics.

1. Have you read Chapter 2, The Art of Creativity, in our textbook?

1. Have you read Chapter 2, "The Art of Creativity," in our textbook? [This is a chapter within a longer work and thus should be placed in quotation marks rather than italicized.]

2. Have you read Chapter 2 in our textbook Thinking and Creating?

2. Have you read Chapter 2 in our textbook *Thinking and Creating?* [This is the name of the book.]

3. The word love has dozens of different meanings.

3. The word *love* has dozens of different meanings. [word referred to as a word]

4. Paul's handwriting is hard to read because he doesn't dot his i's or cross his t's.

4. Paul's handwriting is hard to read because he doesn't dot his *i*'s or cross his *t*'s.

5. Wouldn't it be très romantique to cross Europe on the Oriental Express?

5. Wouldn't it be *très romantique* to cross Europe on the *Oriental Express?*

6. Did you read the reprint of Lincoln's Gettysburg Address in last week's Sunday edition of the Hill City Gazette?

6. Did you read the reprint of Lincoln's *Gettysburg Address* in last week's Sunday edition of the *Hill City Gazette?*

7. Did you know that the Gospel of John in the Bible is influenced by a Greek view of life?

7. Ok [By convention, neither the Bible nor books of the Bible are italicized.]

8. My little brother can't pronounce aluminum.

8. My little brother can't pronounce *aluminum.*

9. Where did the expression keep on truckin' come from?

9. Where did the expression *keep on truckin'* come from?

10. All in the Family, along with MASH, was one of the greatest television series of all times.

10. *All in the Family,* along with *MASH,* was one of the greatest television series of all times.

Exercise 32-2   Mastery exercise: Capitalization, numbers and abbreviations, and italics

In the following sentences add capital letters or italics (underlinings) where needed. Also spell out any numbers or abbreviations that are necessary in order to make the sentence appropriate for a formal essay. Make required changes neatly in the spaces above the errors.

Example:

Ms. Joanne W. williams asked about her copy of faulkner's As I lay dying, & she also wanted to know where the last

23 issues of newsweek were.

1. After assigning shakespeare's as you like it to our literature of the english renaissance class, prof. Jane hollyman

    gave us 34 pp. of literary criticism to read, including some excerpts from dr. c. l. barber's book shakespeare's

    festive comedy.

2. 7 days a week, 52 weeks a year, I hear myself saying the same words over and over: "if you don't like this job, get

    another one."

3. "knowing when to use the correct fork," says grandmother ross, "and when to make a faux pas on purpose is

    what gives you power to be part of society without being commanded by it."

4. "do you live at 25 24th ave. or at 24 25th ave?" my cousin alice ridenour, a dr. of chiropractic, asked. "Neither," I

    replied. "my address is 24 25th st. if you get the streets and ave.'s mixed up in this town," I went on to explain,

    "you'll get so lost an irish setter hunting dog couldn't find you."

5. Rev. Johnson and her brother Lt. Col. Johnson, a distinguished army officer, both arrived in Boise, Id., on May

    21st, 1982, according to a report in the idaho daily statesman.

6. In ch. 12 in Geo. Smith's crime and punishment: a study of punishment as deterrent to crime during 100 years of

    american criminal justice, smith makes the argument that the ancient greek sense of hubris, or pride, still

    remains a motivating force for many criminals.

7. How many s's are in mississippi?

8. How many people are in mississippi?

9. "Does the roman catholic church interpret the biblical stories in the book of genesis differently from the way the southern baptist church interprets them?" asked dr. Wong Tan Su, visiting professor of eastern philosophy at our university. He was quite interested in western religions, particularly christianity as practiced in the u.s., but he had trouble understanding the theological differences among all the denominations.

10. Although uncle charlie was born in the old south while uncle ben was born just north of boston, mass., in the spring of the year they would bury the hatchet, declare a temporary pax romana, and drink mint juleps, their chairs facing west toward the broad expanse of the pacific ocean, as they sat, smoking their english pipes, glad to be alive in southern california.

appendix
Progress Chart for Sentence-Level Errors

Starting on page 1 of your essay, number in the margin of your essay each sentence-level error noted by your instructor. (By *sentence-level error* we mean errors of usage, grammar, and sentence structure, such as comma splices, fragments, dangling modifiers, and nonparallel constructions. Exclude spelling errors and errors dealing with paragraphing or larger rhetorical concerns.) Make an entry on this log for each error noted in your essay.

Fill out the following chart:

Error number	Marginal symbol used by instructor	State in your own words the rule that you didn't follow, and indicate page number in workbook or handbook that explains rule	Rewrite sentence from your draft with error corrected

ACKNOWLEDGMENTS

Text quotations have been excerpted and, in some cases, adapted from the following works.

Buckwaller, Leon. "Music Magic on the Road." Reprinted from *Mechanix Illustrated* mgazine. Copyright © 1979 by CBS, Inc.

Feverstein, R., and Mogens, J. "Instrumental Enrichment: Theoretical Basis, Goals, and Instrument," *Educational Forum,* 1980. Used by permission of Kappa Delta Pi, publisher and copyright owner.

Jordan, William. "The Bee Complex," from *Science 84* magazine. Copyright © 1984 by the American Association for the Advancement of Science.

Menosky, Joseph. "Videographics and Grand Jetés," from *Science 82* magazine. Copyright © 1982 by the American Association for the Advancement of Science.

Morris, Desmond. *The Naked Ape.* Copyright © 1967 McGraw-Hill Book Company.

Olney, Ross R. "Ten Car Noises You Shouldn't Ignore," *Reader's Digest,* April 1983. Reprinted by permission of the author.

Rosenthal, Elisabeth. "M.D. versus Healer," *Science Digest,* July 1983. Adapted by permission of the author.

Thomas, Lewis. "The Medusa and the Snail." Copyright © 1977 by Lewis Thomas. Originally published in the *New England Journal of Medicine.* Reprinted by permission of Viking Penguin, Inc.

Von Doniken, Erik. *Chariots of the Gods.* English translation copyright © 1969 by Michael Heron and Souvenir Press. Adaptation by permission of G. P. Putnam's Sons.